PONZI !

The Boston Swindler

also by Donald H. Dunn:
The Making of "No, No, Nanette"

PONZI!

The Boston Swindler

DONALD H. DUNN

McGraw-Hill Book Company

NEW YORK   ST. LOUIS   SAN FRANCISCO   TORONTO
MEXICO   DÜSSELDORF

123456789KPKP798765

Library of Congress Cataloging in Publication Data

Dunn, Donald H
    Ponzi! : The Boston swindler.

    1. Ponzi, Charles. I. Title.
HV6698.Z9P53   364.1′63′0924 [B]   74-32253
ISBN 0-07-018270-1

for
BARBARA SUE KRAMER
"Bobbie"
whose persistence, patience, and love
kept me alive
to write this

AUTHOR'S NOTE

Incredible and fanciful as they may seem, the events recorded in this book are as factually true as nearly two years of research and reporting can make them. Although treated novelistically, *what* happens is grounded thoroughly in reality, and I would like to credit the institutions, individuals, and various texts which furnished details and assistance.

Of great significance was a rare copy of Charles Ponzi's privately published autobiography, *The Rise of Mr. Ponzi*, and special thanks goes to Marc Cheshire for his aid in making the work available to me from the Library of Congress.

The library of the Columbia University School of Journalism, with its prize-winning entry of the *Boston Post* in the 1921 Pulitzer Awards, was extremely helpful.

In addition to the *Post* files, and those of other Boston papers of the day, considerable information was gleaned from *The New York Times* files at the New York Public Library; *The New Yorker*, May 8, 1937; "The Ponzi Bubble" by Albert Hurwitz, the *Herald* magazine of the Boston *Sunday Herald Traveler*, August 30, 1970; "New and Old South Sea Bubbles" by A. B. Reeve, *World's Work*, November 1920; "For Exposing Ponzi . . ." and other articles, *Literary Digest*; *The Scandalous Scamps* by Harold Mehling, published by Henry Holt & Co.; *Great Swindlers* by A. F. L.

Deeson, published by Drake Publishers; *Strange Tales of Amazing Frauds*, published by Garden City Publishing Co.; "Ponzi's Dupes," *The New Republic*, September 8, 1920; *Life*, January 31, 1949; "Bubble Bubble—No Toil, No Trouble" by Francis Russell, *American Heritage*, February 1973; and *Only Yesterday* by Frederick Lewis Allen, published by Harper & Brothers.

A special bow of appreciation to Mrs. Barbara Kelly at the Office of the Clerk, U.S. District Court, Boston, Massachusetts, for locating and providing numerous court documents—transcripts of Ponzi's bankruptcy hearings, copies of indictments, and other material.

On a personal note, I want to thank Mrs. Lucy Meli Cristoforo; Albert Hurwitz; Paul D'Espinoza; Ann Ray Martin of *Newsweek*; Richard Burgheim of Time, Inc.; Martha Palubniak Freire of McGraw-Hill World News (and Henry Johnston in Rio); Bob Grunin of the Boston University School of Journalism; Flo, Christopher, Paul, Elena, and Carrie Dunn; my editor, Joyce Johnson; Lewis H. Young, editor-in-chief of *Business Week*, whose casual reference to a "Ponzi scheme" provided inspiration; Robin Carlson; Tessie Mantzoros; Jerry Raboy; Sally Powell; Dr. Robert Naiman; Elizabeth McKee; Anne Colamosca; Fred Lounsbury; William Wolman; Peggy and Vincent Ferraro; Phil Osborne; Sandy Teller; Jason Miller; Jim Abernathy; the Harvey A. Viens of Tavares, Florida; Adele Adelson; and Peter Hann, a friend.

—**Don Dunn**
January 1975

Throughout the twentieth century, financial deviltry has had a thoroughly disreputable history, from the robber barons to such stock manipulators of the 1920s as John Raskob and Joseph P. Kennedy, and on to the giant Equity Funding scandal that broke in 1973 when a securities analyst discovered what numerous auditors and regulators had failed to note: That the company had for years created an illusion of growth by loading its computer with imaginary insurance premiums from nonexistent customers. But few swindlers have captured the imagination of the public quite like Charles Ponzi, who was conning people almost from the moment he was born and whose huge fraud in Boston in 1920 became the talk of the nation.

Though it was a type of swindle that had been worked repeatedly for centuries, Ponzi's name became synonymous with it in American lore. Indeed, the adventures of the Boston master are particularly instructive today because Ponzi games have come back into style with a vengeance. In the 1970s there have been so many around the U.S.—literally dozens—that there appears to be an epidemic. Some economists believe swindles proliferate in cyclical patterns through history, and they have noted uncanny economic parallels between the 1970s and the 1920s that make both decades fertile eras for fraud. Most importantly, inflation is rampant, as it was following World War I, and people desperate for ways to beat soaring prices are quick to take a swindler's bait. And, as unemployment mounts, men without jobs seek to profit by investing their savings—just as veterans of World War I sought to put their mustering-out pay to work when they found American industry did not have jobs for them upon discharge. There's no shortage of credulous folk ready to tumble—even the most sophisticated bankers and financiers can be hoodwinked into giving their money to a modern Ponzi operator.

What sets Ponzi schemes off from more intricate swindles is this: The money that investors put up isn't invested in anything, and "profits" are paid out of new money from subsequent investors. Eventually there aren't enough newcomers to keep the snowball process going, and the game collapses. No one knows if a Ponzi operator has ever found a way to close out his swindle successfully. Perhaps some men who are wealthy and respected have done just that.

When a Ponzi game collapses, all of the latecomers lose. Only early investors can win, but many of them frequently lose, too, because they reinvest with the expectation of making even fatter gains. They become trapped by their own greed. To profit from a

FOREWORD

An intriguing tale of financial chicanery never fails to entertain me, but I'm reluctant to explain why. It's a pleasure that doesn't want to be scrutinized too closely. For one thing, those of us who delight in stories of great swindles indulge in a gymnastic delusion: We persuade ourselves that we are not like the suckers who get taken—an example of self-cozening if there ever was one. For another, we tend to identify with the swindler, a clear case of ethical confusion. Fraud, after all, is not an admirable or even comfortable pastime, and real-life swindlers are rarely endearing.

Yet when it comes to yarn-spinning, there is something vastly appealing about the figure of The Swindler—cunning, independent, and flamboyant, mocking the rules-keepers as well as the rules.

The Suckers are, by contrast, a mindless lot, as colorless as sheep, and we can't help feeling that they deserve to have the wool pulled over their eyes. The "public" is very different from you and me. Besides, as every con artist knows, a mark must have a little larceny in his own soul to be conned. People are swindled because they are after a quick-and-easy profit in the first place. Those who plunge their life savings into a fast-buck scheme are the victims, really, of their own folly—or so we rationalize it.

Ponzi fraud, it's not enough to be the first one in; you have to be the first one out as well.

The commonest versions of a Ponzi game are chain letters and pyramid sales schemes, but the swindle can take an infinite variety of subtler forms. Virtually any investment vehicle can start out legitimately—and then turn into a variation on Ponzi's original.

In recent years the flim-flam boys have worked Ponzi operations in everything from offshore mutual funds and private hedge funds to real estate, commodity contracts, and gold coins. Hundreds of small investors around New York were recently stung by a Los Angeles crook who sold them some $9 million worth of 270-day notes, presumably invested in real estate and guaranteeing returns of 20 to 30 percent. But the $9 million vanished. There has been a whole string of companies that have peddled paper representing commodity investments without having any commodities or futures contracts to back them up. One such swindle to emerge recently was worked in investment contracts for gold coins and silver by Las Vegas' Western Pacific Gold and Silver Exchange Corp. The "company" was run by James Ray Houston, an unsuccessful candidate for Governor of Nevada who sometimes goes by the name of Sun Ray Star.

The juiciest scandal uncovered within recent memory is the fabulous Home-Stake Production Co. swindle. Home-Stake, based in Tulsa, purported to be an oil-drilling company run by an Oklahoma lawyer named Robert S. Trippet. Home-Stake sold tax shelter partnerships to hundreds of wealthy investors eager to avoid paying taxes. To disguise the lack of oil-drilling operations, Trippet and his cronies fooled investors with a variety of maneuvers, even including painting irrigation pipes orange to make a California vegetable farm look like an operating oil field. When the company went bankrupt in 1973, unsuspecting investors lost $100 million or more.

The list of investors was astounding. It included scores of the biggest names in U.S. industry, finance, law, and show business. Among the show-biz crowd were Barbra Streisand, Liza Minnelli, Walter Matthau, Candice Bergen, Bob Dylan, Mia Farrow, Barbara Walters, and the late Jack Benny. Andy Williams alone sunk in $538,000. The Home-Stake roster of top executives of U.S. corporations who invested included Donald M. Kendall, chairman of Pepsico; David J. Mahoney, chairman of Norton Simon; and James R. Shepley, president of Time. But where the tears ran heaviest was at General Electric. The smooth Trippet got to more than twenty officers of GE for amounts ranging up to $570,000.

Bankers and financial experts should have been the most embarrassed. Hoyt Ammidon, chairman of U.S. Trust, and Paul L. Miller, president of First Boston Corp., bought into Home-Stake. So did George J. W. Goodman, who wrote two best-sellers about Wall Street's fast-money players, *The Money Game* and *Super-money*, under the pseudonym "Adam Smith."

So those who get taken in a Ponzi racket have one consolation: They can always boast that they're in the same league with the nation's financial elite.

Once the essential characteristics of a Ponzi game are grasped, it's easy to become a little paranoid and suspect that there are swindles all around you. You might be right. Huge as the Home-Stake swindle was, for instance, many investors argue that it is far from the biggest. Some people insist that the Social Security system is only a giant Ponzi game, because money that you pay into Social Security is not invested for your retirement. Rather, it is immediately paid out to the elderly who are collecting now—that is, to the people who got in earlier. By the time the post–World War II population bulge reaches retirement age, so the skeptics worry, everyone else will have to ante up so much in Social Security taxes that the whole system may fall apart.

Far-fetched? Perhaps, but only a little more than the idea that the stock market itself is a kind of giant Ponzi scheme. That is, when an investor buys in during the late, speculative stages of a bull market, such as occurred in the late 1960s, prices only continue to rise because subsequent investors are eager to come in at higher prices. No matter how healthy the economy or corporate profits may appear, the stock market must have new buying to propel it higher. After the last influx of money, as in a Ponzi game, the market can only keel over and go down. Millions of investors who bought stock at astronomical prices in the last few years now realize that they got in too late and stayed in too long—precisely the mistake that Ponzi's dupes made in Boston, 1920.

William G. Shepherd

Wall Street Editor, *Business Week*

PONZI !

The Boston Swindler

Almost as soon as August, 1919, gave way to September, a brisk and swirling wind hurried into Boston. It tore the leaves, which had only just begun to turn color, from the maple and sycamore trees in the quiet suburbs. Then it raced through the narrow streets of the business district with force enough to lift the heavy ankle-length skirts of secretaries and shopgirls an inch or two, exposing a glimpse of black stocking to the appraising gaze of nearby males, and all too frequently compounding the mischief by wrapping the unshrouded limb in a sheet of dirty, discarded newspaper blown from the gutter.

If there was one thing that the wind had declared war on, however, it was that popular element of male attire, the straw skimmer. All over town, from North Reading to Randolph, from Cohasset to Lincoln, closet doors were opened and the beloved—but lightweight—hats were tucked carefully away on upper shelves to hibernate until the following May.

The instantaneous and mass disappearance of the skimmer made the one worn by Charles Ponzi that windy September day all the more noticeable. It sat atop his head like a crown, and he wore it with an assurance that no wind would dare disturb it. As he strode purposefully along the street, Ponzi even tilted the disc of straw back to a more rakish angle, revealing a flash of sandy hair above his high, lightly furrowed forehead, and adding that much more height to his stature. Today, he wanted every fraction he could obtain. Only five-foot-four, he knew well that he lacked an imposing physical appearance—a helpful quality to possess when a man is out to get money.

Charles Ponzi was out to get money. A lot of it. And in the sixteen years that he had been trying to get rich in America, he had

1

learned that any number of things could compensate for limited stature and physical strength. A confident tone of voice, for example; a tone that indicated its owner knew precisely what he was doing at all times. A dapper appearance, too; an appearance that said—from the well-shined shoes, the pristine celluloid collar above the tightly knotted tie with its small diamond stickpin perfectly centered, the casual breast-pocket handkerchief, and the rakish straw hat—that here is a man who, if he is not already successful, will latch onto success at any moment. And then, of course, there was the smile. Always, the smile; for a smiling man is obviously not worried—and who would give money to a worried man?

Ponzi was smiling as he stepped through the doorway of the small Italian restaurant at the corner. Although it was midafternoon, a few candles in winebottles covered with drippings had already been lit in a vain attempt to dispel the chill of the overcast day. It took a minute for him to focus his eyes in the flickering gloom. Then he saw his uncle, not in his accustomed place behind the massive mahogany bar, but slumped over a thick stack of invoices at one of the tables.

"Uncle John," Ponzi called affectionately.

The older, heavier man looked up, blinking his eyes at the silhouette against the frosted glass door. "Carlo? Is that you?"

"Of course it's me," said Ponzi, moving toward him, arm outstretched and the smile as wide as it could be. "I took the trolley halfway here to see you—and let the wind blow me the rest of the way."

His uncle was pumping his hand now. "Well, you lookin' fine," he said, "You ain't been here in a long time. Six months, no? How's Rose? How's she feel? No baby yet?"

Ponzi laughed. He pulled a chair from a table and sat easily, sliding a Murad from its pack and lighting it in the flame of a candle. He drew deeply on the cigarette, then let the smoke glide from his lungs.

"Your niece is fine, just fine. And the babies will come. Give us time. We've been married just over a year."

"Sure, sure, Carlo, I know. But my wife—Rose's aunt—she want things fast, like back home. Everybody want the big family."

Ponzi watched his uncle move to the bar and fill two glasses with a deep red wine. "You have a big family already," he laughed. "There are more Gneccos in Somerville and the rest of Boston than mosquitoes in New Jersey!" He waited for the older man to grin before he added casually: "Besides, I don't want to start raising kids until we're all set financially."

2

His uncle set one of the glasses before him. "You no working, Carlo?"

Ponzi threw his head back. "I'm working," he said, "on something that is going to make me rich—and make your niece rich—in a very short time."

The older man's voice was suspicious. "Carlo, I been in the liquor business, the restaurant business twenty-five years now. I know nothin' else. My English, you know it, it ain't good. But you been sayin' since you marry Rose that soon you be rich. First, you a clerk at that company with exports and you say you be rich—"

Ponzi held up his hand. "The only thing J. R. Poole gives its employees is promises. I could have been there fifty years and I never would have gotten my hands on anything besides my salary! Old man Poole sees to that, all right." He gulped the wine, emptying half the glass. "Nobody's going to get a piece of his sardine factory in Maine or his meat plant in Kansas City. I didn't leave my mother in Parma, I didn't come here and knock all over the country, picking up English along with nickels and dimes to eat on, so Poole could have me translate his letters about million-dollar deals into Italian." He paused to look around the restaurant.

"Look, Uncle John, you've got this place of your own. You know you don't get rich working for other people."

The older man sighed. "Sure, sure," he said softly. "I got my own place. I make the good money. Then 'long come the goddamn prohibition! Carlo, how I make the money when I don't sell the liquor no more? You tell me that, hah?"

Ponzi shook his head. All over the country, restaurant owners and liquor distributors were pondering the same question. His uncle, like others, had talked many times of wholesaling foodstuffs to other restaurants. But the profit margins on food were a fraction of the ones on liquor. And the business was highly competitive, with massive problems of spoilage, agricultural shortages, and slow distribution. Ponzi was well acquainted with the difficulties in selling food. His first job after marrying twenty-year-old Rose Gnecco had been to assist her father and brothers in their business of supplying fruits and vegetables to the pushcart vendors and stands that dotted Boston. Within a year, the Gnecco Brothers operation was bankrupt.

Ponzi's uncle remembered, too, suddenly. "You had the chance to run a business, Carlo, with the fruits and vegetables. You would make the big money, you said."

"What about the time I got the three carloads of matches at half-price?" Ponzi snapped. He smiled over his glass and drained it. "I ordered them, knowing our company didn't have the money

3

to pay for them when they'd arrive. But then I sold them before we took delivery—and got cash in advance. We made $800! That's the way to do business!"

"But suppose you ain't found a buyer so soon? How you pay for 'em when they come?"

Ponzi shook his head, laughing. "You never think that way, Uncle John. You just know you're going to find a buyer—and you do. When Rose's father put the company into bankruptcy, I told the judge that if he'd let me have the $6,000 we still had left, I could double it in a year. Then I could pay off the $11,000 we owed. I could have done it!"

He went to the bar and stretched for the wine, returning to fill the two glasses precisely to the brim. Then he sat across the table from his uncle and looked straight into his eyes.

"The judge wouldn't let me have the money," he said softly. "He decided it made more sense to pay our creditors fifty cents on the dollar. The judge was stupid, Uncle John. I could have doubled that money. I could have doubled it then, and if I had it today, I could double it now."

"Carlo," said the older man thoughtfully, "you got a new business idea, no?"

The straw skimmer tilted back once more as Charles Ponzi nodded his head slowly, forcefully. He did not want to be rushed. He wanted another glass of wine—or two—to go down his uncle's gullet and befuddle his brain before the latest Ponzi plan was laid out before him. He stalled for time.

"Years ago, when I first came to this country, Uncle John, I swore that I would be as wealthy as the Carnegies! The Mellons! The Rockefellers! I nearly made my fortune—several times—but it always slipped away. This time it won't."

"Carlo, my boy, my niece's husband, my nephew," his uncle sighed, "how many times now you make this speech to me?"

"Why, not more than once a week, Uncle John," he answered brightly, hoping for a laugh in response—and getting one. "But—"

"But this time she is different? Yes? And how many times I hear that?"

Now Ponzi laughed. "Enough, obviously, so that you can tell me what I'm going to say before I say it." He made his tone sincere. "But, uncle, this is serious. I'm in business, an important business that's all my own. There are no brothers to share the profits with, no bosses to keep the beef and give me the watery gravy. Look, let me show you—"

He reached into his inside pocket and unfolded a sheet of stationery. With the deft, practiced movements of a stage conjurer,

4

he slid it onto the table. His grin reappeared as the portly restaurant owner leaned forward to look.

"Here," said Ponzi, spinning the sheet of expensive, water-marked paper around. "This says *The Trader's Guide*. And, underneath—you like the way the lettering curves?—this says *Published by the Bostonian Advertising & Publishing Company*. Then the address, *27 School Street, Boston*. Rose told you I had an office? I took space on the second floor of the Niles Building."

"Hmm-mm," grunted the older man. "By the Parker House, no?"

"And I can look right into the windows at City Hall. The Five-Cent Savings Bank is right next door. That should prove this is a real business venture, don't you think, uncle?"

"Isn't it?" The voice was wary.

"Wait until you hear the details, that's all. Then you make up your mind."

His uncle nodded, leaning forward.

"When I rented the office, I planned to do the same kind of thing I was doing at Poole's," Ponzi began. "You know, find buyers in this country for foreign concerns with goods to sell. Or work the other way around. But how could I make the contacts? Mail a circular to thousands of companies here and overseas—but every one would cost me at least five cents, with printing and postage. Too much. Understand?"

He did not wait for his uncle's slow nod. "Then I thought of putting an advertisement about my company in one of the journals read by merchants all over the world. And this is where I hit on something! The leading journal wanted $500 for a one-page notice, and it only goes to fifty thousand readers!"

"Carlo, I no understand. You go too fast."

"Not at all, not at all," Ponzi said, bringing a pencil from his pocket. "Every month this magazine is mailed to fifty thousand people—the same people every month—who pay to get it. And the publisher charges advertisers $500 a page! But I thought it should be possible to create a journal that would go to *more* people—say, two hundred thousand all over the world. And a journal which would not charge advertisers so much money. Why, they'd come flocking to me!

"So, uncle, I have created *The Trader's Guide*." He touched the letterhead proudly. "Now my plan is to get the names of two hundred thousand businessmen overseas from the Bureau of Commerce and the Consular Service. They'll give me all the names I want, free. And I'll mail half the businessmen a loose-leaf binder, free of charge. I've already picked it out—an inexpensive cover with screw posts. Once the readers have the binders, every six months I'll mail them inserts that contain reading matter and advertisements. See, everybody won't get the *same* magazine. For one thing, it will be printed in different languages—I think English, French, Italian, German, Spanish, and Portuguese will be enough. And, another thing, businessmen in Iceland wouldn't be interested in electric fans any more than a Mexican would be interested in fur coats. Each will get what he wants, *free*."

Ponzi's uncle stared at the figures scribbled on the letterhead. *$500. 50,000. 200,000.* He glanced up. "You give everything *free*? You give *free*?"

"Everything but the advertising," Ponzi said jubilantly, rushing on. "Don't you see? When journals go out each month to readers, the old issues get thrown away. If a company pays $500 for an ad every month, it costs them $6,000 a year. But my *Trader's Guide* is a permanent reference book, and each reader gets new pages of interest to him every now and then. So he keeps it. For $500, my advertisers get more than twice as many readers, and they get *permanent* display!"

The restaurant was silent now, except for the buzzing of a half-dozen weary flies. Ponzi stared into his uncle's eyes, waiting.

"But, Carlo, you know nothin' 'bout this kind of business. How you sell—"

"Easily! For every page of reading matter, I'll sell three pages of advertising. If other journals can do it—and they are *doing* it—there is no reason why I can't. Don't you see, I have more to offer, for the same money. For less money, in fact. My selling arguments cannot be beaten, Uncle John. They can't even be matched."

"How much you think you make with this?"

Ponzi's pencil flew across the paper. "One issue will cost about thirty-five cents. That's with fifty pages of reading matter and a hundred and fifty pages of advertising. The ads will bring in $75,000, and a hundred thousand copies will only cost $35,000 to print and mail. Figure office expenses and such, and the first issue will have a net margin of $15,000 profit in six months. Toss in another $5,000 worth of ads I can sell on the cover. And after the initial expenses are taken care of, the net should get better every six months. Well?"

His uncle's finger tapped the penciled figures. "On the paper, Carlo, it sound fine. But up here"—he tapped his damp forehead—"it no sound right." He waved his hand to cut off Ponzi's protest. "For Rose, I like to help you. But now I save every damn penny. In January, when the prohibition really start, I need it."

6

"If I gave you half-interest in the *Guide* for $5,000—"

A roar of laughter rumbled suddenly from the older man's stomach. "I know the liquor business, the restaurant. That's all. What you give me for $5,000? You put my name there on the paper? I no need that, Carlo. I got trouble already."

Ponzi reached out, carefully lifted the letterhead, folded it, and returned it to his pocket. With a flourish, he snapped his shirt cuffs an inch below his jacket sleeves. His voice was jocular, steady, brimful of confidence.

"I'll tell Rose you're in good health, Uncle John."

"Fine," his uncle said, but Ponzi had already turned his back and was moving easily toward the door. The heavy-set, balding Italian watched him go, trying to remember what his nephew had said earlier. Something about almost making a fortune since coming to America, but having it slip away. Was it true? The young man—*how old was he now*? thirty-five—certainly talked as if he stood always on the edge of something big, something important. But when Rose had first brought him home to meet her relatives, several weeks after her music teacher introduced them at a Pops concert, he had been so vague and, yet, at the same time, so boastful about his past accomplishments that everyone had found it hard to determine precisely how and where Charles Ponzi had spent the years between 1903 and 1917.

2

Leaning into the wind, hurrying to the trolley line, Ponzi told himself over and over that the idea for *The Trader's Guide* was a good one. It would never make big money, but it could produce a comfortable return. Furthermore, it was one of the less criminal plans that his fertile brain had devised since that drizzling Sunday morning, November 15, 1903, when he stepped from the gangplank of the S.S. *Vancouver* with hundreds of other Italian immigrants to look for gold in the streets of America.

With his countrymen, he had been disappointed to find the thoroughfares near Boston Harbor paved only with cobblestones. Ponzi was particularly impoverished at the time. Although his beloved mother and an uncle had given him nearly a hundred dollars in American money and a railroad ticket from Boston to Pittsburgh when they saw him off at the dock in Naples, the money was quickly confiscated aboardship by a swarthy Sicilian gambler. Ponzi felt no anger at the man who cheated him—only admiration for his skill. Flattered, the gambler had suggested that he might teach the twenty-one-year-old youth some tricks of the trade.

Ponzi shook his head. "I'm after more in America than you can make playing cards," he said. "Public school, boarding school, three years at the University of Rome! With my education, I won't have to depend on gambling for my fortune!"

The Sicilian raised an eyebrow and the others at the card table laughed. "The University?" he sneered. "And you speak no English?"

Ponzi shrugged. "Can I help it," he said casually, "if my family was so wealthy I spent all my time at the cafes and theaters when I should have been studying?"

Now the players laughed in unison. "Friend," said the Sicilian,

8

"if you can learn to lie like that in English, you should do all right in America."

Hungry, exhausted from a jolting, eighteen-hour train ride, young Charles Ponzi had already begun to build an extensive English vocabulary by the time he reached the home of a distant cousin in Pittsburgh. Dockhands and railroad clerks taught him a few words almost immediately—*greenhorn, wop, dago*—but an inquisitive schoolgirl who shared his coach seat on the train had been more helpful. When Ponzi got off at the grimy railroad station, he greeted his relative in carefully pronounced English.

"Glad—to meet—you, cousin Giuseppe."

The older man looked at him. The boy was slender, probably not more than 110 pounds, and short. But his brown eyes were warm and the smile on his lips was friendly. The word from Parma, Ponzi's home in northern Italy, was that relatives weary of paying his fines for gambling, petty theft, and forgery, had put up the money to get the young man out of the country. Joe DiCarlo had not wanted him, but as a second cousin of a third cousin, he had little choice other than act as a one-man welcoming committee. Besides, he had been told Ponzi was good with figures. If so, he had work for him.

On the way to the weatherbeaten frame house where he lived with his wife, DiCarlo explained his business. "I ship stuff on the railroad for the food companies, takin' it off at this end and splittin' it up among the stores or movin' it on east. It's paperwork mostly. 'Cept now and then I do a little sellin' of my own." His merchandise, he added as Ponzi cocked an eyebrow, consisted of miscellaneous goods—"a crate o' tomatoes here, a barrel o' flour there"—that frequently and inexplicably got lost in transit. "There are ways to cover it up, if you got the right papers. The letter I got says you had enough schoolin' to be good with numbers. You'll be helpin' me."

Working for his cousin, Ponzi mastered both the English language and the mechanics of falsifying shipping orders in less than a year. And with his growing skills came growing profits—profits that seemed only to vanish in his employer's pockets. When he announced in late fall that he was leaving for New York, DiCarlo nodded understandingly. But he held up a cautioning hand.

"I gotta warn you, Charlie, you speak the language like a professor—but some of the tricks you can get away with in this ol' Smokey City won't work in New York. I tried 'em. They got different kinds o' suckers there."

"I'll learn about them, Joe," Ponzi replied. "The filthy air here makes me sick, and the financial rewards are not quite what I promised my mother I'd find. I'll write and let her know I'm heading east."

His cousin's wife looked at him admiringly. "Your mama's such a nice lady. And you're a good boy, writin' her so much. But she'll worry 'bout you gettin' a job—"

Ponzi shrugged. "I'll find something," he said. "Something for which I'll be underpaid for my needs, no doubt, and overpaid for what I'll deserve at first. But there must be plenty of opportunities in New York."

DiCarlo laughed loudly. "There's plenty of money there, that's for sure. An' a smart man can get his hands on it. There was a fellow a couple years ago—'bout three years 'fore you came over, I guess—named Miller. He told people he could pay 'em ten percent interest a week, every week, and the fools gave him 'round a million dollars, no questions asked."

Ponzi's smile widened into a grin. "I'll have to read up on him."

During the next three years, however, he was too busy trying to keep himself alive to remember Mr. Miller. In New York; Paterson, New Jersey; New Haven, Connecticut; and a half-dozen other cities, he grabbed whatever job presented itself. He sold groceries and insurance. He worked in a factory. He repaired sewing machines. He pressed suits in a tailor shop. He waited on tables in cafes and hotels. His vocabulary grew, but his bankroll did not. Occasionally, hoping to enlarge his weekly wages of eight dollars or ten dollars in a sudden splurge of luck, he turned to dice or cards—only to find himself cheated again and again. At first, he accepted his losses philosophically; he lacked the size and strength to do anything else.

But then, angry, he resolved to practice his own card deceptions until his skill surpassed that of his opponents. He gave up that idea in Providence, Rhode Island, one hot July afternoon in 1907. Cleaned out the night before in a game of poker with a deft-fingered Neapolitan, Ponzi had spent most of the morning trying to imitate the sharp's near-invisible method of dealing from the bottom of the deck. But his own hands were too small to grip the cards properly, his fingers were slick with sweat, and the cards were damp and greasy. Suddenly, he threw the pack against the wall in exasperation.

Hoping for a stir of fresh air, he leaned far out the second-floor window that stood wide open in invitation to a breeze that never called. An ice wagon groaned slowly by on the street below, and the ancient horse pulling it left a trail of manure clumps on the dusty pavement. Ponzi in disgust turned to look around his dingy, rented cubicle. Almost retching, he knew that he had to get out of the hot New England town. Quickly. *Now*.

Beneath a small mound of underwear in the top drawer of the decaying dresser alongside his narrow bed, he had hidden a few dollar bills. He unfolded the tight packet and counted them. There was just enough there for a ticket to Montreal. It would be cool there and, in a cafe, a few evenings earlier, a dishwasher had told him about a fellow countryman who was doing well in Canada.

"Louis Zarossi's opened a bank, Ponzi. Imagine that! You talk all the time 'bout makin' the big investment. Why you not go work for Banco Zarossi, where all the money is?"

The following morning he arrived in Montreal.

Two blocks from the city's railroad station, up St. James Street, the sign of Banco Zarossi hung well-braced against the wind over a pair of glass-paneled doors. From across the street, Ponzi studied the building. He could make out the painted-over letters that once had identified it as *Zarossi Cigar Mfg. Co.*, and he smiled. Then, smoothing the ends of the straggly mustache he had grown to appear older than his twenty-five years, he glanced down at his suit. It was clean and well-pressed—he had taken care to sit carefully throughout the eight-hour train ride so his trousers would not get wrinkled. He stamped the dust from his shoes, took a deep breath, and crossed the street.

"I'd like to see Mr. Zarossi," he told the secretary. "Tell him that Charles Ponzi has business with him."

The command in his voice impressed the young woman. She rose from her desk and disappeared into the office behind her. In a moment she was back. "Mr. Zarossi will see you—" she began, but Ponzi was already gliding by.

The bank president put a thick cigar into an ashtray on his mahogany desk and thrust out a huge hand. "Mr. Ponzi," he boomed. "Welcome!"

Ponzi shook the hand, smiling, and sized up Zarossi and his office. The man looked like a fat fool, the office like that of a man with money but without taste.

"Well, well," Zarossi said, "and what can we do for you?"

"I've been hearing about you—in several cities I've visited recently."

Zarossi was flattered. He extended a box of cigars. "We've been growing by leaps and bounds," he said modestly.

"Yes," Ponzi replied, taking a cigar. "That's why I'm here."

"To open an account," said the smiling banker.

"No," Ponzi said. "I'd like to work for you." He was grinning.

"Work for me? Work—?" Suddenly Zarossi was laughing. "You want a job?"

"Want one, and need one," Ponzi said, returning the laughter. "What I own is on my back, and I rode all night from Providence to get here."

Zarossi's laughter was a roar now. "But my secretary, she said it was business. She thought you were—somebody! A depositor!"

Ponzi blew a cloud of smoke from the fine cigar. "I have the ability to give a good account of myself. An excellent account. I think I could be of use to you, Zarossi."

The banker settled back into his leather-padded chair. His eyes looked Ponzi up and down. "You speak and write both Italian and English?"

"I know your needs. I said I've heard of you."

Zarossi's eyes stared into his. "I require someone right now who inspires confidence among the people of the community. Various businessmen have asked me to invest the bank's funds, and our deposits are—" He caught himself. "We can talk of that later. You're hired, you're hired. Anyone who can come in here and get me to—"

He laughed again as he scribbled on a scrap of notepaper. "Here, Mr. Charles Ponzi, give this to that girl out there and she'll pass you on to the chief teller. Let's say twenty dollars a week to start?"

Ponzi allowed himself another laugh, also. "Fine," he said, "and I hope to hear more about your investments. They sound interesting."

Zarossi's eyes were clouded now, worried. "We'll see," he said.

It took Ponzi only a short time to learn what was on the bank president's mind. As an assistant teller, cheerfully taking in the hard-earned savings of the predominantly Italian residents of the neighborhood, he had ready access to the records of Banco Zarossi. They showed that Zarossi, unaccustomed to sudden wealth, had placed much of the bank's assets into highly speculative real estate ventures. Now cash reserves were depleted to the point that any loss of confidence on the part of investors, any large demand for money by a creditor—and the entire operation could go under.

There was an opportunity there, Ponzi knew. He just had to figure out how to take advantage of it.

He was pondering the problem a few weeks later when his

thoughts were interrupted one afternoon by a giggle behind him. He turned to see Angelina Zarossi, barely turned seventeen, the eldest of his employer's three children, plump and long-legged.

"Charles," she said, "don't you ever think of anything but profits and interest rates?"

He smiled up from the column of figures that he had been adding, and looked into the girl's mischievous brown eyes. Slowly, he touched the tip of his mustache and ran a hand over his thick hair to slick it handsomely back from his forehead. His voice was soft.

"Yes," he said, "I occasionally think about flirtatious young women, Miss Zarossi."

"Oh," the girl squealed, "I must tell my father what you called me!"

Ponzi watched her flounce giggling through the inner office door. *Let her tell her father I'm interested in her,* he thought. *There's no quicker way to move up here.* He saw Zarossi's door open and pretended to concentrate on his figures, waiting for the booming voice.

"Ponzi! Ponzi, my boy, you've worked long enough this day. Angelina has taken pity on you. Would you be our guest tonight at dinner? My wife makes such a sauce for the macaroni!"

Dinner with Zarossi! Dinner with the president of a bank—a small bank, to be sure, but still a bank! Macaroni drenched in sauce! And only a few months before, he had kept himself from starving by begging for bits of broken macaroni at a New Haven factory!

The memory of the hearty meal at Zarossi's home and the coy glances of Angelina remained with him the next afternoon while he sipped a glass of wine in a crowded cafe. All at once a sharp voice rang through the noise and confusion. He thought he recognized it immediately, and when he turned to see a short, ferret-faced man pushing through the crowd, he knew he was right.

"Carlo! Carlo, old friend!" The man was facing him now, extending a greasy hand. "Carlo Ponsi! It's been five years at least."

Ponzi pulled his own hand away quickly after a brief squeeze. "The name is Charles Ponzi now," he said, emphasizing the anglicized syllables.

"Gone American, huh? I'm sticking with Angelo Salvati, like always. Unless the law is after me."

Laughing, Ponzi was tempted to say, "Like always," but caught himself. "Same old Salvati, I see." He ordered a bottle of wine for the two of them while he studied his old schoolmate from

13

Rome. Five years had not changed the watery eyes, the long nose with its pointed tip, and the white scar from an old knife fight that ran an inch along Salvati's right cheek.

At the same time, Salvati was eying Ponzi's heavy suit, gauging the silk of the tie, searching for a sign of soil on the high celluloid collar. "You're doing all right for yourself, Charlie," he said flatly.

Ponzi shrugged. Of course. Banco Zarossi was one of the fastest-growing financial institutions in all of Canada, he explained, with new branches in Ontario, Alberta, and British Columbia. He himself stood in line to marry the president's daughter and take over the whole thing someday.

Salvati glanced sideways at him. "Someday can be a long time off."

Instantly, Ponzi felt a plan spring full-blown into his mind. There was no need to wait for an eventual "someday." With Salvati's help, he knew how to gain control of Banco Zarossi almost at once. He leaned across the table, lowering his voice.

"Zarossi's in trouble, Angelo. He confided to me last night, but I knew it anyway. A bunch of dimeless promoters and sponges have been buzzing around him, the kind who can smell a sucker faster than a buzzard can sight a corpse."

Salvati grinned. "He's put money in some bad deals?"

"Very bad deals. And a lot of money—a lot from the depositors' accounts. He asked me—imagine!—to speak to my family in Italy to help him raise some cash."

A snort of laughter. "How much?"

"He needs about $50,000—and promised a partnership in the bank."

Salvati choked on his mouthful of wine. "You're giving it to him, I guess?" he sputtered. "All $50,000!"

"I couldn't give him fifty cents, old friend. But if you want to work with me, I know how we can get more than a partnership. We can get the whole damn bank."

Louis Zarossi tapped his fingers nervously on the top of his desk a few days later and surveyed the man Ponzi had brought into his office. An old schoolmate, Charles had said. With wealthy connections in Italy. A man who might be able to help him restore the missing funds before the depositors got wind of what was happening to their money.

"You need $50,000, I understand," Salvati said in a matter-of-fact tone.

A flush of embarrassment spread across the banker's face. He gestured animatedly, "At least that much. When the investments began to go bad, I—er—borrowed from some accounts. I can repay it all, in a few months, but meantime—"

Salvati cut him off with a puff of smoke from the cigar in his thin lips. "I can get you the money, but it will take several weeks for my friends in Italy to send it. And it will cost you ten percent."

"Anything," Zarossi answered. "Anything. But I can't wait that long. I don't want a run on the bank. It would wipe out five years of work."

Salvati seemed to think it over. From the corner of the office, where he leaned casually against the wall, Ponzi said, "Mr. Zarossi's a friend, Angelo. You must have some ideas."

"Hmm," said Salvati. "I know how you could insure yourself while I get the money. It's been done before, at other banks in similar situations, and the risks are small—"

"Tell me," Zarossi urged.

"You merely increase your interest rates for depositors," Salvati said. "Most banks in Montreal are paying two percent or three percent, just as you are now. What if you said that you would pay ten percent—?"

Ponzi answered before Zarossi could open his mouth. "Why, depositors would practically break down our doors with their money!"

"But I don't understand," Zarossi gasped. "We can't pay that much."

"You don't have to," replied Salvati, lighting a fresh cigar. "A lot of people will give you money to send to their relatives in Italy, right? Take the money, tell them you're adding ten percent interest—but don't send it. Use it to pay off your debts. By the time word gets here from Italy that nobody's received any money, you'll have enough cash to send it over. Simply say the first dough must have been stolen in the mails, and make it good."

"Nobody would lose in the long run," Ponzi said quickly. "It's a brilliant plan."

"I—I don't know—" the banker mused.

Salvati shrugged. "It's up to you. I'll contact my friends tonight if you want, and the money will be here within two weeks."

"We'd only have to raise our interest rates during that time, Louis," said Ponzi. "Just long enough to coax in some big deposits."

15

Zarossi chewed his lower lip in silence for a moment, then held out his hand in agreement. He did not see the quick glance that passed between the two visitors in his office. "Mr. Salvati, you must join us for dinner this evening. Charles here can testify to my wifc's cooking!"

"So I've heard," Salvati said. "And I'm anxious to meet the daughter he talks about, too."

Much of the worry had left Zarossi's eyes a few weeks later when he sat in a barroom on St. James Street with two of his close associates. The assets of Banco Zarossi had increased greatly with each passing day, as Salvati and Ponzi (who used the name Bianchi to conceal his connection with the bank) moved through the Italian neighborhood, chatting quietly about the bank that paid its depositors 10 percent interest.

Now Zarossi peered at the letter Salvati placed on the table before him. It was written in a sprawling Italian hand. "I can't read it," the banker said. "It's too dark, 'n I've been drinkin' too much. We're celebratin' 'cause the money's comin'? That's what it says?"

Ponzi refilled Zarossi's glass, then nodded at Salvati to go ahead.

"It's coming, friend, but there's going to be a delay. Maybe a month."

Zarossi, his eyes bleary, stared into the thin face oposite him. "A month? But—"

"That's why we called this emergency meeting, Louis," Ponzi said quickly. "I don't think we can wait that long. Maybe not even a week. Two banks sent messengers yesterday to collect on some checks. They wanted cash. Our credit is about to be shut down, and there are rumors all over the city. I've been practically begging small depositors not to withdraw anything. All we need are a few big ones to follow, and we're in real trouble."

Suddenly there was perspiration on Zarossi's face. "I know," he said softly. "But your friend here—"

Salvati picked up his cue. "This letter from back home gave me an idea. The money is on the way, but we have to stall for time. Zarossi, you ought to get out of Canada right away. If you wait, they'll have you on charges of embezzlement—and if you're in jail, we'll never get things straightened out."

"Jail? But I can't—I haven't—" He was sputtering now, incoherent. "I have a business, a family—"

"Family!" Salvati said loudly. "A lot of good you'll be to them in jail!"

Ponzi reached out to touch the banker's arm. "We have an excellent plan, Louis, one that solves everything. Before you leave, you sign a receipt for the $50,000 loan. That makes Salvati the bank's major creditor. Once you're safely out of the country, he declares you bankrupt. The judge gives him control of the remaining assets of Banco Zarossi."

"And I offer to settle with the other creditors for two cents on the dollar," Salvati said. "We pay off your debts and split the rest fifty-fifty. You'll be a rich man, with enough to live on comfortably the rest of your life."

The bourbon had turned the banker's face redder than usual. "I don't know," he said.

Now Salvati sneered. "Friend, there's no time to argue. You can stay here and go to jail, or clear out and live happily on what's left."

"Louis," Ponzi said, as he saw the hesitation in Zarossi's eyes, "I'll be here to keep an eye on things. And you know how I feel about Angelina. I'll take as good care of your family as you would."

Zarossi turned to him, trying to focus his gaze. "I believe you, Charles. I trust you."

Ponzi fought to keep the grin from appearing. After all, this was supposed to be a sad occasion. But as Salvati pulled some papers from his pocket and began to guide Zarossi's hand across them, it was difficult not to laugh out loud.

The plan appeared to work beautifully. Zarossi disappeared for a few days and then—as an embarrassed Ponzi explained to one angry, suspicious creditor—seemed to have fled to Mexico. Within hours, the bank was closed. Arrest warrants were drawn up. Depositors wrote angry letters, some that threatened harm to Zarossi's wife and children. Auditors began poring over the books of Banco Zarossi, and creditors lined up to file petitions for payment.

"It's going to take a little time, Carlo. But we're going to be rich," said Salvati, chewing on a thick corned beef sandwich, while Ponzi sipped a glass of wine in a cafe on St. Catherine Street.

"I can wait," he replied. "But not too long. You at least have a room of your own. Zarossi's kids are driving me crazy."

Salvati shrugged. "It looks good that you moved in with the family. We don't want Zarossi comin' back up here from Mexico. 'Sides, this way, you get all the macaroni you can eat. And that little Angelina's somethin' nice, too."

"You forget, old friend, that with the bank closed, there's no money coming into the family. I'm out of a job myself. And God knows how long it will take for things to cool down, for the court to start releasing the bank's assets."

"We'll just have to hang on until they do. But you're right 'bout the law working slow."

"Good thing it does," Ponzi smiled. "Otherwise there would be more bank executives hanging from tree limbs than smoking dollar cigars behind mahogany desks."

A laugh escaped Salvati's lips. "I've been thinkin' of a way to get some cash to tide us over," he said. "What about tapping the branch banks before the courts grab them?"

Ponzi slapped his high forehead. "Christ," he whistled. "I should have thought of that. As a major creditor, you could go out and demand payment at once—or else threaten to close them up."

Salvato protested. He didn't want to leave Montreal, he said. He spoke no French, as Ponzi did, and he was not familiar with the officials at the branches. Besides, such a trip would take a month. His testimony might be needed at the bankruptcy hearings meanwhile.

"You go, Carlo," he said. "Say you're my agent. Get whatever you can to reduce the debt Zarossi owes me."

Ponzi thought it over swiftly. "It would do me good to get away from those kids for a month."

"And by the time you're back, I should have my hands on Banco Zarossi!"

"I could catch the train Monday morning."

Salvati nodded quickly. "The sooner the better. How's the cash situation? You'll need tickets—"

"And hotel expenses."

"You'll need a couple of hundred, at least. You can't walk into a bank and demand money if you look like a tramp. Any ideas?"

Ponzi smoothed his mustache thoughtfully. "I have a check," he said.

"Whose?"

"Founier, the shipping broker at Canadian Warehousing. I've called on him for Zarossi. One day he left his office and I tore a check from the back of his book. For a rainy day, who knows? It's on the Hochelaga Bank."

Salvati's eyes were gleaming. "It's Saturday evening, and there's a Hochelaga branch down the street that's open late. Make out the check to cash for—what? $400?—and I'll cash it. You'll be gone Monday before the check even gets to the main office. Nobody will know until the end of the month when your broker pal gets his statement."

Grinning, Ponzi glanced through the dirty window of the cafe. Outside, the sun was going down in a cloudless blue sky. "Well," he said, "it's not a rainy day, but let's go."

He was carefully folding a pair of new trousers into the small steamer trunk he had purchased Saturday night when there was a knock on the door of his room. Ponzi dipped his hand into his vest pocket, taking out the new expensive watch he had also bought. *Angelina,* he thought. It was 11:30 Monday morning, and he had less than a half-hour before the train left. Not much time to bid that pesky girl a lingering farewell.

The knock came again, harder. Hurriedly, Ponzi opened the door. Two men were standing outside.

He had seen enough policemen to know these were plain-clothesmen even before the taller one flashed a badge inside his coat. "What is this?" he said as the men hurried into the room. Already, one had placed a huge hand on the stack of dollar bills atop Ponzi's dresser. The other man tossed the new clothing out of the trunk.

"What is this?" Ponzi repeated.

Now the tall policeman was staring at him, grinning with a wide smile. "You're under arrest, Charles Ponzi. You'll come with us."

Ponzi, looking up at him, had no intention of challenging the towering officer's order. But there was a question that had to be asked even though he thought he already knew the answer.

"What is the charge?"

The shorter policeman replied at once. "Forgery's prob'ly as good as anythin'. Looks like there's plenty of evidence."

They hurried him out of the room and down the stairs. At the bottom, Angelina, her eyes wide with fright, stood with her mother.

"Charlie," she called as the two detectives hustled him toward the door. "Who's going to take care of us?"

Despite the pain from the strong hands gripping his arms, Ponzi smiled. "Maybe Salvati!" he called over his shoulder. "He seems to have taken care of everything else!"

From his cell in Canada's St. Vincent de Paul Penitentiary, Ponzi wrote his mother a letter in late October, 1908. "Dearest mother," he began, "your son has at last stumbled on excellent fortune in this country. I have taken a position as special assistant to the warden of this institution, who can well use my fluency in language in conversing with some of the inmates. It is a three-year contract, darling mother, and during that time I shall not have to worry where my next meal or warm bed is to come from . . . ."

He knew there was little to do other than try to smile at the situation. In prison, at least, immigrants and native-born citizens alike had equal opportunity to succeed or fail. There was no favoritism, no prospect for advancement other than what could be earned from a graft-minded guard. Bankers, laborers, thieves—all had to start at the bottom and work their way up.

"Three years! Three years for forgin' a $400 check! Ponzi, that's a helluva sentence."

Ponzi put down the heavy mallet he was using to pound lumps of rock into gravel, and wiped his forehead with a dirty bandanna. Inside the rock shed, the air was so grey with dust that he could hardly see the figure of Louis Cassullo next to him.

"It's a helluva sentence when you figure that bankers who steal thousands can get out of here in six months, Cassullo."

"Damn! 'N I got three years for liftin' a few hundred green-backs from a lumberyard I worked in!"

Ponzi swung the mallet angrily as a guard glanced in through the open door. "The Crown's justice isn't any better than that of Italy or the States," he said over the noise of other hammers all around.

Cassullo coughed through the dust cloud. "How'd you get caught?"

"I can't swear to it," Ponzi puffed between swings, "but I think a 'pal' turned me in. I'm sure of it—enough to make me plenty wary about working with partners in the future."

Cassullo turned to look at him. "Maybe you just ain't had luck pickin' the right partner." His gaze caught the guard at the shed door, and he set to work industriously. "Let's talk about it—after we're finished making all these big rocks into little ones."

"I tell you, Cassullo, if they ever let me out of here, I'll be practiced enough to flatten all of British Columbia smoother than a pancake!"

"I ain't interested in your talent at this kind o' thing. You're a man with a mind for bigger jobs, Ponzi. I bet you was after more 'n $400 with that check, too."

Ponzi's grin spread slowly across his face. Flattered at Cassullo's recognition of his style, he related the story of Banco Zarossi in detail. "Then Salvati decided to cut both of us out of the deal—Zarossi first, and then me. I should have figured him out sooner. But there was so much cash involved—waiting for the two of us—that I forgot how greedy some people are. I'll remember next time."

"And now you're in here and he's back in Montreal with the money."

Ponzi shook his head. "I don't think so. They kept me in jail there for a couple of months—what a place that was! Filthy, infested with lice! I pulled the old trick. Curled up in a corner of the bed and chewed on a towel. When the guards came, I tossed a fit and got transferred to the hospital, to a nice, quiet bed and good food."

Cassullo's narrow eyes widened in appreciation. "*You* can get away with that kind o' thing, Ponzi. You're an actor."

Unable to resist an audience, Ponzi went on with his recital even though he distrusted the other convict's fawning tone. "While I was waiting for my trial, I heard the court refused to turn over the bank to Salvati. He headed out west with whatever he could lay his hands on, and I don't think I'll see him again."

"You could kill him, eh?"

"With one hand!" And he smashed a handy stone with a demonstrative swing.

Except for an occasional meeting in the mess hall or exercise yard, Ponzi saw little of Cassullo in the next months. During that time, his affability won him a promotion to a clerk's job in the prison blacksmith shop. Later he was shifted to the chief engineer's office, and soon afterward to the prison records department. On the humid morning of July 13, 1910, he learned that he had been pardoned.

When he ran into Cassullo at supper, he couldn't resist the impulse to tell him about it. "The warden walked right up to me with this paper and says, 'Charlie, I want you to make a copy of this right away.' Well, I've typed dozens of them, and I knew what it was—a pardon from the governor general's office. Then I get down to the name—and it's mine, friend. It's mine."

"Sonofabitch, Charlie! When you gettin' out?" The jealousy in Cassullo's voice was evident.

"Saturday. It'll be twenty months."

"Where you goin' to head? Back to Montreal?"

"For the present. Christ, I'll get out of here with a suit from the tailor shop and five dollars. Where else can I go with that? It's going to be mean starting all over again, like a greenhorn off the boat."

"You'll have trouble gettin' work in Montreal. Less you want t' change your name again." His eyes narrowed with an idea. "Listen, if you want to head back down to the States, I got a friend that maybe can help you out. Name's Yacovelli. He's got some kind of labor agency. Puts men on at the railroads and the lumber camps."

Ponzi nodded. "I think Zarossi used to send men to him. The bank would keep their salary on deposit while they were away on the jobs."

"Look him up, then. And tell him Cassullo knows you. Maybe someday you can pay back the favor. Maybe we can work together?"

Ponzi had shrugged, thinking that Cassullo as a partner might make his relationship with Salvati look good in retrospect. Still, he presented himself at the office of Alfredo Yacovelli a week later. The only work he had been able to find in Montreal was washing dishes and sweeping out stores. There was nothing to be lost by following up Cassullo's tip.

Yacovelli eyed him suspiciously. "Hell, son, you ain't tall enough to swing a hammer or cut a tree!"

"I thought maybe a camp might need a timekeeper. I'm good with figures. Or an interpreter? I speak four languages."

The old man shook his head. "I got no calls for that sort of work—good pay, and no muscles needed. There ain't many jobs like that. 'Course you could go down to one of the camps and see what they got."

Ponzi nodded. "I'd do just that if I had the price of a railroad ticket. Cassullo thought you might be able to help out, otherwise I'd—"

There was a gleam of interest in the other's red-rimmed eyes. "Cassullo sent you?"

Ponzi stared back at him evenly. "We spent the last two years together."

Now the old man was talking quickly, confidentially. "You speak English and Italian? I got a job for you, then." He dug some crumpled bills from a shirt pocket. "Here's the cash for a ticket to Norwood. There's a camp there, right across the border. On tomorrow's train, I've got five Italians who are supposed to show up farther south. You take 'em in hand and make sure they change trains at Norwood. That's all. They don't speak English, and they ain't too bright, so just keep an eye on 'em. You get the ticket and twenty bucks."

He held out the bills, but Ponzi did not reach for them. "The job sounds so simple, it should be worth more," he said. The old man pressed his lips into a knowing grin, and added a ten-dollar bill to the others. Still Ponzi did not take the money.

"All right," Yacovelli said, wearily adding another ten. "Take this, and keep those guys quiet."

The five men, seemingly frightened and confused despite their obvious physical size and strength, were huddled in a corner of the depot when Ponzi arrived. In painstaking Italian, he explained that they were simply to follow him aboard the train and sit quietly. When he handed his ticket to the conductor, he said, they were to do the same. The men, smiling now, agreed.

Crowded into a dusty coach, the group stared silently through the oily windows as the train jolted southward. At noon, it ground to a halt at the last station on the Canadian side of the border and remained motionless for long minutes—long enough for an immigration inspector to ask Ponzi a few brief questions about the men. Then he waved the train across the border into the U.S. At Moers Junction, New York, it stopped.

"All right, you wops! On your feet!"

The Italians did not understand the words, but the tone was clear. Ponzi looked down the aisle to see the inspector striding toward them. "On your feet! Let's go! Off the train!"

The workmen were standing now, talking excitedly in rapid Italian, already following the inspector. Ponzi started to protest, but it was too late. He herded the group along. The inspector led the way to a wooden shack near the station. Behind a cheap desk sat a round-faced man wearing steel-rim spectacles. He ruffled a sheaf of papers busily, then looked up at Ponzi and the group.

"You've brought these men into the U.S. in violation of the immigration laws," he said.

"I did nothing of the kind. They came of their own accord. We were all merely traveling on the same train."

"None of you has a permit to enter."

Ponzi's face reflected true misunderstanding. "I did not know a permit was necessary. I left the U.S. for Canada several years ago and went back and forth a half-dozen times. Never was I asked for a permit."

"Maybe you've been out of touch," the official said. "The fact is that you have illegally entered the U.S."

Ponzi searched his memory for phrases from some of the lawbooks that he had studied in the library of St. Vincent de Paul. "I concede nothing," he snapped. "We were interviewed by the inspector on the Canadian side of the border. The train was not in motion. If we were inadmissible for any reason, it was his duty to tell us."

"We don't need you, Mr.—" and he looked at the papers before him—"Ponzi, to tell us our duties."

Now, Ponzi drew himself to his full height. Behind him, the five Italians were restless, muttering. "Your man led us into a violation, knowing that we were ignorant of the facts, so he can make a record for himself!" He turned, as if to walk angrily from the shack. "Well, I have no earthly use for that sort of public official! *He's* the one who should be charged with smuggling aliens into this country!"

The jail at Plattsburg, New York, was a fraction the size of the Canadian penitentiary where Ponzi had spent the last twenty months, but it was every bit as uncomfortable. Two months passed, during which he ate, slept, and read and reread old magazines. In late October, he met with a boyish assistant U.S. district attorney. "It's my sworn duty to preserve the constitution—" the young man began.

"Preserve it! Christ, it's been preserved so long it's pickled!"

The lawyer looked pained. "It'll be best if you plead guilty," he said.

24

"What? I will, like hell!"

"Look, the men you brought in are in custody as evidence against you. If they testify, they'll be permitted to remain in this country. You've got a record, so the judge is not going to take your word against the inspector's."

Ponzi thought it over for a moment. "But if I'm convicted, I won't be any worse off than if I plead guilty—and there's always a chance I'll get off."

"If you make us go to trial—*Charlie?*—the judge won't be inclined to leniency. We've got enough other business, important cases, to worry about." He held out a pack of Sweet Caporals and lit the one Ponzi took. "The penalty is two years and $1,000 fine for each alien. You could get ten years and $5,000."

"And if I plead guilty?"

"I'd recommend a fine. It could be as little as fifty dollars."

The little Italian laughed, looked down at his filthy uniform, saw the dirt on his delicate hands. "I couldn't pay *twenty dollars*!"

"Then you'd have to work it out. It would mean a month in jail. Probably the time you've already put in here would count."

Ponzi shoved back his chair. He walked to the window and looked out at the autumn-brown New York countryside. "All right. I'll take you at your word. Plead me guilty."

Before the judge less than a week later, Ponzi watched the young attorney pass some papers over the bench. A few low whispers followed. The judge squinted at the prisoner before him.

"Two years and $500," he said.

And Charles Ponzi, along with four other federal prisoners and a pair of deputy marshals, suddenly found himself on his way to the United States Penitentiary in Atlanta, Georgia, where he was to spend twenty-four hours a day in company with the best criminal brains from all over America. It was there that he learned that there existed no shortage of ideas on how to make money in the land of opportunity. The trick was merely to select the good idea, the best idea, the safest idea, from all the others.

Uncertain as his prospects were, Ponzi was at least confident that his view of himself as a dashing figure—diminutive, perhaps, but dashing—was shared by his twenty-year-old bride, that she seldom saw him in any light but an admiring one.

"Did you say something, Rose?" he asked, without turning away from his reflection in the glass as he carefully adjusted his necktie and smoothed his hair before the wavering bathroom mirror of their cramped apartment on Powder House Boulevard in Somerville. Over his shoulder he saw Rose brush her hand against the jet-black mass of curls that framed her round and pretty face. Ponzi smiled at the gesture. Rose, he felt certain, once again was wondering if she should cut her hair short—the way that film actress, Madge Kennedy, had taken to wearing it.

He stepped out of the bathroom and put on his suitcoat. "Leave your hair long," he said in amusement, repeating a familiar argument. "It's like Lillian Gish's in *Broken Blossoms*, and I thought you loved that picture." If she cut it, he continued with a laugh, next she would be smoking cigarettes as so many young women were doing. And then, at the beach, she would want to wear a one-piece bathing suit without shoes or stockings.

He had to grin at Rose. Her heritage—Italian, Catholic, and Bostonian—would hardly permit her to imagine such offenses. As the breakfast dishes were cleared away, he thought how lucky he was to have this patient and unquestioning young woman as his wife. It was her nine-hours-daily job as an apprentice bookkeeper that was sustaining the two of them just now, and yet she also handled the housework both dutifully and cheerfully. Rose would have to be repaid for her efforts and her loyalty, thought Ponzi a few moments later as the two of them hurried to catch a trolley. He would have to find some money quickly.

Not only for Rose, of course. The telephone bill at his small office was two months overdue. He was behind in his rent. To succeed in any business enterprise, he would have to have a skeleton staff of some sort—an office boy, a girl to answer the phone—and that required at least enough cash to pay the barest of salaries. When he had first conceived *The Trader's Guide*, there had been enough money on hand to hire the two employees, but they had been let go after two fruitless weeks. Now, Ponzi sat alone each day in the empty office, staring out the window at City Hall across the street, and scratching incomprehensible figures on the lined yellow pad that lay on his second-hand desk.

While he and Rose waited on a windy corner for the trolley, he bought a morning newspaper. The single column of Stock Exchange transactions made him shake his head in mock discouragement. "Look at that," he said, as much to himself as to his wife. "General Motors has gone up to 180. Steel's up to 100. Whoever said a recession would follow the war sure didn't know what he was talking about."

Rose stood silent, near him. It would have done no good to ask Ponzi what the numbers meant, or how he expected to profit by them. His ready answer would inevitably be the statement that complicated business maneuvers could never be understood by a young and pretty girl.

It was obvious as Ponzi studied the newspaper that nothing besides the financial news had meaning for him. Other men might read about the riots that the Bolsheviks were stirring up all over the country. Or about the Klan lynchings in the South. They might turn to the sports pages to learn of the young baseball pitcher, George Ruth, who had been sold by the Red Sox to New York. They might argue with the editorials berating the entire Boston police force for having gone out on strike, leaving the city wide open to thieves until Governor Coolidge ordered volunteers and vigilantes into action. But there was little profit to be made from such news, Charles Ponzi knew. He folded the paper and placed his hand at his wife's elbow to help her up the trolley step, almost regretting that he had to tear his gaze from the reports of financial dealings in New York and around the world. *Money*, he thought. *Everything revolves around money.*

His wife, he was sure, was aware that she was vitally important to him. As important as his beloved mother, Imelda Ponsi, in far-off Italy. But was either as important—more important—than money itself? That was a question.

Ponzi strode swiftly along the streets of the business district on his way to his office. He had wasted enough time trying to tap his wife's relatives for the funds needed to start up *The Trader's*

27

Guide. The newspaper in his hand fairly burst with details of overnight millionaires. Landlords were profiteering from exorbitant rents as the doughboys came back from Europe, married, and set up homes. Prices on everything—milk, steak, clothing—were shooting upward, and manufacturers were raking in the money. And Ford, whose ugly Model Ts were everywhere, had begun with what Ponzi had right now—only an idea.

The thoughts raced through his mind, over and over, as he crumpled the newspaper. In front of the Hanover Trust Company, he paused long enough to throw it into the gutter and take several deep breaths. When he pushed through the bank's door, he appeared completely at ease, as if he had just stepped from a chauffeur-driven limousine, rather than having walked nearly two miles.

"You can tell Mr. Chmielinski that Mr. Ponzi is here," he said to the pinch-faced assistant outside the president's office.

"Er—uh—does he know you? I mean, you have an appointment?"

"Charles Ponzi needs no appointment, I'm sure."

"Mr. Ponzi?" said the Polish bank president a moment later, his eyes wary. "I don't believe I know you."

"There's no reason that you would know me," he began. "I've had a small checking account here for several months. To be frank, you probably consider it more of a pain in the neck than an account." His soft laugh met with no response. "Almost every day I've had to drop by at nine in the morning to cover checks I've written the night before. I seem to have kept ahead of your bookkeepers, all right, but I must admit it's been close at times."

Chmielinski said nothing.

This was no Zarossi, Ponzi realized. No fellow countryman, waiting to greet him warmly.

Ponzi took his notations for *The Trader's Guide* from his breast pocket. "If I could just have a minute—" He talked swiftly but it seemed an eternity before he said, "And there is no conceivable way it can fail to make money. All I need to get things rolling is $2,000."

The banker's voice was a growl, incredulous: "That's what you've come for? A loan of $2,000? With what security?"

"My personal note. In six months—three months if you prefer—the loan will be repaid with whatever interest you require."

Chmielinski began shuffling some papers on his desk. "Sorry, but I can't approve anything like that. It's the bank's policy to accommodate our depositors whenever we can, but lending $2,000 on your word, Mr.—uh—*Ponzi*, yes? It's out of the question. Good day."

As if by prearranged signal, the office door opened. The young assistant, showing the way out, had a cocky grin on his face. Ponzi fought back the urge to whirl and mutter a threat—something like, "I'll have you birds eating out of my hand someday."

He hurried down the street toward the Niles Building, quickly regaining his jaunty step and wide smile. Al Ciullo was sweeping the sidewalk in front of his jewelry shop on the ground floor. He waved his broom in greeting.

"Ponzi, you're looking well."

A nonchalant shrug. "Why not? I've just been discussing a loan with Chmielinski at the Hanover."

"The Pole? Doing business with you?" The jeweler's eyes were questioning, anxious for the details. "If he's backing one of your schemes, you must have something."

Ponzi stepped around him and started up the narrow flight of stairs to his office. "It's something, all right," he said. "But Chmielinski has made me swear not to let anyone else in on it until the papers are signed and sealed." He glanced back down the stairs. "By the way, Al, those bracelets and rings you loaned the cash on? Don't let anyone have them. I'll be taking them back from you any day now." At the landing, he called back loudly, "Next week, for certain."

He opened the door—its glass panel covered with lettering that read *Charles Ponzi, Export & Import* and *The Boston Advertising & Publishing Co.*—and stepped into the empty office.

Perhaps there was still room on the panel for a few more names. If he rented the desk space to one person, maybe two—there would be money enough to cover the rent. True, the door might look like a directory, but there were young lawyers around, and tradesmen, who would take space if the price were low enough. And, thought Ponzi, what their rental money would cost in dignity would be offset by the gain in peace of mind. *Money! Money makes for peace of mind.*

He moved through the outer office to the large back room. There his desk waited for him in blank expectation. On its surface stood an upright telephone—which had rung only a few times since the day it was installed—and several sheets of correspondence covered with a thin layer of dust. Ponzi hung his jacket on the clothestree in the corner, then pulled the sturdy, uncomfortable wooden chair to the desk and sat down. Across the street, shadowy but important-looking figures moved behind the windows of City Hall. He forced his gaze away from them. No doubt they were politicians and businessmen, conniving, bribing one another for favors, talking big money. Big money.

He looked at the letters in the thin stack with reluctance. One, he knew all too well, was in his mother's faint, wavering handwriting. It had arrived nearly a week before, and he ached to answer it, to tell her how marvelously her only son was doing in America, how he soon would send for her and see her again, for the first time in nearly seventeen years. But how could he write any more lies? Any more "soon" and "perhaps" and "if only"? *The Trader's Guide!* If only he had the few thousand dollars he needed to launch it!

Forget it, Ponzi told himself. The *Guide* was a dead issue now. The trick was to move on, to find something else. He had never lacked for ideas. *Christ, ideas were cheap enough!* His cellmate in Atlanta, a counterfeiter named Ignazio Lupo, had had plenty of ideas—enough to get him a thirty-year sentence. Lupo had wanted to teach Ponzi the ins and outs of every violent crime short of murder, but had found him a reluctant pupil. Atlanta had a reputation as the Biltmore, the Ritz-Carlton of prisons, and Ponzi had prowled through it for a more respectable breed of criminal.

He found one in the person of Charles W. Morse, an investment banker who had been sentenced to fifteen years for misappropriation of funds. An Ohio political boss, Harry M. Daugherty, had served as Morse's lawyer, reportedly for a fee well above $100,000. And the story had it that Morse would receive a check for a cool million upon his release from prison—as a token of appreciation by several judges, Congressmen, and members of the cabinet who preferred not to have certain information made public during his trial. Morse did not even need the money, according to the rumors; he had another seven or eight million dollars tucked away in various bank accounts and safety deposit boxes.

Small wonder that the illustrious convict seemed relaxed at all times, that he seemed to delight in the clerical job that gave him the run of the prison, that he mixed well with prisoners on any level and was always liberal and friendly. Sometimes when they played chess together, Morse would give Ponzi advice in sure, positive tones: "It's all a matter of keeping your sights high, my boy. There are millionaires outside who make mistakes every day, but their sights are high and when things go right, the money is there to cover the errors.

"Always have a goal, Charlie, my boy. A goal that keeps getting bigger. If you think a thousand dollars is enough the first time around, an hour later you'll realize that you might as well go for ten thousand. In another hour, you'll see that you might as well go for ten million. The risk is the same, isn't it? If you have the nerve to go for the first bundle, you have the nerve to go all the way."

Ponzi knew that he had nerve, all right. Charles W. Morse might hobnob regularly with Wall Street bigwigs, he told himself, but he did not have one ounce more assurance or pride in his own capabilities than Charles Ponzi. If Morse could pull in seven million, or eight million, or whatever the real figure was, Ponzi could, too. Someday, he would prove it to them all—to the bankers and the brokers, to the rabble fresh off the immigration ships, to the stupid Canadian police and their equally stupid cousins in the U.S.

But, most of all, he would prove it to his mother—thin, greying, tiny, but oh, so beautiful still, back in Italy. Someday, someday, he would send for her, mail her a prepaid ticket for the finest stateroom on a transatlantic steamer, along with a thousand dollars cash for a new wardrobe and incidental expenses. Charles Ponzi's mother would come to America like a queen.

In his silent office on the second floor of the Niles Building above busy, narrow School Street, Ponzi searched his brain for the big idea. It was there, he knew. *The big idea.* For his mother.

For Rose, too. Of course. And her slow-thinking, suspicious father and brothers who had refused to let him show them how to turn their failing fruit-peddling business around. All he had to do to show all of them was . . . *find . . . the . . . big . . . idea.*

He sent his thoughts back into the past, trying to remember every syllable that Charles Morse had spoken. But nothing fresh came to the surface. Morse had not been in Atlanta long enough for Ponzi to probe him deeply on the techniques of Wall Street stock manipulation. A fifteen-year sentence! That was all that had been handed down to Morse, who had made off with millions! But dissatisfied with even that, the wily financier had spent a fraction of his spare time each day eating bits of soap from the washrooms. It was not long before he had fallen ill, was certified by three doctors to be in a hopeless condition, and pronounced in imminent danger of death. Wheels had begun turning, and a pardon—delivered virtually on Morse's deathbed—had come down from President Taft. It brought about a miracle: Morse had promptly recovered and lived for a number of years afterward!

With the money, Ponzi thought. Morse had lived, *with* the money. A pardon from the President of the United States—*that* was really thinking big, that was keeping your sights high. Morse, sent to Atlanta to serve fifteen years, was out in less than two. While he—Ponzi—had actually served an extra month on top of his two-year term in lieu of paying his $500 fine.

31

When he had been released, Ponzi found few opportunities to set his sights at higher levels. In Birmingham, he ran across a friend who was operating a small infirmary and cheating insurance companies on medical payments for miners with fake injuries. "Penny-ante stuff," Ponzi said, and moved on to New Orleans. There he teamed with a minister of sorts to organize a "secret society" that told local newspaper editors it would fight criminal elements that were terrorizing the business community. The mayor and city council were asked to provide $10,000 to help the society's efforts, but then word leaked out that the organization had only two members. The minister fled in one direction; Ponzi—working as a signpainter—in another.

The School Street office was growing warmer by the moment as the morning sun forced its way through the rain-smeared window. Ponzi pushed his chair away from the desk and turned to strain the window open a few inches. A slight breeze slipped through the narrow crack and fluttered the papers on his desk. One letter slid forward, dropped over the edge to the floor. Ponzi glanced disinterestedly down at it, then turned his attention to the street below where several delivery men and messenger boys were laughing, clustered around a balky four-passenger Maxwell. Its driver seemed unable to cope with the intricacies of the vehicle's folding top.

I'll have a closed limousine, Ponzi thought, *as large as any war profiteer's.*

The driver had managed to get the top down, and pumped the car's self-starter. The motor caught with a sudden growl, and the sound of the gasoline engine struck a chord in Ponzi's memory. An engine like it—a nonexistent engine—had figured prominently in another unsuccessful scheme in Blocton, Alabama. He had worked there as an interpreter and part-time accountant for local merchants who dealt with the community of Italian miners. In a short time, he had professed to have come up with a plan to provide the growing town with both electric light and running water. He explained his idea at a town meeting: A gasoline engine at the top of a hill would pump water from a nearby creek and also operate a small dynamo for electric current.

"I have no figures to submit at this time as to the cost of the plant, the piping and the wiring," he had told the respectfully silent crowd. "I have no money to pay for any of it. What I propose to do is to get an estimate of the cost. Then I will form a corporation and ask each member of this fine community to subscribe to one or more shares of its preferred stock—enough to pay for the cost. For my services, I intend to retain a controlling interest of the common stock. The town council can set rates for water and electric current as soon as I am able to submit figures for the running cost of the plant and amortization of the preferred stock. The rates should leave a reasonable margin of profit for the common stock. I ask that a resolution be put to a vote of the meeting, endorsing my activities and directing the town council to give me a deed to the land needed . . ."

The speech was impressive, Ponzi was certain. Charles Morse would have been proud of him. There even had been a line in it about his being "desirous to promote the welfare of the community." Of course, he had added with an easy grin that he felt he was "entitled to some returns for my time, energy and service."

And it had almost worked. The resolution had been passed. It looked momentarily as if the town council would acquire the needed property from several owners, and would give it—free—to the literate newcomer. Then, as a landowner, he would be in a position to sell his shares in the Ponzi Power and Water Company! Obtaining estimates, drawing up engineering plans, construction of a practical plant—it might take years, Ponzi knew—but, meanwhile, he would be in control of both land and money!

It all had ended with a sputter. The owner of the desired acreage on the hilltop refused to sell. If a power plant were going to be built on his property, he decided, why shouldn't *he* own the controlling share of it? After all, the only thing this young Ponzi fellow was putting up was the idea! The landowner and the town council got together, and—without including a certain third party—began calling in engineers to survey the feasibility of the plan.

Now, eight years after the abortive power-plant episode, the landowner's sarcastic voice came back to Charles Ponzi, as clearly as the sound of the Maxwell engine in the street below. "After all, the only thing Ponzi is putting up is the idea!"

The fools! Didn't the fools realize the idea is everything? Ford's assembly line. Edison's phonograph. Bell's AT & T. And all the other schemes that had led to millions. The idea, first—and then the money to turn it into reality. Someone with the idea starts things rolling, and everyone benefits. But the idea—first!

Ponzi slammed the window shut, muffling the engine sound below. Again, absently, he sat at the desk. Again he glanced at the few sheets of correspondence, seeing and yet not seeing the inquiries about advertising rates in his unborn publication, *The Trader's Guide*. There was an idea somewhere. He *felt* it. It had not appeared in Blocton, Alabama. Nor shortly afterward in Mobile, where he worked briefly as a librarian at a medical college. Nor in

Pensacola, Florida, where he took a job as a painter on a coastal steamer, just for the free transportation, just to be going somewhere where opportunity might lie. Nor in Texas, where he handled foreign correspondence for the Wichita Falls Motor Truck Company, owned by Kemp & Kell, two invisible industrialists who seemed to own half the town.

Wait. In Wichita Falls, he remembered, there had *almost* been the idea. On weekends, several times, he had joined a truckload of company clerks to picnic on fat bullfrogs netted in the numerous prairie pools. Capturing the frogs frequently meant that the men went wading knee-deep into water which gleamed with iridescent patches of floating oil. *Oil!* It was inches underground, practically in plain view. The land that could have been snapped up for five dollars an acre then, in 1916, was worth *millions* now, only a few years later.

It seemed that he had been in the School Street office for an eternity. The afternoon sun, so bright not long before, now was blocked by neighboring buildings, and the office air was shadow blue. Ponzi did not bother to turn on the large overhead light in its dusty yellow globe. As it was, there was no money for the long-overdue electric bill. He sighed, uncharacteristically, and shoved the stack of letters to the center of the desk again, placing it precisely in the spot where he had placed it the afternoon before. Out of the corner of his eye, he glimpsed the single sheet that had blown to the floor. With a grunt, he bent down and caught the edge of the page. It was a letter from Spain, with a small scrap of yellow paper pinned to one side.

Before Ponzi straightened in his chair, the familiar smile was already spreading across his face.

He had the big idea.

A bored clerk lounged behind the wide expanse of counter, too lazy to care that the elbows of his shirt were turning black from the fresh newsprint on the sports pages of the *Boston American.* Why bother to roll his sleeves higher—the cuffs, at least, were held halfway up his forearms by elastic bands looped over them—when it was late in the afternoon, and City Hall would close in a few moments. The shirt, worn two days already, would go into the weekend's wash.

Someone's heels clicked on the marble floor, the sound growing in volume, obviously approaching him—but the clerk did not look up. Idly, he turned a page and continued to read. Ordinarily, he would not have been studying the results of distant horse races and college football contests; it took something like Jack Dempsey's third-round knockout of heavyweight champion Jess Willard the previous July to interest him in sports at all. But, on this dreadfully dull day in the registrar's office, he had already scoured every other page of the newspaper. The noise of footsteps stopped, and the large room was still.

Perhaps, the young man thought, *if I ignore him, he will go away. I could say we're ready to close, and he should come back tomorrow.*

"Ah-hum," said Charles Ponzi, forcefully clearing his throat—and vocally forcing the clerk to raise his eyes. "This *is* the registration department?"

The youth straightened to his full height so as to look down at the dapper figure before him. *One of those self-important Eye-talians,* he thought. "Oh—excuse me, sir," he said. "I didn't hear you come in."

35

Ponzi smiled in all-too-obvious disbelief. "I need a registration blank," he said.

Reluctantly, the clerk folded his newspaper. "What sort of blank?" he asked.

"For a business venture," Ponzi replied. "A partnership."

Breathing a sigh of relief, the young man turned to open a steel drawer. It was simple to register a partnership. Thank heavens, it wasn't a corporation with all those legal certificates and red tape. He slid the form out of the drawer and across the counter in a continuous motion.

"If you can complete it immediately, sir," he hinted, "it can be filed before closing time."

Ponzi smiled disarmingly at him. "You read my mind. I really don't want to waste a minute."

He took the pen from the inkwell and bent over the counter. With a firm, broad stroke—on the line where the form asked for the name of the partnership venture—he wrote *Securities Exchange Company.* The name had come to him in a burst of inspiration as he crossed School Street from his office to the municipal building. *Securities Exchange Company.* It was perfect. It described his new business reasonably accurately and sounded unmistakably official.

He paused over the next line of the form. "Is there a problem, sir?" the clerk asked, noticing that Ponzi had stopped writing.

"No, no, I just want to be sure of the spelling—here, on the names of my partners." *Partners*? He had not been prepared for the question, planning only to list himself as manager of the Securities Exchange Company. *Partners? Damn!*

It would have been simple enough to start up as the Charles Ponzi Company without notification of any kind to anyone. But who would invest in a company named for a man known by too many Bostonians to have failed in several previous business efforts? Incorporation of the Securities Exchange Company would have been safer than a partnership arrangement—the head of a corporation would not be personally liable for its debts—but Ponzi lacked the legal skill to draw up the articles of incorporation himself. And he also lacked the funds to pay a lawyer for his services.

"Might I suggest, sir, that you might want to take the form to your attorney? You could bring it in tomorrow."

Ponzi flashed his smile. "I have some advice for you, young man, should you ever choose to go into business of a confidential kind. The lawyers you can trust, you will not be able to afford;

36

those you can afford, you will not be able to trust. Until you have the legalities all locked up, stay away from lawyers—or they'll steal you blind."

With a flourish, he added two names as his partners. Under his own name, he wrote *John S. Dondero, 77 Dexter St., Medford, Mass.* And beneath that, he wrote *Guglielmo Bertollotti, Parma, Italy.*

"There you are," he said, handing the page across the counter. He watched carefully while the clerk checked it over. As the young man wrote in the date and signed his own name as a witness, Ponzi chuckled at how the names of his "partners" had popped into his mind. John S. Dondero, his wife's uncle, was the only person he knew in the area who had money; and, should the Securities Exchange Company run up any debts, well, Uncle John might just have to be stuck with them. As for Bertollotti, he had been a boyhood friend in Parma, a ruffian whose brute strength had saved them both several times when Ponzi's fast tongue failed to talk their way out of difficult—and criminal—situations. Ponzi had not thought of Bertollotti in nearly twenty years! His old friend was probably dead by now, strangled by a member of the Black Hand or shot down by the police. *Well,* he thought as the clerk extended his hand and collected the fifty cents registration fee, *if Bertollotti is dead, he's perfect as a silent partner.*

His receipt folded carefully in his breast pocket, Ponzi hurried outside. It was nearly five o'clock, and he would have to move fast to catch the last mail pickup at the box on the corner.

But there should be a moment of celebration, he thought. After all, the Securities Exchange Company now was officially in existence. It had little other than a name and an address, a manager, two unknowing partners (one perhaps among the departed), and some inexpensive office furniture. But it existed, Charles Ponzi's latest brainchild—and its future had as much potential as Carnegie's first steel plant or Rockefeller's initial oil well. Celebration was called for, and celebration there would be.

Charles Ponzi decided to buy himself a fresh, full pack of cigarettes.

He had gone nearly a week now without smoking, not through any exercise of willpower, but because he knew that fifteen cents laid out for a pack of Murads might well leave him without carfare one evening. But the money could be spared now—even though his wallet contained only a few dollars to last until Rose was paid on Friday. There would soon be many bills, large ones, in it, he felt certain. So many that the cracked and dry leather would bulge and stretch. Yes, he would celebrate with a pack of Murads today, but he soon would use dollar bills to light thick black cigars from Havana!

Still, he passed the pharmacist's where most of the City Hall employees bought their cigarettes and headed for the United Cigar outlet in the next block. No sense wasting money at this stage of the game—and although the United Cigar Stores charged the same fifteen cents for Murads as other places, they gave with each pack a coupon good for various trinkets or discounts on future purchases. Besides, it was never too early to let a friend know that Charles Ponzi was onto something big.

"Good afternoon, Vincenza!" he called as he came through the front door. "A pack of Murads—and make sure they're fresh!" He flipped a dollar easily onto the counter.

The shopkeeper laughed and held up a hand of protest. "Have I ever sold you a stale pack, Ponzi?"

"No, I admit that. But we both know why, don't we?"

The proprietor rang up the sale and held out the change to Ponzi. "Why's that?" he asked.

"Because, friend, Vincenza, you accept me for a countryman—even if I'm not Sicilian, like you. But I'll bet you sell plenty of stale smokes to the Jewish merchants and the Irish who come in."

Again the shopkeeper laughed. "Perhaps," he agreed, "but not all the Irish. The police—they get fresh packs."

Ponzi scooped up several books of matches from a glass bowl and lit his cigarette. He inhaled deeply and blew a cloud of smoke into the air, then began to hum a Victor Herbert tune as he repeated the process. He made no move to leave.

"Something else, Ponzi?"

Absent-mindedly, he shook his head. "No, no, I was just enjoying myself. It's fine to end a busy day like this."

The shopkeeper rose immediately to the bait. "A busy day?"

"Very busy. While you stood behind your counter dispensing tobacco to shoeclerks and tradesmen, friend, I embarked upon a major business venture. I've just come from City Hall, where I discussed the organization with some officials who are—and I tell you this in confidence, Vincenza—placed quite high up."

Ponzi felt the man's eyes studying him. He inhaled once more and let the smoke escape his lips with a grunt of satisfaction.

"High up, you say!" There was no question in the shopkeeper's voice. "I always said that you are a born businessman, Ponzi."

"It is not something you are born with. You acquire it, after years of study, after efforts that succeed more often than they fail. I'd like to tell you more about the Securities Exchange Company, but—"

"The *what* company?" interrupted the other.

"Oh—uh—sorry, Vincenza." He appeared momentarily flustered. "I should not even have revealed the name at this time—not until my partners at City Hall have told their own financial contacts. Just let me say one thing before I get back to my office to settle some final details: I'd appreciate it if you'd lay aside—oh, let's say a dozen boxes—of your finest Havanas for me to give at Christmas. I think any member of the board will appreciate a box of cigars, don't you?"

The Sicilian raised his eyebrows in suspicion. But to sell a dozen boxes of Havana cigars! Losing the sale was not worth the risk. "I think they all would. I'll have them fresh for you the first week in December."

Ponzi reached for his billfold, opened it just far enough for the shopkeeper to see the edge of several bills. "Here," he said, "let me put a deposit on them." He caught the corner of a bill, then suddenly withdrew his hand to snap his fingers. "Oh, no, dammit, I just remembered that I promised to take Rose to dinner and the vaudeville for her birthday tomorrow. And I won't be able to cash a check over the weekend." He smiled, replaced the worn case in his inside pocket. "It's no problem. I'll see you many times between now and December."

Back in his office—that cramped inelegant space connecting rooms 227 and 228 at the top of the stairs—Charles Ponzi cheerily snapped on the overhead light in its flyspeck-encrusted globe and began typing the first of three letters on a much-used Woodstock machine. Weeks earlier, when his attempts to raise money for *The Trader's Guide* had ended, he had let go the young woman he had briefly employed as a typist. (The girl, who had thought her employer warm, humorous, and a perfect gentleman at all times, had sobbed at the news of her dismissal—and sobbed louder still upon learning that Ponzi could not afford to pay her the two weeks back salary, at fifteen dollars a week, that she was owed.)

Ponzi smiled to himself as he finished the first letter and read it over. It was simple and direct. It gave only instructions and provided no details. There was no chance that its recipient—an old friend from Rome who had moved to France—would discern his intentions.

He rolled a fresh sheet of paper into the typewriter, and wrote the identical letter once again, addressing it to an acquaintance in

Spain. A third copy went to a distant relative in Italy, and to this one Ponzi added a few solicitous questions about the man's health. Quickly, he addressed the three envelopes.

He was moving now with precise, easy gestures, not bothering to proofread the letters or the addresses. His years as a clerk—in and out of prison—had filled him with confidence in his own abilities when it came to such mechanical duties as typing and filing. Into each envelope he inserted the appropriate letter, folded around a single one-dollar bill, along with a return envelope addressed to Charles Ponzi, 27 School Street, Boston, Mass., U.S.A. Far back in a desk drawer, he found part of a sheet of stamps and affixed one to each of the envelopes.

He glanced at his pocket watch. There was still time to catch the last mail, if he moved smartly. Each day would be precious now. The sooner the letters came back to him, the sooner he could begin to grow rich. Even with the newest transatlantic steamers, it would be several weeks before he could expect replies from the three countries. He was eager now, anxious to keep going on the business, and he wondered if he could wait without growing impatient. Those slow, damned steamships! Only a few weeks before—the papers had been full of the news—a dirigible called *R-34* had flown from England to New York and back in a matter of days. The builders of the airship predicted that someday even larger craft would ferry passengers, mail, and cargo across the Atlantic and Pacific oceans in a fraction of the time required by the fastest ship afloat.

The shadows caused by the sun dipping below the horizon roused Ponzi out of his brief moment of mental meandering. He put the stamps away, gathered the letters, and had just switched off the light when the telephone rang. *Rose*? Perhaps. She might be wondering when he would be home, ready for dinner. But there was no phone in the small apartment. Had she gone downstairs, asked to use the landlord's? She knew that her husband did not like that, did not like the crotchety and unpleasant owner knowing that the Ponzis could not afford a telephone. No, the ringing phone—it was ringing for the third time now—had to be a creditor. He debated picking it up, thinking that it would be better to slip out and let it ring. But, then, it *could* be Rose. Perhaps with an urgent message.

"Hello."

"Ponzi? Where the hell you been? I've been trying to catch you for a week!"

He recognized the voice immediately. It was the man he had once described to Rose as "that little runt that sold me the office

40

furniture." He wished that he had obeyed his instinct to let the phone ring unanswered.

"I've been in and out, Daniels. My business takes—"

"I don't give a shit about your business, Ponzi. What I care about—'n all I care about—is you payin' for that damn furniture!"

For a moment Ponzi considered pressing down the receiver hook and clicking it in the pretense that he was being cut off, and then simply hanging up. But hadn't he tried that on Daniels once before? He kept his voice businesslike instead.

"By furniture, Daniels, I assume you mean these white pine desks and chairs that you palmed off on me as quartered oak?"

"Goddammit, that stuff *is* quartered oak, Ponzi. You know it is! Stop the stalling, f' Christ's sake! You goin' to pay up, or do I come in there with the boys and haul the stuff out?"

"Wait a minute, just a minute," Ponzi said hurriedly. It would not do to have the office stripped bare, not when he was about to make a fortune with the newly established Securities Exchange Company. "When did I make the last payment? Let me get my bookkeeper in here—"

Daniels was ready for him. "Don't bother. I got the papers right here." The rustling of bills and receipts carried through the wires to Ponzi's ear. "On May second, you leased $230 worth of furniture, and paid fifty bucks. You gave me five more a week later on May twelfth. And that's it. I sent you a bill every week, 'n you damn well know it. You're duckin' my calls, Ponzi, but I'm givin' you warning—"

Ponzi waited until the irate furniture dealer wore himself down. He gave an understanding sigh. "Daniels, we're both businessmen, right? I know what it is to have someone owe me money, just as you do. But no one is going to profit if you take this furniture out of here. You'll lose the money I owe you, and you'll have to sell this second-hand junk to someone else—and they would have to be a bigger fool than I was to take it in the first place. Am I right?"

There was a second of silence at the other end of the line. "I guess so. But what—?"

"I'm onto something that can be very profitable. It won't take long—just a few months at most. I need the furniture, and if you can wait—"

"Wait! Goddammit, I been waitin'—"

"I know. I know, and I appreciate it. But, look, let me get something to you next week, at the end of the month—"

"It better be a helluva lot more than five bucks."

"It will be, I promise you. I'll get at least a third of what I owe you paid off. If I don't, feel free to come in here and take your quartered oak desks and chairs, and do whatever you want with them."

Again, a pause at the other end. Then, a weary sigh. "I'm a damn fool, Ponzi. But all right. Get that money to me, fast."

Ponzi brought the positive tone into his voice once more. "Don't worry about it, Daniels. Charles Ponzi, manager of the Securities Exchange Company, would not default on an inconsequential debt of a few hundred dollars." He hung up the phone even as Daniels' "Manager of *what*?" was crackling from the earpiece.

Daniels was curious, just as the cigar store owner had been when he heard the name. *Securities Exchange Company*. It was a name with prestige, all right. And as soon as he heard from his friends in Italy, Spain, and France, that prestige could be converted into cash. A lot of cash.

If he had wanted to, he could not conceal from Rose the fact that he was onto something.

Always talkative, always cheerful, always ready to dismiss his wife's infrequent doubts and worries with a smile or a story, he suddenly seemed even gayer than before. Whatever Rose wanted to do—stay in if she came home tired from her job, visit her relatives in Somerville, spend a Sunday afternoon walking across the snow-covered Common—he agreed to, willingly. Time and again, he professed his love for her, often in highly romantic and surprising ways. One day, for example, he put his thoughts on paper:

"I am grateful and thankful to America for the gift of my wife, who is ample reward for everything I have suffered, justly and unjustly, during my years in the United States. I cannot bear any grudge, any malice, against a country which has been so lavish and generous as to place within my reach to pick, from a whole garden-full of beautiful flowers, such as American girls are, what has been for me the most exquisite of all blossoms. An American Beauty. My Rose!"

The words were not written in honor of any birthday, any anniversary. "Must there be a reason for me to let you—or the world—know that I love you?" Ponzi asked, smiling at his young wife. Then, he shrugged. "Actually, dear, things were a bit slow at the office this afternoon, and I decided that it was as good a time as any to begin work on my memoirs. That page was the only one I got written. It shall be the first, my dedication to you."

She was amused, incredulous. He laughed and rushed on. "Too young to be thinking of my memoirs? Not at all, Rose. Not at

43

all. So much has happened to me already, I could fill a volume. And now that I'm on the threshhold of——"

He caught himself. It was not the first time in the last few weeks that he had left a sentence dangling in midair. He leaned across the dinner table to touch her hand. "It's best that you don't know the details," he said. "Not just now, anyway. Not until everything is final, and the money is coming in."

He turned the conversation quickly to the failing health of her father. There was no point, he implied strongly, in her asking questions. For weeks he had seemed on the verge of announcing a surprise—a business venture, a job, an investment, something that would solve their problem of unpaid bills and end their pinch-penny shopping. He had dropped enough hints to make her feel secure that his boasts of future riches were promises that soon would be fulfilled. But he would not provide any details. And there certainly were no signs of activity at his sparsely furnished office—the few times she visited it to bring him a forgotten sandwich wrapped in newspaper or to meet him before attending a concert—that indicated something important was about to happen.

But Ponzi's ebullience, his half completed statements, his air of anticipation, all added up to a certainty. Something big, some-thing major, was ahead. He was waiting for it. And when it happened—whatever it was—Charles Ponzi would show Rose and the world that he was a man to be reckoned with, a man of power.

Ponzi's waiting ended suddenly in the third week of Novem-ber. It had lasted much longer than he had anticipated that September evening when he sent off his three letters. One reply had come quickly, two weeks later. The second followed in a week. But the third seemed to have gone astray—until almost six weeks after its author received Ponzi's strange request, it arrived at 27 School Street. Ponzi tore open the envelope, ignoring the brief letter inside, and withdrew several small squares of colored paper.

Hurriedly, he crossed the office and slid back the grooved cover of a roll-top desk. From a pigeonhole in the rear, he removed several other colored squares and separated them into two stacks, then placed them on the cleared surface of his own large desk—one on either side of the packet he had just received. From a drawer, he took a pad of notepaper and a freshly sharpened pencil. Then, he began to examine the colored squares.

All three stacks appeared identical on first glance. About three-inches square, each piece of paper carried a simple legend imprinted on both its front and back surfaces in several languages. In English, the wording read: "This coupon may be exchanged at any post office of any country in the Universal Postal Union for a postage stamp of the value of _____ or its equivalent."

At the top of each coupon and in the main legend appeared its value in the specific country that had issued it—thirty centavos on the one from Spain, five lire on the one from Italy, and ten centimes on the one from France—and at the bottom appeared the name of the issuing postal department.

On these bits of paper, Charles Ponzi realized, he could build a business that would make him rich. His mother, his wife, the world, would watch and marvel; and wealthy bankers, manipulators, and financiers would grind their teeth in envy at how simply he had generated a fortune.

During his weeks of waiting for the coupons, he had studied the regulations governing their use and the authority that had brought them into being. It had not taken much research. In the last decades of the nineteenth century and the first of the twentieth, emigrants in ever-growing numbers had moved from the older and fading capitals of Europe to America and other countries where, they believed, greater opportunity awaited them. As they corresponded with families and friends left behind, in an ever-increasing flood of mail, problems arose. All too often, a young man grown prosperous in a new land could afford the postage necessary to write his parents overseas—but his relatives, living only slightly above poverty levels at home, were hard pressed to come up with the extra few cents needed to reply to his letters. In 1907, to ease the situation, an International Postal Congress had been held in Rome.

Out of the meeting had come the Universal Postal Union and its product, the International Reply Coupon. Such coupons made it possible for the writer of a letter to prepay the postage for a reply. All he needed to do was purchase a coupon in the proper amount at his local post office and send it along with his letter. The recipient could exchange the coupon at his own local postal department for stamps. Signatories to the Universal Postal Union agreement, Ponzi determined, could neither refuse to sell coupons nor redeem them. And there were no limitations on the amounts of coupons that could be purchased or turned in for stamps.

Ponzi had learned all this simply by asking a few questions at the Boston Post Office, browsing through the newspaper files at the Boston Public Library, and practically memorizing page 37 of the latest copy of the *United States Official Postal Guide.* Now, with one dollar's worth of coupons from France, Spain, and Italy before him, he was ready to test his theory.

45

Quickly, he opened his copy of the morning newspaper to the financial pages, searching for the table that listed the value of foreign currency in comparison to the American dollar. Minutes later, before his pencil had half-finished his computations, the grin on his face stretched from ear to ear.

It would work. Dammit, the simple, simple plan would work!

That day, the Spanish monetary unit—the peseta—was equal to only fifteen cents in American money. The dollar he had sent to a friend in Spain had been exchanged for six and two-thirds pesetas, or 666 centavos, which in turn had purchased twenty-two International Reply Coupons, each costing thirty centavos. Ordinarily, the peseta was worth twenty cents American at its par value, and one dollar would have been converted into five pesetas or 500 centavos—which would purchase only sixteen coupons. But each coupon Ponzi had received could be exchanged at the Boston Post Office for a five-cent U.S. postage stamp. And twenty-two coupons, purchased for one dollar, could buy a dollar-ten in stamps. A 10 percent profit!

It beat the banks, of course. And the interest rates on bonds. But it was not enough. He began to figure the value of the coupons from Italy, a country whose currency had depreciated far more than Spain's since the war. The lire, ordinarily quoted at twenty cents American, was now only worth five cents. His dollar had purchased twenty lire, or 2,000 centesimi—which had brought him a thick packet of sixty-six coupons worth thirty centesimi each. And each coupon would buy one five-cent stamp. *$3.30 in stamps*, Ponzi wrote upon his pad. And then, *Gross profit: 230%*!

He could hardly believe it, although he had been sure it would work. He looked at his figures, checking them over quickly. There was hardly any point in computing the value of the French coupons. In any country where currency had depreciated, the system would work. And he had not even begun to figure the profits that could be made by shuttling coupons from one European capital to another!

Only one thing still remained to be proved. Whistling softly, happily, Ponzi gathered up the handful of coupons, donned his worn topcoat, tightened a muffler around his neck to ward off the wind that whistled an altogether different tune, and made his way to the post office, through snow-covered streets. He stood in line behind a half-dozen weary citizens buying stamps one or two at a time, and then shoved his coupons through the grillwork.

"All of these?"

Ponzi stared straight into the eyes of the elderly clerk in his grey work uniform. He felt a momentary pang of doubt, but then realized that the man merely dreaded the task of counting the coupons.

"Yes," he said, "all of them."

The clerk sucked air between his stained teeth, shrugged tiredly, and licked his thumb before bending to the task.

Moments later, Ponzi strode from the government building. The stamps—far more than he could have bought for three dollars if he had purchased them in the standard fashion—were safely in his inside breast pocket. Again, he felt the need to celebrate. And this time, he would not settle for a pack of cigarettes. Charles Ponzi had two dollars in his pocket and a glass of wine at a fine cafe could still be found, despite the spread of the Wartime Prohibition Law throughout the country.

One glass to celebrate with, Ponzi smiled to himself. *And one to plan on.* At most, with a tip for the waiter, it would cost a dollar. Besides, it might be his last chance for a drink in public before the Eighteenth Amendment caused the liquor pipelines to dry up everywhere. Then, too, now that he was sure the coupon system worked, from this day on, he would be too busy raking in the greenbacks to think about enjoying himself.

As he sipped the heady red wine, he mulled over the elementary problems that would have to be considered. Could the postage stamps, once received in exchange for coupons, be turned back a day or so later at another post office for cash? If not, could they be sold to businesses—through a black-market operation—at a discount? How much would that cut into his profits? What sort of international network of agents would he need on the payroll or commission in order to buy hundreds of thousands—perhaps millions—of coupons to make profits on a large scale?

His glass was empty now, and he waved a hand imperiously for a waiter to fill it, his mind busy tying up the loose ends. The questions, of course, were entirely theoretical. He did not have to worry about redeeming the stamps for cash. Or about taking a reduction in profits. Or about hiring others to buy and sell for him.

He merely had to have ready answers, in case anyone asked for them later. But Charles Ponzi had no intention of buying any more International Reply Coupons.

He tossed a dollar casually on the table and strode confidently from the cafe, oblivious to the long-skirted stenographers and derby-crowned businessmen hurrying by. The plan had a solidity that few of his schemes (or anyone else's, for that matter) had ever had before. In his mind he thought over the dozens of tales of instant wealth that he had heard during his prison days, and he recalled that every one of them had a simple, basic flaw: each was based upon a means of making money that, if actually and honestly followed, could not possibly work, at least not as well as its progenitor promised.

Oil, for example. If investors' money actually went into exploration and drilling, what guarantee was there that oil would be found? Or that it could be produced and sold for astronomical returns?

Or, take the stock market. No one could put money into stocks that unfailingly would show high profits. As he thought about that, Ponzi shook his head, musing on the escapades of William F. Miller—"520 Percent Miller"—at the turn of the century. His cousin long years before had mentioned the man, Ponzi remembered—and eventually he had looked up the records himself. From his home in Brooklyn, the twenty-year-old Miller had told hundreds of people that he could invest their money in Wall Street securities so profitably that they could make 10 percent interest every week on their original stakes. A few early investors told friends of the high returns they received, and the friends poured money into Miller's hands—enabling him to pay off more of the initial investors, who told *their* friends, and so on. The scheme had grown to the point where more than a million dollars had been virtually thrown at the young financier. Then, the *Boston Post* denounced the man who ran Miller's Boston office as a "fly-by-night stock operator" and the story sent hundreds of people rushing to demand that they be shown the shares their money had purchased. When the stock could not be produced, the angry investors demanded their money back. Few got it. The slippery Boston manager fled to Europe with $175,000 in cash, while the unsophisticated Miller paid several hundred thousand dollars to a lawyer before the man would defend him. He had been convicted of fraud and served half of a ten-year sentence in Sing Sing before being released in poor health. The entire investment scheme, which lasted only eleven months from start to finish, had left its originator ill and without a penny.

The fool, thought Ponzi that cold afternoon. All the work, all the effort, all the thinking that went into the creation of a scheme to separate people from their money—and then to have the whole thing collapse like a house of cards, merely because it became obvious that a true investment would not produce high-profit results.

That was why the Ponzi system was different. By buying and trading International Reply Coupons, astronomical profits *could* be achieved. It *could* be demonstrated on paper, in black and white, to

48

any skeptic. It had not only the legitimacy of the Securities Exchange Company behind it, but that of the United States Post Office, the Universal Postal Union, and the postal systems of every major country in the world.

And, thought Charles Ponzi, *whenever I have sufficient capital—one million, two million, ten million—I can buy enough reply coupons to produce profits of 50 percent, 100 percent, 500 percent, before anyone knows what has happened!*

Feverishly now, his mind flooded with final details. He would need new stationery emblazoned with the name *Securities Exchange Company*. Once the investors began calling on him in numbers, he would have to hire a stenographer, and certainly a cashier of some sort. The investors would need receipts for their money—some sort of note would do. And there would have to be a small initial bankroll to pay off the very first group of greedy participants.

To make money, Ponzi realized in an all-too-familiar flash of awareness, he needed money. Not much, a few hundred dollars at most. But he was deeply in debt as it was. On his desk lay three successive missives from the Fidelity Trust Company, calling attention to an overdue loan of $279 since the previous February and (in the most recent one) threatening suit. *Let them sue*, Ponzi had thought. *You can't get blood from a stone.*

But now, now that he was so close to starting something that could easily become the biggest venture of his career, he could not afford to be hauled into court as insolvent. The bank and other creditors would have to be stalled once more, would have to be promised additional interest—exorbitant interest—if they waited patiently just a bit longer. They would wait, Ponzi felt sure. And they would not care how he got his money, ethically or otherwise, just so long as he got it. *Nobody gives a rap for ethics. Possess the dollar, and you're beyond criticism.*

For the next few weeks, he moved around Boston and its outlying townships, calling on friends and acquaintances, desperately trying to borrow a hundred dollars, fifty dollars, ten dollars—and getting nothing. Christmas was coming, he was told time after time. Inflation was driving prices high, and extra cash just was not available. He knew that he was at a disadvantage: If he told certain of his friends why he needed fast funding, they might be shrewd enough to latch onto the International Reply Coupon business for themselves. Or, they could spread the word to Boston's financial community, to the postal authorities, or—worst of all—to the police. Ponzi revealed just enough of his plans to whet people's greed and curiosity, but refused to give details. And his unwillingness to part with full information turned potential lenders against him.

On a bright morning in the second week in December, a discouraged Ponzi slowly climbed to his office. His hands jammed deep in his coat pockets and his chin tucked far down into his collar, he almost collided with the man waiting for him on the second-floor landing.

"Oh, Daniels," he said in surprise. "Decided to come in person, did you?"

The caller's florid face looked ready to explode. "Damn right I come in person, you deadbeat. I come for my money or my stuff."

Ponzi was in no mood for a lengthy argument. "Daniels, my man," he said wearily as he fitted his key to the lock and swung open the door, "come in and sit down. We'll see what we can do."

The furniture dealer hesitated, then stepped through the doorway. "There's nothing to see about," he grumbled. "You don't pay notice to my letters, you hang up on my phone calls. Now, if you don't want the police in here, Ponzi, let's settle the bill."

With a casual shrug, Ponzi turned toward his back office. An idea had started to form. "Come on in here and take a seat, will you? I have a proposition for you."

"Proposition?" Daniels snorted. "Have you got the money, that's all I want to know!" He stood straight just inside the door, ignoring Ponzi's wave toward the empty chair near the roll-top desk.

"For the love of mike, sit down!" Ponzi shouted. "That chair is still yours. Sitting in it won't place you under any obligations."

Daniels began pulling documents from his pocket. "I got everything right here, your mortgage on the furniture, the bills, the receipts. If you want to—"

"I waive presentation of the evidence. What do I still owe you?"

Daniels looked at him in surprise. "You ordered this load of furniture last spring, and—countin' the thirty dollars in the October payment, the last one you made—you still owe ninety dollars. Maybe it ain't much to you, Ponzi, but Christmas is coming and I got plenty of shopping to do."

Ponzi nodded, deep in thought. "Ninety dollars, is it?" He studied Daniels' face. "I'll tell you frankly, the thought of losing the furniture does not appeal to me. I'd pay you if I had the cash, believe me. But, I can offer you the next best thing—my promissory note."

"Your personal note?" Daniels growled. "What good is that to me? I have your mortgage note now, and you can't meet the payments on that."

"This would be a different kettle of fish entirely," Ponzi said. He ticked off several seconds, then lowered his voice. "I'm going to have to take you into my confidence. In a short while, I expect to have plenty of money—to pay you and a number of others hounding me. You've waited this long, so why lose out on the ninety dollars and a sale of additional furniture to me in the future?" At that, Daniels' eyes showed a spark of interest, and Ponzi went on hurriedly. "If things go the way I plan, I'll need more desks, chairs, files, and cash drawers, and I'll need them in a hurry. Naturally, I'll call you."

The dealer drew a cigar from his coat pocket and stuffed one end of it into his mouth. He was intrigued but wary. "You'd call me, you say? And I'd end up chasin' you for more money!"

"Not at all, not at all. I swear that you'll be paid, and you'll be paid C.O.D. for anything else I order. This is what I propose: You take my personal note for $200 to your bank, and discount it there. They'll give you the cash, and you apply ninety dollars of it to what I owe you. The rest you hold for me, and I will give you instructions to pay some other bills as they come due. In sixty days, upon the maturity of the note, I'll pay the bank the $200 plus any interest due."

"And when you don't take up the note, I'm stuck for $200 to the bank, right?"

Christ, the man is dense. "Would I make such an offer if I wasn't certain I can pay off the note in sixty days? It's bad enough having you on my back now. Do you think I want the bank after me, too?"

"But where's the money comin' from, the money to take up the note?"

Ponzi drew a deep breath. It was as good a time as any to find out if anyone could punch holes in his story. If there were flaws in the International Reply Coupon business, Daniels was the sort of man who would grind his teeth until he found them, before investing a penny. Ponzi slid open his top drawer.

"Do you know what this is?" he asked, tossing a coupon from Italy onto the desk. Nodding, Daniels moved close in to study the slip of paper.

"Sure," he said. "It's a stamp coupon. What about it?"

It took Charles Ponzi fifteen minutes to outline his plan to trade coupons and profit on the open market. Scribbling figures

51

furiously on a lined yellow pad, quoting current rates on currency exchange from the financial pages, and talking without seeming to draw a breath, he began with the treaty at Rome in 1907 and continued right up through the rules and regulations laid down in the 1919 edition of the *United States Official Postal Guide*.

Daniels fought to understand. "Three hundred percent profit? You can make three hundred percent?"

"Easily. That's why I'm prepared to pay investors forty percent, perhaps fifty percent if their amounts are sizable enough."

The other man was almost convinced. Almost, but not quite. "Once you've got the stamps," he asked, "then what?"

It was the question that Ponzi knew would have to be faced on all sides. "You mean, how do I turn them into cash? That—I'm afraid—must remain my secret."

Now Daniels nodded knowingly. "I knew it," he said. "You can't answer that. The whole thing—"

Ponzi cut him off. "Not *can't* answer it, my friend. *Won't* answer it. There's quite a difference. Do you think I would have gone to all this trouble, done all this figuring, checked out the results in Italy, in France, in Spain, unless I had the means to dispose of the stamps? How foolish do you think I am?"

"Then, give me your answer."

"And have you know enough to go into business for yourself?" Ponzi shook his head, smiling. "Not on your life. Don't you see, Daniels, the whole thing is so simple that as soon as I begin operating, the DuPonts and Vanderbilts and Astors could come charging in. That is, they could, *if* they knew how to work the final step that turns the stamps into money. Oh, they'll find out in time, I'm sure. But by then I'll have made my fortune. At this stage of the game, I can no more tell you how I'll do it than I would tell Morgan himself."

Daniels slowly considered the scheme. "But, how—?" he hesitated.

"Just let me say this. I can do it, Daniels. I have the means. There are certain people who must go nameless—whose names are not even known to the police in their own countries—who have agreed to help me. For a piece of the pie, so to say. You know as well as I do that stamps in the right hands are as good as cash. Any other questions that you or my investors might have, I will answer. But I warn you, it is better—healthier—for you not to know too much about the last stage of the operation."

The furniture dealer sat forward to study Ponzi's face. Could the Italian be believed? He had gone to a lot of trouble, and the figures did make sense on paper. Then, too, Ponzi undoubtedly still had friends in Europe. Members of one of those secret societies, perhaps. Or Bolsheviks. Those reds always had schemes of one sort or another to undermine the stock market, and to raise money for their own needs. If Ponzi was teamed up with them—hell, he just might pull it off.

Behind his desk, Ponzi was silent, but he could almost hear the gears meshing in Daniels' brain. And, because he was certain of the furniture dealer's greed, he sensed that the man had taken the bait even before Daniels nodded his head.

"All right, Ponzi, you've got a deal."

The familiar grin spread across Ponzi's mouth. He whisked pen, ink, and paper from a desk drawer in a single motion, and began to write. "Fine, Daniels, and you've got my promise that I'll rely exclusively on your company for any more furniture. Here, now—" With a flourish he signed his name on the page, then held it across the desk. "Here's my note for $200, payable in sixty days. I've made it out directly to you, rather than to Daniels and Wilson Furniture."

Daniels inspected the note carefully. Then, he extended his hand. "I'll get this to my bank—that's the First State—right away, this afternoon, Ponzi. It's them you'll owe the money to in February."

Ponzi could hardly wait for the merchant to get out of his office. There was work to be done. Brusquely, he squeezed Daniels' hand. "If you'll excuse me," he said, "I have business to attend to. Here, I'll walk you down." He pulled on his coat.

On the sunlit, windy street, he moved with quick strides. *The fool*, he thought. *Greed enough in him to risk a hundred more to get a hundred already lost.* As long as there were people like that around, Charles Ponzi believed, he would have a chance at growing rich.

Inside a small print shop on a side street, he outlined his needs to the proprietor. Simple, printed notes. In three colors. Green, for amounts under one hundred dollars. Orange, for amounts up to $1,000. And blue, for amounts above $1,000. Each, with an ornate border, and wording to the effect that on such-and-such a date, the Securities Exchange Company would pay to so-and-so so many dollars.

"I'll write in the names, dates, and amount," said Ponzi. "Just leave the space." He ordered a thousand of the green notes, which were to be imprinted at the corner with the letter *A*. The orange notes, lettered *B*, were to be run off in a quantity of five hundred. "I'll only need a hundred of the blue ones—mark them with a *C*—and have the whole batch ready Thursday, all right?"

The shopkeeper nodded wearily and wiped his hands on his ink-smeared apron. "Rush, rush, rush," he said. "From a young man like you, too, with plenty of time ahead. Why such a hurry?"

"I've spent nearly twenty years trying to make my fortune, friend," Ponzi replied. "I'm getting just a trifle impatient."

7

Other Bostonians—the Irish, the Italians, the Catholics and Protestants, almost everyone—were shopping and making preparations for Christmas, approaching swiftly. But Charles Ponzi, a bundle of International Reply Coupons warm in his breast pocket, spent his days and evenings visiting restaurants, clubrooms and recreation halls—where he knew large groups of people would be found. At one time, he would have begun to operate in bars and taverns. But prohibition had already closed most of them, and their patrons had been driven to membership in private clubs where bootleg liquor could be had for a price. Tonight, as Ponzi pushed through the door of the sporting hall, he was gratified to hear the roar of sound that immediately met him; the larger the crowd, the faster the money would come.

He shouldered his way through the mob of jovial men, grinning as a few slapped him on the back and called his name— "Ponzi! Nice to see you again! Where you been?" He didn't bother to try to answer in the noise. Only when he was in the back room, where a boccie court was laid out against one wall, did he raise his voice.

"How many points, 'Tonio?" he called to a short, barrel-chested player waiting his turn at the far end of the court.

The man looked up, trying to find Ponzi through the haze of tobacco smoke. "Ponzi!" he shouted. "It's been months! Wait a minute."

"How many points?" Ponzi called again, laughing.

The man waved two fingers in the air. "We need two—and I'll get them. Now!" He took one step down the court, swung his arm back and tossed the red boccie into the air. It made an almost indistinguishable arc before hitting the small white jack with a

55

cracking sound. The jack rolled forward and snuggled behind two red boccie lying side by side. A sigh of disappointment came from the two players nearest Ponzi. "You're too good tonight, Antonio," one of them called. "Another game?"

"Not unless my friend Ponzi wants to play."

Ponzi shook his head, and reached to take the hand of his friend. "No, no. I'm only here for a few moments. Rose has me doing Christmas shopping and I have no time for games. Buying presents, the new business, I'm running myself ragged."

An old man, his shoes coated with dust from the dirt surface of the boccie court, held out a pack of Sweet Caporals. "Have a smoke, and relax a while with us, Carlo. I could use your toss in the game. Your wife will survive without you."

Ponzi refused the cigarette, and took a cigar from his pocket. "I prefer these, Barilli," he laughed. Several players and spectators gathered around to see the newcomer and Antonio introduced him. "My friend Ponzi here can make the boccie do tricks," Antonio said with pride. "We must make him play."

"Some other time," Ponzi said. "Really, friends, I was passing by on my way to see an investor and remembered that I had not stopped here in months. Now I must hurry."

"Working?" The old man was shaking his head. "At this hour? Ponzi, you will be a rich man yet."

"It's not late when there is money to be picked up," Ponzi said easily. "And if you were one of my investors, Bertilli, like the ones waiting for me to come around and give them their interest, I doubt that you would care if I came at midnight."

The cracked lips moved into a grin. "If someone comes to give me money, he can even come after I'm dead and in hell," the old man said, and the crowd laughed its approval.

Antonio's voice was curious. "You have investors, Ponzi? For your advertising book?"

"The *Trader's Guide*? Oh, no. That idea went so well that I was offered a good sum for it by a large publisher. I sold out, and put the cash into securities exchange. That's the future, friends. As manager of the Securities Exchange Company, I should know." He drew deeply on his cigar.

A slender youth on the edge of the group tried to roll a boccie up his arm, show-off fashion. It fell to the floor. "Uh, what's your company do?" he said quickly to cover his embarrassment.

"Do?" asked Ponzi. "Why, we exchange securities and pay investors fifty percent interest in ninety days. But you're too young to know finance. Some of your elders here no doubt could explain it to you. Right, Bertilli?"

The old man nodded sagely. "Of course, Ponzi."

56

"Well, I'd better hurry," Ponzi said, glancing at his pocket watch. "Good to see you again, 'Tonio. Give my regards to your pretty little wife. Oh, here—" he added, as if in afterthought, "take a couple of these cigars." As he extended them toward the other man, several of the printed coupons fluttered from beneath his coat to the floor. Ponzi looked annoyed, bent to retrieve them. "Dammit," he muttered, "I'm carrying too many of these things."

The young player had already picked up one of the notes and was reading it. Ponzi's voice was sharp. "You won't understand that, I said. Let me have it."

Antonio snatched the note from the boy. But before handing it over, he glanced at it. "Christ, Ponzi," he said, "that's for $1,200."

Ponzi folded the notes and moved to return them to his pocket. "I imagine so," he said. To replace the papers properly, he had to remove the entire thick bundle of notes, flashing them briefly, casually, before again squeezing them under his coat. "Some investors are doing quite well."

"What interest did you say you're paying? Fifty percent?"

"*I'm* not paying it, friend. The Securities Exchange Company is paying it. The present rates are fifty percent in ninety days. Naturally, as more investors come in, we might have to lower the rates—but right now, it's fifty percent." He could almost hear them calculating as they compared his return with that of 4 percent or 5 percent paid by Boston banks.

One man let out a low whistle. "How many people you have investing now?"

Ponzi tapped his bulging breast pocket. "One for each of these notes, and ten times as many back at my office."

"Sounds like you got a regular stock market going there," said the old man.

Ponzi laughed. "Not quite, not quite. The Securities Exchange Company works very simply. No shares, no dividends, no worry about whether the market is going up or down. You invest your money and get a note in exchange. In ninety days, you turn in the note and get your money back with half-again as much in interest." He pulled his watch from his pocket. "I really haven't time to tell you more now, but if anyone is interested, come to my office. All the facts and figures on International Reply Coupons are there."

"Reply coupons?" murmured his friend. "From the post office?"

Ponzi was turning up his coat collar now. "'Tonio, I really have to make some of these payments tonight. Good to see you again. I'll come by some evening, maybe right after the New Year, for boccie. *'Rivederci*!" He waved, turned, and was gone.

The following afternoon, Ponzi looked up from his desk,

covered now with a multicolored layer of Securities Exchange Company notes made out in a variety of amounts to entirely fictitious persons—and saw the youth from the boccie court standing before him.

"Uh, Mr. Ponzi," the boy began, "I wanted to learn about your business."

Ponzi's eyes measured the slim figure carefully. The boy had an honest look about him, but he seemed nervous. He rubbed one hand swiftly over his upper lip where a shadow of a mustache was sprouting. It reminded Ponzi of his own early attempts to make himself look older.

"You're not old enough, son, to understand the investment business."

"I'm twenty-two, sir. I might not look it, but it's true. I've got a little money put aside. And what you said last night—"

"A little money? What kind of work do you do?"

"I'm a stitcher, at a shoe factory. It's hard to save on eighteen dollars a week, and I'm supposed to get married."

Ponzi nodded. The boy's savings probably didn't amount to much, but they would do as a start. "Very well, young man, you've come to the right place if you're interested in making money quickly." He spread several Securities Exchange Company notes in a neat row on the desk, and then took a packet of reply coupons from a drawer. "I won't be able to give you all the details of this operation at this time," he said, "but you can see for yourself the kind of money there is to be made if you act quickly."

The boy's eyes already were looking at the amounts inked in on the notes—$750, $1,500, $3,500. Ponzi grinned and said, "Now if I go a little too fast, stop me and I'll try to answer any questions. Some of this might seem complicated. Undoubtedly, the first thing that pops into your mind is how can the Securities Exchange Company pay fifty percent interest in ninety days when the banks are paying five percent in a year, right? Well, that's because banks put their money into bonds and stocks and low-interest loans. Why? Because bankers are conservative and afraid to try anything different. This company, on the other hand, puts its money into these—International Reply Coupons . . ."

It took him ten minutes to go through the story. The young man listened quietly, apparently doing his own mental figuring. Ponzi realized halfway through his explanation that his listener was not going to ask questions. He was too busy pyramiding some imaginary investment at 50 percent.

"The notes," Ponzi concluded, "can be had in any amount— from ten dollars to $10,000, and payment is guaranteed by the

Securities Exchange Company. How much, Mr.—uh—Mr.—?"

"Giberti," the youth said. "Ettore Giberti."

"How much, Mr. Giberti, were you thinking of investing?"

"I got maybe a hundred, or a little more, Mr. Ponzi. But it all gets me a little mixed up, I mean, the coupons and the notes and the different countries. You're right, I guess. I got to learn more about finance."

Ponzi tried not to answer too swiftly. "The company can take a hundred dollars, young man—and would pay you $150 in ninety days. Let's see, that would be about mid-March."

The boy thought it over for a moment too long, and Ponzi realized he had lost him.

"Uh, no, Mr. Ponzi, I—uh—I don't think I should. It took me months to save it up, and I'm going to have some bills to pay, y'know." He started for the door. "Sorry I took so much of your time."

For an instant, Ponzi thought of trying to stop him, of pointing out that in a few months the young man could increase his savings dramatically. But he caught himself. After all, a man who obviously was giving out thousands of dollars on all sides would not care whether a green kid invested a hundred or not. He nodded indifferently.

Then, suddenly, an impulse made him call out. "Giberti, just a minute." The boy turned, his eyes questioning.

"At the factory where you work, there are probably friends of yours who also need money?" The boy nodded, puzzled. "How would you like to tell them about the Securities Exchange Company? There's no reason that only the town's wealthiest men, bankers, brokers, should be in on this deal. As manager, I can bring anyone into it that I choose. If you told your friends about it, they could pick up a nice piece of change. And you could make enough on commission to settle your financial worries."

The young man moved back to the desk. "What would I have to do?"

Ponzi spread his hands. "Merely tell anyone interested that you can place their funds in a safe investment, a highly profitable one. I'll give you a supply of notes with my signature in various amounts. Sell the fifteen-dollar ones for ten dollars, the hundred-and-fifty-dollar ones for one hundred dollars, and so on. You keep ten percent of whatever cash you're given as your commission, and bring the rest to the office."

"Bring you the cash?"

A nod. "It will be placed with the thousands of other dollars that pour in each day, and sent to our agents overseas. But you don't have to explain that. Just tell your friends to bring in their notes ninety days after they're issued—you fill in the date here—and they'll get their money."

The boy smiled. "It sounds easy."

"It *is* easy. But let me give you a one-lesson course in salesmanship and psychology. This investment is a good thing, and being a good thing, it needs no high pressure selling. You don't have to stress its advantages. What you are doing is selling a perfectly good dollar for sixty-six cents. If someone is interested, fine. Just tell him the details of the coupon transaction. But don't go beyond that point—or we'll find so many people in the business that the bottom will fall out of the market. And don't try to force notes upon a prospect in order to increase your own commissions. Force always creates suspicion, rather than confidence."

The boy reached out to examine some of the notes. He studied the impressive border that framed the words, rubbed the paper between his finger and thumb to test its weight. "I got confidence," he said, laughing.

"There's no reason you shouldn't have. Enough men are already getting rich to prove what I've told you, and in a short time you will know the taste of wealth yourself."

"I keep ten percent? That's what you said?" As Ponzi nodded, the boy stretched to shake his hand. "Maybe I'd better just take a few to start with."

"Of course. You can always get more. When you bring in the investments, let me know the amounts that others have promised, and we'll make out notes for them." He took a pen and signed several notes in each color. "The name goes here, the date here, and the amount here. Fill in the investors' names and amounts on the stubs, with the date."

The young man was nodding now, eager to get to work. "And they collect in ninety days? Three months?" he asked.

Ponzi started to agree, then changed his mind. "I'll tell you what," he said. "Profits already are running higher than anyone expected, and we can use more funds to expand the program into several countries in South America. Tell your friends that if they invest promptly, within the next few weeks, they can get their money and fifty percent interest in forty-five days."

A whistle. A quick nod of the boy's head. "You'll hear from me, Mr. Ponzi. You'll hear from me quick."

After the young man had gone, Ponzi sat silently behind his desk. He had not planned on cutting others into the business this early. But he knew instinctively that he had made the right

60

decision. Rather than take a hundred dollars from Giberti, he would get ten times that amount. The boy's friends would be suspicious at first. But some would be intrigued enough by the proposition to test it. All it would take would be a ten-dollar bill. It might look extremely unsound as an investment—but as a gamble, it was extremely attractive.

It would be easier this way—with a third party between the investor and the Securities Exchange Company. Not that Ponzi did not have acquaintances and friends who had money to give him, but they also had memories of his previous business forays that had gone awry.

With Ettore Giberti, thought Ponzi, a small snowball had been started downhill. All he had to do now was wait until it gathered momentum, grew larger, and became an avalanche.

On December 20, 1919, Giberti sold his first note, a green one, for fifty dollars, to a foreman at the factory where he worked. The foreman felt secure in his purchase, positive that if he did not receive seventy-five dollars on the fifth of February as promised, the young salesman would lose both his job and a few teeth.

Giberti used his boss' purchase as a lever to induce other workers to take the notes. If the foreman, a tight man where money was concerned, had confidence enough in the remarkable investment scheme, why should anyone else have doubts? Several other buyers opened their wallets or withdrew small sums from their treasured savings accounts, and Giberti found that the green notes moved so briskly that he hardly thought to ask for amounts over fifty dollars. Then, a few days after Christmas, a senior bookkeeper who had received a bonus of one hundred dollars decided to risk it—"if it isn't too much trouble, Ettore?"

Smiling ruefully, Giberti wrote out a green note that promised to pay the bearer $150 in mid-February. Word of the relatively large investment went around the factory and brought a handful of minor-league investors scurrying to buy notes for themselves.

On New Year's Day, when the majority of Boston businessmen were nursing hangovers, Ponzi surprised his wife by announcing that he had to stop by the office. Rose, weary after welcoming in 1920 with her family, let him go resignedly. The evening before, one of her brothers had asked Ponzi what he did all day, every day, at his office, and had laughingly suggested that he make a resolution to work less hard and spend more time "makin' the *bambino*."

Ponzi, chuckling, had promised that the new year would be different. "I won't be going to the office so much myself," he had said. "If I need anything, I'll send one of the servants."

But now, at ten o'clock in the morning on the first day of what was to be the most eventful year in Charles Ponzi's life, he sat behind his desk and watched young Ettore Giberti take some papers from his pocket. They were the last of the stubs from the eighteen notes sold in the final ten days of December. Next to them on the large desktop, which had been cleared of all other papers, Giberti placed a stack of dollar bills. Casually, Ponzi moistened the tip of his thin forefinger and began to count. He looked up.

"I get," he said, "a total of $870." He compared the amount with the total from the stubs, and nodded. Then, from the stack of bills, he took several fives, tens, and twenties, and slid them toward the young man who stood with eyes gleaming before the desk.

"Here," Ponzi said, reaching for his billfold, "we owe you some singles—and that makes exactly eighty-seven dollars. Not bad for ten days work, is it?"

"It's a knockout, all right."

Ponzi started to put the cash on the desk into a brown manila envelope. Then, casually, he said, "Would you want to invest your earnings? In six weeks you'd have half again as much."

Giberti stared with youthful suspicion into Ponzi's steady gaze.

"No?" Ponzi said, smiling. "Well, I've always gone along with the idea that every man and woman is a born gambler, craving for easy money. Still, the best gamblers know when to quit." He sealed the envelope with a flourish.

"If I can make money as easy as this," the young man said, tucking his bills into a pocket, "I won't worry about investing."

Ponzi moved to turn off the overhead light. "Come, I'll walk with you to the trolley," he said. "There's something I want to say about your work."

Heading for the Common, he explained that the Securities Exchange Company was doing so well, expanding so swiftly, that a manpower shortage had developed. There were not enough clerks and bookkeepers on the payroll to process all the small amounts from numerous investors. For that reason, and until more people could be hired and trained, it had been decided by the board of directors that only sizable investments could be accepted.

"Sizable? What do you mean?"

"Absolutely nothing under $300. No more of this ten-, twenty-, and thirty-dollar stuff."

"But the bozos I work with don't have $300. Hell, Ponzi, that $870 I brought you came from fifteen of them. And Hallahan's hundred was the largest of the lot!"

Ponzi stopped walking suddenly. "My young friend," he

smiled, looking into the other's face, "I'll wager you will find more people who have $300—or more, much more—than you can imagine. Everyone's investing in something these days. People are pulling money out of mattresses and tin cans and putting it into the stock market or gold mines. You know as well as I do that as appealing as gold mines are, anything connected with foreign exchange is better. You're a good salesman. We both know that. But a good rule for a good salesman is, always ask for a little more than you think you can get. If what you're selling is worth nothing, ask ten dollars; if it's worth ten, ask twenty, and so on. Then, if a man refuses to buy until you cut the price, you'll still be ahead. Understand?"

Giberti nodded slowly, and the two walked on. "I think I understand," the youth said after a moment. "You want more money, from fewer people."

"You *are* very bright. More money from fewer people is exactly what I want. For the next four weeks only, however."

The young man's voice snapped sharply in the cold. "Because at the end of that time, you'll owe my fifteen investors fifty percent interest on their money. Let's see, on $870, you'll have to pay out—thirteen hundred!"

"Thirteen hundred and five, to be exact. But *I* won't pay it out, Giberti. The Securities Exchange Company will pay it out. And we're as solid as Gibraltar, have no fear."

Now the boy studied him. A thin smile tightened his mouth. "No fear, Ponzi? My job depends on it, and my life, perhaps. But I think you know what you're doing."

Ponzi returned the smile. "I know human nature. You might say that I'm a better salesman by instinct than others are by training. And you will find when you get back to work this week that others who have heard of the company from the fifteen people who bought the notes will be coming to you. Your selling will actually get easier. Outline the coupon proposition, don't crowd, and they'll throw money in your lap."

"And when I tell the men with a few dollars that I don't want their money—"

"Larger investors will want to get in, just to show how smart and important they are. Remember, though, tell your little investors that it's only temporary. The company is hiring and training extra help right this minute. It's a massive investment of our own. And very shortly, we'll be taking investments of any size again."

"Ponzi," said Giberti, just before he dashed to catch a departing trolley, "I bet you will." A grin flashed across his face, echoing the one Ponzi wore.

There was nothing to do now but wait once again. It was the most difficult part of the entire plan. There was no scheming to do. The thing was whole. Complete. All the loose ends were tied up.

Ponzi busied himself for a few days by using $600 of the money given him by Giberti to open a dozen bank acounts in as many different banks. Small sums, all in his name, went into the Fidelity Trust, Hanover Trust, Tremont Trust, and Old South Trust, among others, and, after short side trips into neighboring communities, into the Merchants National Bank of Manchester and the Lawrence Trust Company. Ponzi enjoyed filling out the forms and watching clerks check his figures carefully. It gave him something to do.

Afterward, almost daily, he slid open the bottom drawer of his immense desk as soon as he entered the office in the morning. There, in a neat stack bound with a narrow pink ribbon, lay the bankbooks. Ponzi hefted them in his hand, ran his finger along the edge of the stack to make sure there were exactly twelve, and then returned them to the drawer and locked it. Soon, there would be even more bankbooks, and each would have its pages covered with the careful penmanship of dozens of clerks as they recorded deposit after deposit after deposit.

Then, to occupy idle hours, Ponzi made frequent journeys to the public library. There, he pored over tattered newspaper files that recounted the further exploits of "520 Percent Miller," Cassie Chadwick, and others who had reaped fortunes from an unsuspecting public. Between 1904 and 1911, an old copy of *Financial World* revealed, more than $83 million had been poured into 41 fake oil companies and $528 million had gone to the promoters of 119 companies ostensibly set up to mine gold, silver, copper, and other valuable minerals from the earth. The more he read, the more certain Ponzi became that his inspiration—the Securities Exchange Company—was the most masterful scheme ever devised to separate greedy investors from their cash.

Unlike Miller's phantom Wall Street investments, Mrs. Chadwick's package of "Andrew Carnegie's Caledonia Railroad bonds" that proved to be nothing more than scraps of brown wrapping paper, and numerous nonexistent oil wells and gold mines, Charles Ponzi's "securities"—the postal coupons—could be seen, touched, counted. Each had a cash value. Each actually could be purchased in one country for a certain amount of money, and each actually would be worth more in another country. There was no reason in the world why investors would question the basis of the proposition.

But he had to wait.

The tension was so great now that he could hardly bear it. What was more, it was a struggle to keep his anxiety from Rose. Each evening when he came home from the office, he wondered if she knew what an effort it was for him to begin his jaunty whistling as he climbed the stairs. One night he had been so lost in thought as he walked down the street, his hands clenched uncharacteristically behind his back, that he had glanced up just in time to see her peer out from the bedroom window. Instantly, he smiled and waved cheerfully, but he wondered if she had seen his concern.

Several times he considered telling her a few of the details of his scheme. But he did not want to excite her or worry her. There was worry enough, he knew. The bills that were unpaid last month were still unpaid, and new ones were piling up. No, it was best merely to display confidence. Assurance.

"Tell the butcher he will definitely be settled with next month," Ponzi scoffed when the danger of a meatless table was pointed out to him. And when a collector from a department store called at the front door one afternoon, his answer was the same. "Next month—without fail."

But where the money was to come from, that was a matter he shrugged aside. When the situation appeared too grim, or Rose's questioning silence seemed too intense, he would suggest taking in a movie. Or something more expensive.

"The devil with a motion picture!" he exclaimed. "Have you seen the signs for *Irene* in town? Isn't that where they sing 'Alice Blue Gown?' You'd like that, Rose."

He stopped, seeing the look in her eyes. "I know," he said. "A movie is cheaper, and we really can't afford either." He reached out to touch her hair. "You're right, of course. But next month—I promise you, Rose—next month everything we owe will be paid. And in a short time, we'll go to the theater as often as you like. And you'll wear an Alice blue gown of your very own."

He could not tell any longer if his wife shared his enthusiasm. His promises, he knew, had fallen on her in such profusion— almost from the evening she first met him—that it might be hard for her to continue having faith in him. Still, she was a young girl, a very young girl, and it was difficult for young girls to keep from dreaming.

An Alice blue gown. To wear to an afternoon tea, or perhaps to a lesson in the new rage, auction bridge, at a smart restaurant like the Union Oyster House. A player piano from Steinert's, with

66

dozens of Mel-O-dee music rolls—that was what the wealthy Mrs. Charles Ponzi should have. A dozen pairs of satin slippers with Louis heels in all the colors of the rainbow. And something marvelous to put on the dinner table—a thick steak or huge roast—instead of the codfish cakes she had prepared two nights in a row.

Ponzi had remarked about the cakes, then had laughed at the newspaper ad for them. "'Gorton's Codfish Cakes,'" he had said, reading. "'A delicious meal for three for twenty-five cents.' No wonder there's enough for three, Rose. Two of the three can't get them down."

He was still laughing as they prepared for bed. He waited while Rose, with the bathroom door modestly closed, scrubbed her face clean of the light dusting of powder she wore. Some of the younger and more sophisticated girls in the offices and shops of Boston had taken to applying a touch of rouge to their cheeks and lips, but Ponzi preferred his wife's unadorned beauty. Besides, rouge was the identifying beauty mark of a scarlet woman—everyone knew that.

When Rose, in a flannel nightgown, stepped into the darkened bedroom, her husband, already in his pajamas, glided wordlessly past her and closed the bathroom door behind him. Then, as he waited for his wife to begin drifting off into sleep, he busied himself with the ceremonious preparations for the next day's work. First he stropped his razor repeatedly, honing its gleaming edge so that it would float smoothly over his skin. Then he meticulously washed his hands, taking great pains to remove every trace of the city's grime from beneath his nails. He brushed his teeth and gargled with a strong mouthwash, trying to do it quietly so Rose would not be disturbed.

He was sure that she would understand why, more and more often, he let her fall asleep before he joined her in bed. It was not a question of physical rejection, of course. Charles Ponzi had always liked women—"all of them, God bless them!" he stated. "In a sort of good fellowship way."

But there was so much that had to be done before he and Rose could think about having children. Despite her Catholic upbringing, his wife would surely understand that a brood of Ponzi youngsters was out of the question just now. In addition to the all-important matter of money, there was the fact that Ponzi himself was naturally weary at the end of each day; he *had* to be, since his every effort—all his mental and physical energy—was devoted to getting his new business off the ground.

And he was doing it all for Rose.

And for his mother.

At times, when his wife had trouble falling asleep, Ponzi might sit on the edge of the bed and stroke her hair while he told tales of his childhood in Italy and of the marvelous, wonderful things his mother had done for him. In soft and soothing tones, he wove stories that seemed to put his mother only a step away from sainthood. And surely, as he told it, the Church could do no less than canonize this unselfish, kind, and loving woman within moments of the Last Rites. That event was not too far off, Ponzi said sadly, explaining that he himself was racing against time. He had gauged from his mother's feeble handwriting in her increasingly infrequent letters that she was aged and ill, and he was hurrying to make his fortune to ease her final days on earth.

Ponzi spun out the stories, and the promises, and the dreams—until he heard Rose's deep, regular breathing. Then, carefully so as not to wake her, carefully so as not to touch the warm skin of her thigh or breast, he would ease himself into bed beside her.

And he would lie awake for long hours, his eyes wide open, his mind racing.

It was late in the month, after Ponzi could no longer find thoughts to occupy himself, that he began to wonder about Giberti. He had not heard from the young salesman since New Year's Day, when he had laid down the new rules. Perhaps the youth was having more difficulty pinning down large investors than he had figured on, or was ill and unable to solicit new business. Perhaps he had decided to get out of town and leave Ponzi with the problem of paying the initial customers.

He shook his head clear of conjecture. There was nothing to worry about. In nearly thirty-eight years on earth he had learned to recognize the opportunists and the sheep, the slightly dishonest and the outright crooks, as well as the totally innocent. Giberti, he told himself, was precisely the right person for the assignment he had been given: opportunistic enough to want the job and dishonest enough to stay clear of too many questions—and yet not so crooked as to clear out with someone else's money.

No, he was certain his salesman would show up. It was just the damn waiting—

On the twenty-third of January, there were hurried footsteps on the stairs and then an anxious knocking on the door. "Giberti," he breathed as he moved quickly toward the outer office door. But the man outside was older and dressed in the heavy, salt-encrusted clothes of a merchant seaman.

"Silvio! I wasn't expecting you for another week!"

The man stepped into the office, unbuttoning the rope toggles on his thick coat. "We left port a few days early 'n picked up two days more on the trip over," he said. "Ain't many people crossin' the Atlantic in this kind of weather, I tell you. Passenger business is goin' all to hell."

Ponzi checked to make sure the narrow hall was empty, then locked the door again. "But your ship made all its stops?"

The seaman held up a cautioning hand. "Don't worry. We hit seven countries. The whole Mediterranean run. Your goddamn coupons can be had jus' about everywhere."

Ponzi's eyes flashed an acknowledgment. "I knew it. I never doubted it. Everywhere!"

"I only bought a couple at each place. You didn't want more, right? You just wanted enough to make sure they were on sale, right?"

"Exactly right. Just to make sure they were on sale."

"Well, everytime we hit port, I checked the post office. And I talked to enough locals to find out they can be had in the country. Some people thought I was off my bean."

"Even the smallest post office has a reasonable supply?"

The seaman nodded. "Far's I can tell."

"Then probably, with sufficient notice, they could be purchased in large quantities. I'm sure of it. Pay off the right officials, and you can get anything!"

Ponzi paced cheerily, tapping a forefinger against his lower lip. The other man watched him in silence for a moment, then his hand dipped into a pocket and came out with a fistful of the familiar coupons. They were wrinkled, grimy, and damp, but Ponzi accepted them eagerly.

"It's about five dollars worth," said the seaman. "And you promised to pay me twenty for the trouble."

Ponzi nodded and took a checkbook from his desk. A moment later he was alone once more in the office, listening to the fading sound of the seaman's footsteps. As he studied the various coupons from different European countries, Ponzi nodded in affirmation of the wisdom of having his friend determine the availability of coupons abroad. His original letters, of course, had provided enough evidence to suit most men—that coupons could be obtained and moved freely between the United States, Italy, France, and Spain—but if he were going to appear to traffic in millions of coupons, it followed that he would need more than three sources of supply. Now, he could prove to anyone that the rules and regulations of the Universal Postal Union were truly international in scope.

Ettore Giberti came bounding up the dark stairway two days later. He was breathless, virtually beside himself with excitement. He began to speak even as he was striding in from the outer office.

"You were right, absolutely right! It took a little time, but I got three. Here, this is yours!" He made a tossing motion with his right hand and a flurry of bills fell onto the desktop.

Ponzi did not move to assemble the money into a neat pile. He let it lie there, casually, as if seeing dollar bills scattered before him was an everyday occurrence. "Three investors," he asked, "for—?"

"Three hundred apiece. I've already taken my commission. There's $810 there. And here's the stubs."

Slowly Ponzi straightened the bills, glancing disinterestedly at the scrawled names on the orange scraps handed him. Again, he felt a glow of pride. He had told Giberti how easy it would be, and he had been right.

"Two of these bohunks are friends of the foreman," the young man was saying. "And the other one came up to me at lunch yesterday. I don't even know him. He said he had heard about it from somebody else. He had the cash with him. I would have come in sooner, but I figured I'd wait 'til I had three guys at least."

"There is no hurry," Ponzi said easily. "The Securities Exchange Company has been here for some time and will be here for some time." He flashed his broadest smile. "You've done quite well."

Giberti appeared not to have heard him, but went on excitedly. "And what you said about others gettin' mad because I wouldn't take their money—that looks pretty good, too. I turned down at least ten guys who wanted to invest. An' I wasn't even selling! I could o' brought you maybe two, three hundred dollars more."

With an easy gesture, Ponzi swept the bills into one drawer, the stubs into another. "You'll be pleased, then, my young friend, to hear—as I recently did—that, effective immediately, the company is open to investors of all sizes. No amount is too large, no amount is too small. We are fully staffed and prepared to handle whatever anyone wishes to give us. Perhaps you'd better take a few more blank notes with you. You might meet a potential investor on your way home."

Once his youthful salesman was gone, Ponzi took out the stack of bankbooks and began some careful calculations. Certain accounts would get larger deposits, others would get smaller ones. There would even be enough left over to open an account at yet another bank, perhaps two more. What a sweet, sweet system!

Ponzi slid open the top drawer of his desk and felt far back in a corner for a thin sheaf of penny postcards purchased for the specific occasion. In time, he would have special cards printed in rough approximation of the notes, with an ornate border—but for now, the postcards would serve quite well. He dug out the stubs of Giberti's first fifteen investors and searched through them until he found the one with the earliest date. Then, inserting a postcard into the worn typewriter in the outer office, he carefully typed the first of fifteen messages, identical except for the dates and the sums involved:

"If you will present your voucher No. A101 at our offices, Room 227, 27 School St., on or after Feb. 14, you will receive payment in the amount of $75."

He typed his name beneath the words, *The Securities Exchange Company*, and then signed each card with a bold stroke of the pen. Finished, he stacked the cards in order, so that the one with the earliest date was on top. Over the next two weeks, he would mail them—one or two or three each day.

He could visualize the activity that would follow each recipient finding the card in his mailbox. There would be momentary surprise, particularly on the part of those who had invested small sums. A few individuals would hurry to his office immediately to collect their money. But others would take their time, convinced by the mere fact that they had a one-cent postcard that they also had a profit of 50 percent on their investment. They would read the card over, show it to their wives and relatives, visit a restaurant or one of the bootleg clubs that had already sprung up everywhere, and show the card to friends. Some of the friends would be suspicious; some would accompany the original investor to the offices of the Securities Exchange Company to watch him collect his money. And they would leave their own money behind when they left, prepared to return in forty-five days for their own 50 percent profit. Back at their jobs, at the restaurants, at the recreation halls, they would tell others of their stupendous good fortune—and the ones they told would come running. Each satisfied customer would become a salesman, self-appointed.

Like a pyramid, inverted and growing from a single point that was the fertile brain of Charles Ponzi, the Securities Exchange Company would flourish until it rivaled the empires of Morgan, Rockefeller, and Carnegie.

It worked, of course.

Like a swarm of bees following the queen, second and third ranks of investors buzzed eagerly after the first ones. By the third week of the month, Giberti had climbed the stairs on School Street a half-dozen times and poured several thousand dollars onto Ponzi's desk. At his office door one grey morning, Ponzi found another young man waiting for him: Sam Milanese, who had heard that he could make 10 percent commission by bringing in other investors' money. He was promptly made the second agent of the Securities Exchange Company. In two days he was back, with cash and stubs for more than $1,500 in notes. At the end of February, Ponzi added up the sales totals of his two agents, then figured in nearly a thousand dollars that he personally had received from merchants and acquaintances. It came to $5,290 from seventeen people!

He first revealed to Rose that her life as Mrs. Charles Ponzi had changed in the middle of the month, two weeks after their anniversary on February 4th. His announcement took the form of a single strand of pearls that he placed across her dinner plate one evening. Under the kitchen lamp, the necklace gleamed lustrous-white.

"One of the business deals I've been working on has begun to come through," he said casually. "Instead of going out to celebrate, I thought you'd prefer these."

There was a flurry of questions about the money, the unpaid bills, but he dismissed them easily as he helped to adjust the pearls about her neck, where they glowed softly against her dark hair. "We can afford them, Rose. From now on, we can afford almost anything. Just wait and see. I promise, this is only the beginning."

He had first thought of the pearls the evening before. He had left the office and was passing Al Ciullo's jewelry shop when a sudden rapping sound caught his attention. Ciullo was at his front door, pulling down the blind that covered the glass panel, when he saw Ponzi outside. He let the shade spring back into its roller and rapped sharply on the glass. Ponzi waved and started to walk on, then realized that the jeweler wanted to talk to him.

"It's getting late, Al. You'd better lock your door," he said after Ciullo let him into the store. "With a storm coming up, there's not going to be much business this evening."

"In a minute, Ponzi. I've been hearing about this business of yours, and—"

Ponzi held up a hand to shut the other off. "I'm sorry, Al, but I only take investments during office hours. If I didn't handle things that way, I'd be walking around at all hours of the day and night with my pockets stuffed with dollars. Come up tomorrow, and we'll talk about it."

"I'm not interested in investing," the jeweler said. "I understand that you pay ten percent commission to your salesmen."

"That's right. Thinking of getting out of the jewelry business?"

"Not at all. But I have a lot of people come in here every day, Ponzi. People with money. They come to buy my silver and diamonds, but they're all looking for a good investment. What if I talked to them about your company?"

Ponzi appeared to think it over for a moment, then nodded. "I'll give you the details in the morning. You're right, with the traffic that comes through here, you should be able to make five hundred a week." He turned his coat collar up and stepped toward the door when his eye fell on the string of pearls in a display case. He stopped, tapping a forefinger on his lower lip in thought. "Those pearls—"

"A lovely strand, and only three hundred," said the jeweler, instantly sensing a buyer who was not about to quarrel over price.

Ponzi looked him straight in the eyes. "I'll take them for Rose, but you don't want to muddy our new business arrangement by treating me like a customer. Give me the pearls, and merely hold back three hundred from the investors' money that you bring me. I'll give full credit, of course."

Ciullo was confused. "I don't—"

"No problem," Ponzi said breezily. "You'll get your full commission. And the investors will get their full interest. It will save my staff some bookkeeping, that's all. Here, wrap those up for me."

A few seconds later, the pearls tucked snugly into his pocket, Ponzi continued toward the trolley. He had mentioned a staff of employees to the jeweler. It did not exist at the present time, of course, but things were going well enough that he should at least have a secretary. Investors soon would start calling at the office, and they would be suitably impressed if the Securities Exchange Company had a semblance of an office force. He recalled one of the men at the recreation hall mentioning a young friend who had recently graduated from a local business school. The boy was looking for a job. What *was* the name? Porcella! Joseph Porcella, that was it. Hire him for, oh, say, twenty-five dollars a week. The investment would be well worth it.

Young Porcella was interviewed the next morning—and hired on the spot. When a visitor called at the office that afternoon, the new assistant was busily typing postcards to be mailed the following week, after March 3—a date that would mark Ponzi's thirty-eighth birthday—to investors who had paid into the company in early February. Porcella rose from his typewriter and opened the door to Ponzi's inner room.

"Uh, Mr. Ponzi, a—Mr. Dondero—is here to see you."

"Uncle John!" called Ponzi. "Come in."

Blinking, the old man moved hesitatingly toward Ponzi's desk and looked around the sparsely furnished office.

"Carlo," he said. "This is where you make all the moneys?"

Ponzi laughed in agreement. "It doesn't look like much, I admit. But I think my investors would rather have their profits in cash than have to pay the cost of extravagant offices."

Dondero lowered his weight onto a chair as Ponzi asked what brought him downtown. "More than curiosity, I imagine?"

Now the older man nodded his head. "It's the restaurant. The business—it's no good since the prohibition. I think next month I close up. The whole thing. I got the money in the bank. Then I heard 'bout your business here."

Ponzi shrugged. "I'm sorry, Uncle John, but I'm not looking for a partner now. The *Trader's Guide* that I talked to you about last year—that is finished. I'm dealing in International Reply Coupons."

"I know, Carlo. The people, they all talkin' 'bout it. You pay the big interest."

"Fifty percent in forty-five days, one hundred percent in ninety days. I guess you *could* say that's 'big interest.'" Ponzi laughed. "But I'm not looking for a partner any longer, Uncle."

The old Italian ran a heavy hand over his shiny scalp. "I no come to lend money, to be the partner. I make the investment. And maybe I be the agent, too. I know the friends with moneys."

Ponzi's grin flashed. "That's another matter, then," he exclaimed. "An investment I can handle easily, Uncle. But an agency—well, there aren't many territories left open in Boston. I'll have to see about that." He tapped his lower lip. "How much did you want to invest?"

Dondero took a worn checkbook from his pocket. "My wife's," he said apologetically. "She have the check account. I have the savings. But I can sign the check." He studied the figures scrawled on the check stubs. "Maybe I can give $1,000?"

"Whatever you wish, Uncle. On April tenth, $1,000 will pay you $1,500. Invest less and you get less; invest more and you get more. It's up to you. One dollar or a million, the money is safe and sound. And if you have an agency with us, you'll have plenty more from your commissions in a short time. Then you can invest more."

Dondero's eyes narrowed. "If I invest more now," he said evenly, "I get the agency? Yes?"

As a matter of fact, Ponzi told him, the agent in Medford, where Dondero lived, had not been overly productive, and some investors had complained about his impersonal attitude. "If I could prove to him that someone else in his territory was providing better results for the company, I wouldn't hesitate to let him go. Let's see—" He opened his top drawer to consult some imaginary figures, then closed it before Dondero could see into it. "It looks like he'll have brought in about $2,000 by the end of the month."

"I give you $2,000 right now," the older man said, hurriedly inking the figure onto a check.

"And I'll have my secretary prepare a voucher for you, Uncle John. Now, let me explain your role as an agent of the Securities Exchange Company. You obviously have heard the basis of the operation?"

Dondero shook his head. "I hear, but I no understand. I know you pay the interest like you say. Carlo, I long say you smarter than anybody. Now, goddamn, you showin' all the people."

With the addition of his uncle to the field force, the list of investors began to accelerate. At the end of March, the records of the Securities Exchange Company—records kept haphazardly on file cards and a loose-leaf ledger that had lain unused around the office for more than a year—would show that 110 different persons had purchased $28,724 worth of notes during the month and would be owed some $43,000. In actuality, Ponzi had discovered quickly

75

that he had to pay out very little. A person who invested $600 and learned forty-five days later that he now could collect $900 would leave the $900 with the company as an investment that would pay him $1,350 in six weeks more.

Everything was coming in, and almost nothing was going out. Hardly an evening passed that Ponzi did not go home to Rose with a trinket from Ciullo's jewelry store. Each morning on his way to the office he stopped at the United Cigars Store to buy a fistful of expensive cigars, most of which he passed out to the policemen who waved friendly greetings on the corners or to a growing corps of messengers who regularly brought envelopes thick with cash from agents. *Nothing like a good cigar*, thought Ponzi as he handed them out each day, *to establish a man as a person of wealth and breeding.*

Carefully, slowly, so as not to arouse undue suspicion, he began adding other trappings of the successful businessman. A phone call to Daniels, the furniture dealer, brought more desks and chairs for the outer office.

"What about some coat racks?" the dealer asked. "It sounds like you're getting enough people to work in there that you'll need 'em."

"No, I don't think so. There's enough ten-penny nails on the walls to take care of a dozen coats. Besides, spring is on the way."

"What's that got to do with it?" Daniels grumbled.

"Once the weather turns, the help won't be wearing coats. Why spend my investors' money on frills? Just the desks and chairs, Daniels—and your men can collect for them when they deliver. Cash on the line."

Ponzi hung up the phone, satisfied. Daniels was a money-grubbing lout, he thought, even if he was a countryman, and it was never pleasant having to depend on somebody like that. It was too bad that it had taken the furniture dealer's money to prime the pump of the Securities Exchange Company in the first place—but now that the bank's note had been paid, it was all over. There were other details to be handled, other arrangements to be made.

By this time, savings and checking accounts in the name of Charles Ponzi and/or Securities Exchange Company had been opened in some thirty different banks throughout the area. In some, the balances on hand were considerable. It was nearly time to start doing things with the money—to begin putting it into property and good, solid securities. Oh, enough cash would be kept on hand to swing a major deal in International Reply Coupons if one was needed. But more would be pouring in daily, so there was little point in worrying about the coupons. Not now, at any rate.

Wearing a brand new suit, a neatly striped tie, and a fresh carnation on his lapel, Ponzi called on Joseph Fowler, Esq., and offered him an annual retainer of $5,000 to serve as his attorney. "I expect to have a great many legal matters to be handled in the near future. Investments in various companies, purchases of land, a few homes, things like that. There will probably just be a lot of paperwork, but I want to make sure that everything is aboveboard. Agreed?"

Fowler accepted a thick, eight-inch cigar to seal the deal and added Charles Ponzi's name to his list of clients. Then Ponzi walked a few blocks down the street and made an identical offer to another lawyer, John Marcella. That evening a puzzled Rose heard that her husband was now wealthy enough to have two attorneys working for him.

"It's not all that complicated," Ponzi told her. "Each will work on different matters. At times I might have them both involved in the same deal, working against one another to provide me—their client—with the best protection, the most advantageous terms. Each will try to outdo the other, and I'll come out ahead.

"Besides, I've learned that the more lawyers it takes to put something together, the more it takes to take it apart." He saw Rose shaking her head in amused dismay. He started to explain carefully how the Securities Exchange Company had begun to grow in leaps and bounds. Some of the agents, he said, had hired subagents of their own, and were letting them keep 5 percent of any investment money brought in.

"It may seem strange to give them five percent for not actually doing anything, I admit. But so far as the investors who collect their interest are concerned, the agents and subagents alike have done more than enough. They've made it possible for the man with a few dollars to build a fast fortune, and that's worth a small piece of the pie." He grinned at her incomprehension.

"Don't worry about it, dear. You just think about those new gowns I want you to pick out tomorrow."

Tomorrow? But that was a work day. Her job—? He shook his head, amused. He had called her office already, he told her, to say that Mrs. Charles Ponzi no longer needed a job.

"This lawyer Marcella has a secretary who called a girl-friend—Meli, I think her name is, Lucy Meli. She's coming to work for me tomorrow. And when you come in the office from now on, I want you to come in as the lady of leisure that Mrs. Charles Ponzi should be. I don't want the help gossiping that the wife of the manager of the Securities Exchange Company has to earn thirty dollars a week to help pay the bills."

Rose was delighted, almost disbelieving. And she was more incredulous when her husband suggested that on the weekend they might look at a house that he had learned was for sale.

"It's in Lexington," he said offhandedly, knowing that she would be stunned at the mere idea of the exclusive area. "First thing tomorrow, get downtown and buy some pretty things to make my Miss Meli's head spin—and to wear when we drive out to look at the house. Oh, did I mention that I'm going to purchase a car before the weekend?"

There were so many questions to be asked, but he did not give her time. "Let me show you something really important," he said. From a paper bag he took a small machine of metal and wood and placed it proudly on the tablecloth. "It's to number the vouchers," he said. "Automatically." He pumped the handle of the device and stamped a series of consecutive numbers on the cloth. "I've decided to simplify things. The green and blue notes are too hard to write on—you can't see the ink—so we're just going to use yellow ones from now on. With this, I can number them in order for the records. Look how it works." Like a child, he moved the handle rapidly up and down.

Perhaps, he thought, he looked like a fool in his wife's eyes. He, Charles Ponzi, who had talked a moment before of new clothes, new homes, new cars—as delighted with a five-dollar mechanical toy as a child at Christmas. But the kitchen was filled with laughter, and Ponzi went on stamping until the white tablecloth was covered with red numerals.

"Now," he said, whipping the cloth into the air, "put this into the bank. Stamped like that, it's every bit as good as a note of the Securities Exchange Com—" He caught himself, wondering if Rose had glimpsed the truth in his words. *I'll have to watch myself*, he thought. *I'll have to watch everything I say, to anyone.*

It was the second time in a few days that he had told someone close to him more than he wanted to reveal. The previous weekend, one of Rose's brothers, Adolphus, had come to him with a proposition. Since Uncle John Dondero was boasting of the gains that could be made with the Securities Exchange Company notes, why shouldn't the members of the Gnecco family invest along with everyone else? Ponzi had hesitated only for a fraction of a second before agreeing to accept whatever was brought him, and Adolphus undertook to get as much as he could from the interested relatives.

"The more we all put in at once, the more we'll make in a shorter time. Isn't that right, Charlie?"

78

Ponzi nodded. "Just bring the cash to the office. I'll make out the notes there."

"Tomorrow, then," Gnecco said. "I'll get my savings out of the bank tomorrow." He began to count on his fingers. "There's me, and Edward, and Charlie, and Theresa 'll want in, I know. Oh, and I think one of Rose's aunts has $800 put aside for her. If I can get that, you could take it and double it along with the rest, right?"

Ponzi's eyes widened imperceptibly. $800? His wife's money? Then he shrugged and smiled. "Why not?" he said. "Rose's money is as good as anyone else's, and just as safe with me."

Rose was still asleep when her husband—wondering how many April Fools would put their money into his hands this morning—left for his office. He did not wake her to say goodbye. The previous day had been tiring, he knew. There had been the huge new house in Lexington to explore, with measurements to be taken and furnishings to be planned.

Six bedrooms! It seemed an overwhelming number, but he had explained that his mother would take one as soon as she arrived from Parma, and that the servants might need one or two downstairs for themselves. On the broad second-story sunporch that completely surrounded the upper level of the house, he had gestured expansively at the surrounding countryside.

"Only five acres of it belongs to us," he said as if apologizing. "But the view for miles is all ours." He tilted his head and looked at the delighted Rose. "Five acres," he repeated. "I'll have to get a car now. I certainly don't want my wife walking that far."

As he boarded the trolley that morning, he had already decided on the car. A dark blue Locomobile. With a chauffeur, of course. An automobile such as an Astor or Morgan would choose. An automobile suitable for a financial wizard. It was priced at $12,000, or roughly one-third the amount asked for the house in Lexington. *What matter?* thought Ponzi as the trolley clanged its way along the tracks. *This week he would own both.*

He felt sure that he could get the price of the house down to an even $30,000. The seller was a man named Richard Engstrom, who had expressed interest in investing in the Securities Exchange Company. He would probably take $9,000 or $10,000 in cash and a note for the rest. It was all so easy. Nearly everyone who met

Charles Ponzi these days—who listened to his soft, confident voice and looked at his unlined face, his clear eyes, his immaculate clothes—sensed wealth and opportunity. The roster of agents and salesmen was growing as quickly as Pinocchio's nose.

Ponzi tried to keep his mind off his expanding operation while he glanced at the morning paper during the ride. It was full of news about a payroll robbery in South Braintree in which two men had been killed. The police were searching the Italian community for two radicals, Nicola Sacco and Bartolomeo Vanzetti. Their nationality could hurt him, he mused. He tried to concentrate on an article about the coming fall Presidential campaign to find a successor to the ailing and autocratic Wilson. A U.S. senator from Ohio, Warren Harding, seemed the probable choice of the Republicans, while the Democrats were favoring the governor of Ohio, James M. Cox.

It's six of one, a half-dozen of the other, Ponzi thought. *The fat cats will stay fat, and the fools will stay fools, starving while the old fogies in State Street pay 4 percent on their savings—no matter who heads the country.*

He liked to be the first one in the office. It set a good example for his small and growing staff, and convinced investors that he worked hard for their benefit. But this morning the efficient Miss Meli was already seated at her side of his huge desk. In a week's time, the energetic, eighteen-year-old blond, her blue eyes perpetually sparkling with enthusiasm, had proved to be a highly valuable asset. Fluent in English and Italian, she had little trouble conversing over the increasingly busy telephone with agents and investors whose accents at times were thicker than molasses. She was well worth twenty-five dollars a week, Ponzi realized, for he had turned over to her almost all of the simple bookkeeping chores of the Securities Exchange Company.

"Three calls already, Mr. Ponzi," she said as he strode into the office. "A man named Bruno—Joseph Bruno, it is—wants to open an agency in New Hampshire. He's in Manchester. And a Mr. Carlton in Meriden—that's Connecticut—wants to work for us there, and said to tell you he has some friends who are interested, too. Then, a Mr. Frank Pope is on his way to see you."

Ponzi nodded his head in admiration. "Excellent, Miss Meli. Excellent. Write the two prospects—what was it, Bruno and Carlton?—that they may go to work as soon as they notify us of a permanent office address. We'll send them a supply of vouchers upon acceptance, and they'll get the standard ten percent. Did this Pope say what he wanted?"

Miss Meli had no idea. She busied herself at the typewriter while Ponzi searched his recollection. The name rang a bell, and he sensed that Pope was not an investor. He was almost certain of it.

He was still trying to place the name when an angry, red-faced Italian truckdriver stormed into the room. Behind him, two flustered employees from the outer office followed, protesting. Ponzi waved them back to their desks.

"You big crook!" the truckdriver shouted. "These ain't good!" Ignoring Lucy Meli's wide-eyed fright, he tossed several reply coupons onto the desk. "They ain't good! The post office said so!"

Ponzi picked up the coupons and studied them. Coolly, he looked up at the man who stood before his desk with fists clenched and rage in his eyes. Then he lit a cigar before speaking. "They're perfectly good. Do you think I would have given them to you to show people if they weren't? Now, tell me what happened."

His attitude—all calm confidence—made the truckdriver take a deep breath. When he spoke, his voice was lower. He took the coupons, he said, to the North End of town, to the post office substation at Hanover and North Bennett Streets.

"The man said, no, he ain't taking them in! He won't give stamps for 'em!"

Ponzi shrugged in exasperation. "I can understand that, friend. These coupons were purchased here in Boston, in the U. S. of A. They're supposed to be redeemed *overseas*. But there's no reason they can't be exchanged here, too." He looked across the desk. "Miss Meli, get the postmaster at that station on the phone."

In a minute, the young girl handed the phone across to him, and Ponzi began talking in a loud, clear voice. The befuddled driver listened in awe as Ponzi began quoting chapter and verse from the postal regulations, hardly giving the official at the other end of the line a chance to speak. Finally, however, the manager of the Securities Exchange Company shook his head wearily. "All right, sir," he said into the mouthpiece. "I see that nothing short of a bulletin from the third assistant postmaster general will convince you. Thanks for your time. I'll just have to go higher up."

He slammed the receiver back onto its hook. Shrugging resignedly, he said, "I'm sorry, but the post office is not infallible, like the Pope. It hires its share of fools." The driver was staring at him. "I suppose that you would like your investment returned. How much was it? Miss Meli, get this man's file card, please."

"No, no, no," the driver protested. "I got a hundred dollars invested. You keep it, Mr. Ponzi."

"But the postmaster agrees with you. You heard me with him—"

The big man was shaking his head, already backing out the door. "He's wrong. He's makin' a mistake. You wouldn't o' talked to him that way 'less you were right. I see that, Mr. Ponzi. I'll be back for my money in a couple weeks. Sorry I bothered you."

Frank Pope was next, waiting his turn in the outer office—and Ponzi sensed trouble the moment the short, elderly man came through the door. The business card he displayed identified him as the Massachusetts state supervisor of small loans. Ponzi sized him up as somewhere between senility and dotage. "Within a radius of half a mile from the Custom House Tower," he had once told Giberti, "you can run across more mummies at large than you'd find walled up in King Tut's Tomb.

The familiar smile flashed. "Thank you for dropping in, Mr. Pope, but I'm not looking for a loan these days. The company is doing well. Very well, I might say."

Smiling back at him, the official explained that his office had been flooded with applications for loans of $500, $1,000, or more from various parts of the city. Most of the applicants, he said, stated that they wished to invest with the Securities Exchange Company.

"And since we know very little about your company, Mr. Ponzi, I thought I had better talk to you about it. We've heard that you are paying exorbitant rates of interest."

Ponzi nodded. "The kind that would make your Pilgrim forefathers get restless in their graves. But what exactly did you want to know?"

A half-hour later, the caller left. He was a bit skeptical, perhaps, about the amount of interest that Ponzi was paying, but he was apparently convinced that his business—unorthodox, to say the least—was legitimate. Ponzi leaned back in his chair, swinging around to place his feet on the radiator beneath the window, and looked over his shoulder at Miss Meli.

"I had the feeling when I was talking to him, Miss Meli, that he did not know whether the Postal Union was a merger of the Postal Telegraph and Western Union, or a branch of the American Federation of Labor."

The young girl grinned back at him. "I'm not sure I understood everything you said, either. But if it's all there in the postal guide—"

"Why, he practically saluted, didn't he, when I pulled that out. I thought he was going to sing 'The Star-Spangled Banner.'"

The phone rang, and Ponzi gestured to the girl to get it. She picked it up, murmured a few words, and then held it out to Ponzi. "It's for you. He won't give his name."

83

"Charlie, there's a warrant out for your arrest," crackled the voice in the earpiece. Ponzi's feet came down from the radiator. For an instant he was shocked, but then his mind flashed back across the years and he recognized the voice. He laughed.

"Cassullo, you sonofabitch! What the hell do you think you're doing? Where are you, anyway?"

"Right here in Boston, old friend. Want to have a steak with me and fill me in on what you're up to these days? Christ, it's been years, hasn't it?"

There was an ominous tone in his old prisonmate's voice, something just below the surface of the words that spelled danger. Ponzi knew that he would have to talk to Louis Cassullo, whether he wanted to or not. "It's been ten, almost twelve years, I guess. Sure, I'd like to see you again. What brings you to Boston?"

"Business, friend. Business. Where can we talk?"

Ponzi named a cafe around the corner on Tremont Street. He was there a good five minutes before Cassullo sauntered in, and he studied him intently as he wove his way between the tables to a booth in the corner. The wiry Italian had put on a little weight, but he still bore an unmistakeable prison pallor. His eyes, if it were possible, were even duller than Ponzi remembered them being during the months together at St. Vincent de Paul Penitentiary. Nevertheless, Ponzi flipped the smile into place and held out his hand.

"Scared ya with that warrant business, did I, Charlie?" Cassullo was laughing.

"Not a bit," said Ponzi, returning the jest. "But I *was* thinking of calling up Sheriff Kelliher at the Charles Street Jail and asking what he was serving for lunch. Maybe telling him to keep it warm for me."

A waiter appeared, handed menus to each of them. "Damn," Cassullo snapped, "since you can't get a drink any more, they practically throw the food at you. How's a man supposed to relax and enjoy a meal?"

They studied the menus and ordered, with Ponzi waiting until the waiter was beyond earshot before he spoke. "What've you been up to, Cassullo, since I last saw you—and you gave me a tip on a job that led to a lengthy stay in Atlanta."

"I heard 'bout that. Tough luck. I ain't had much better, though. I been in and out, up and down, you might say. I was just down in Jersey and really onto something. In Trenton, three of us ran across this Polish immigrant and got him to take all his bank notes out of the vaults—we'd heard he had a fortune. We

84

pulled the envelope switch, all right, and opened the goods. It was all there—all the big bills we'd heard about. But the damn things were German marks, Russian rubles, Austrian crowns! Since the damn war, they're not worth twenty-five cents a ton!"

Cassullo tore into a porterhouse steak hungrily. "Worst part of the whole thing," he growled through huge mouthfuls, "was that we'd loaded our envelope with a couple o' twenties on the top and bottom so's he'd be sure to go through with it. Dumb Polack made dough off us!"

Ponzi sat silently while Cassullo cursed the war, the foreign mints, the "lucky" victim. It was painfully obvious why his old friend sought him out. With investors beginning to be heard from throughout all of New England, it was a certainty that the Italian underworld on the East Coast would be tipped off about Boston's new financial genius. Ponzi realized that he was lucky he had operated this long without hearing from some less savory acquaintances from years gone by.

"Tough luck, friend," he said as Cassullo uttered a final "Damn!" "But what are your plans now?"

"I—uh—heard that you've got a big business going here. An' I thought maybe you could use some help."

It was that simple. There was no indication of blackmail, no threat that a word or two about Ponzi's past might be delivered to the proper authorities. The two men read each other perfectly—and Ponzi knew that Cassullo was the sort who would relish an opportunity to show his hand. He had no choice.

"It's fortunate you arrived when you did. The business has been expanding by leaps and bounds. I have a half-dozen people working at the office already, and will need more very soon. You might just fit into the Securities Exchange Company nicely."

Over a cup of thick, black coffee, Ponzi provided the details of his transactions in International Reply Coupons. "It's absolutely legal," he said with conviction. "I've been straight for years." Cassullo listened intently, neither arguing nor accepting—merely listening. He knew only that Ponzi's scheme, legitimate or not, was making money. A lot of money. And he would have part of it. Perhaps a large part.

It would not do to have Cassullo around the office, Ponzi realized immediately. There was something about him—the smell of prison—that would create suspicion among investors and catch the eye of the police.

"Louis," he said, "I'll tell you how you can be most useful to me. Each day I get requests from people in other cities—all over

New England and as far south as Philadelphia—who want to open agencies. How about serving as my advance agent and checking out branches?"

Cassullo nodded readily. "How much?"

"Fifty a week to start, a hundred next month when we see how things are going."

"Make it a hundred now, two hundred next month. And I'll need a car."

Ponzi grimaced at Cassullo's pettiness. The man could have asked five hundred and gotten it! "A car it is, then. Come with me. We'll go talk to my Miss Meli about putting you on the payroll. She's got quite a collection of names of possible agents. In fact, a couple of new ones called this morning, and you might as well get up to visit them. One in Connecticut and another in New Hampshire, I believe."

He knew that the more he kept his new business associate out of town, the better it would be. Already, he sensed difficulty explaining Cassullo to Miss Meli and the others at the office. Thus far, he had taken pains to hire clean-cut and ordinary-looking employees, the kind who might be seen behind the teller's windows at a bank. Perhaps if he hinted that this was an old friend, down and out, who needed help—yes, it wouldn't hurt to start establishing himself as a philanthropist. There would be publicity value in that later. *Ponzi, Retriever of Lost Souls.* He could see the headline.

At the office he introduced Cassullo to the surprised Miss Meli, and added a wink that indicated he would relate more afterward. Then he said that an errand had to be run—"I must see a man about a car"—and went out into the warm spring afternoon.

Cassullo's automobile would wait—at least until after he had purchased his own Locomobile. Right now there was something more important to do, something that Cassullo's first words on the phone had suggested to him. He turned into Pemberton Square and walked up the steps of police headquarters.

"Warrants?" said the officer behind the desk. "That's downstairs, the basement."

In the lower level of the building, he faced another blue uniform. "Officer, I've come for a warrant," he said.

The policeman looked at him. "Who's the party?" he asked, taking a sheet of paper from a pile before him.

"No one. I was told that you have a warrant out for me."

The cop looked at him in astonishment. "You're surrendering? Who the hell are you?"

Ponzi drew himself up to his full five-foot-four. "Ponzi's the name. Charles Ponzi. P-O-N-Z-I."

"Oh, ho," the policeman said in an impressed tone. "The investment company! We *have* got something on you in here—but there's no warrant out that I remember." He began leafing through a book the size of a cardtable. "Here," he said, stopping at a page. "A couple of people have asked that we look you up, that's all. Nobody's registered a complaint."

Ponzi was not surprised. He had studied or been involved in enough similar ventures, both legitimate and otherwise, to know that it was impossible to grow to any size at all without attracting skepticism. Between December and April, it would have been unusual if the police had not received a few routine calls for a check into his operation.

"No warrant?" he mused. "Some damn fool playing an April Fool's joke on me, I guess." He paused as if in thought, then delivered a practiced chuckle. "I must say, officer, enough of your fellows have been investing their paychecks with me that I'd really be an idiot to try anything slippery." He dipped a hand into his pocket. "Here, this is my card. Pass it on to your inspector and tell him I'm in my office every day. I'd be delighted to have him over any time."

The officer took the card and tucked it into a corner of his desk blotter. He watched curiously as Ponzi casually laid a fresh cigar on the desk.

"Mr. Ponzi!"

"Yes, officer?"

The man's face was flushed. "Uh—I was wondering—I heard, that is, some of the boys said you pay ten percent on any investment money brought in. There's—uh—plenty of men here who have a little saved up, but don't have time to come 'round. If I was to talk to them—?"

Ponzi nodded, seeming to consider it. "I hadn't thought about opening an agency in police headquarters—but—well, you have my card . . . ." He almost laughed aloud.

Lucy Meli looked up from the typewriter at her employer and waited for him to finish yet another in a string of calls that kept the telephone busy from nine to five each day. It was hardly past ten in the morning, but there were already a half-dozen people—laborers, an Army officer in uniform, a young shopgirl—lined up at the counter out front to put down their cash. At noontime, when other offices closed for lunch, the crowd would grow to twenty or thirty people, practically climbing over one another to make their investments and still have time to eat. And the stubs from the notes, along with the cash, flowed from the front office to Miss Meli's desk like an endless river. Quickly, efficiently, she checked one against the other, filled in the simple master record book of investments, prepared deposit slips for various banks, and bundled the money under Ponzi's watchful eye.

He had told her to keep a tight rein on the practices of the Securities Exchange Company. All money passed across the dark oak counter of the front office was to be handled with the precision of a well-run bank. If the four tellers who had been hired could not keep up with the growing crowd of people waiting to buy notes, more would have to be employed. "Get what you need to keep order, Miss Meli," Ponzi had told her. "Don't bother me with details."

For a young girl, fresh out of Burdett Business College, it was just about the most exciting job imaginable! She was part of the world of high finance—and she was aware that of the dozen or so people working in the office and more than twenty agents in ten different cities, only she and her considerate and kind employer, Charles Ponzi, knew that money was pouring in at the rate of $5,000 a day!

"Something wrong?" she asked, as Ponzi hung up the telephone, an uncharacteristic frown on his face.

"The Locomobile agency—they still don't have the car in. The salesman tells me the only dark blue model for miles around is being made to order for a banker in New York. I'll have to wait another month for one like it. Meanwhile, I bought a little Hudson."

The secretary shook her blond curls. "That's too bad."

"No problem. I told the Locomobile agency I'll pay an extra thousand if I get the car and the banker waits. They'll call me back." As if on cue, the telephone rang. "If that's the salesman, tell him I'm out," Ponzi said with a smile. "Let him stew awhile wondering if I've changed my mind."

Miss Meli took the call, putting down the receiver a few seconds later. "You were right," she said. "He says to tell you that *your* car will be ready in two weeks. Oh, Mr. Ponzi!"

He looked at the letter she had ready for his signature. It was to Carlton, the new agent in Meriden:

I am in receipt of your favor of the 13th of April and wish to thank you for the check for the account of Mr. Sommer, and am enclosing a voucher for same. I am also enclosing a book of temporary receipts which are self-explanatory. Mr. Coit and Mr. Brown came to Boston yesterday and I have made arrangements for them to open an office in New Haven. I am planning to go there myself on Monday. I have agreed to allow them a commission of 10% in addition to what I will allow you.

It is pretty hard for me to tell you how long this thing will last. The exchange rate is very uncertain and after rising up to 27 came down again close to 22.

As per your request, I am also enclosing you a couple of coupons.

He couldn't help being amused by the second paragraph. He could visualize Carlton trying to figure it out. *The exchange rate, up to 27 and down to 22! What the hell does that mean?* The man didn't have to understand it—no one, Ponzi included, had to understand it. All that Carlton had to do—and all that Coit and Brown in New Haven and the other agents anywhere had to do—was collect the money, take out ten percent, and send it in. Their job was that simple.

He signed the letter perfunctorily. Watching Miss Meli seal the envelope and then turn back to her typewriter, he realized that something was bothering him.

It was all too simple, that was the problem. The money was

coming in and he was spending it—but it was coming in faster than it could be spent. He had put a dozen people on his payroll, paid off all his old debts, spent cash for the house, sent Rose out to Boston's finest furniture stores with instructions to buy nothing on credit, purchased one car and ordered another, and cabled his mother enough for an entire new wardrobe and a first-class steamship ticket to America. And still the bank accounts were growing, growing, growing until they threatened to drown him in a green tide.

The solution, he knew, was to begin spending larger amounts, to buy into banks themselves so that he could control yet more investors' dollars. *That* would pit his brain against the top financial men of the community. *That* would be a challenge. Thus far, it was all too easy. Outwitting simple-minded immigrants and minor-league postal officials, verbally dazzling housewives and dock-hands who could barely read—there was nothing to that. It was, practically speaking, by this time, a bore.

But what really bothered him was the thought that it might be just as easy to pull the wool over the eyes of the so-called financial wizards as it was to fleece a greenhorn from Naples.

He realized that one of the clerks from the outer office had called his name—*once, twice, how many times?*—and he snapped out of his reverie.

"Mr. Ponzi, some people want to see you. It's—uh—I think, policemen."

Instantly his mind was fully alert. Someone must have caught up with the news he had read in post office bulletins two weeks earlier: at the end of March three countries—France, Italy, and Rumania—had withdrawn from the postal agreement and had ordered an end to the sale of reply coupons. He welcomed a confrontation, particularly if the interrogators had done their homework.

But when he held his hand out to the trio who came through the door, he sensed yet one more easy victory. Oh, well, it would occupy the morning.

"Yes, gentlemen, what can I do for you?"

Two of the men were plainclothes officers from police head-quarters. The other was a postal inspector, who opened the discussion. "I understand, Mr. Ponzi, that you had some kind of conversation—almost an argument—with the postmaster at the Hanover Street station?"

Ponzi smiled inwardly. So that was to be the opening gambit. *Argument, my eye, gentlemen! You're looking for evidence of fraud.*

"I think that tack will waste a lot of my precious time," he said

90

aloud. "The postmaster's report of his alleged conversation with me is not evidence that the conversation itself occurred. If it did, and if you have reason to believe it constitutes a violation of the law on my part, bring charges and we'll thrash the matter out in court."

He saw, out of the corner of his eye, Miss Meli's blue eyes widen in admiration. It must have seemed for her a courtroom performance by Clarence Darrow, he realized.

"We're not contemplating any action against you," one of the officers said. "We're interested in some points you made with the postmaster, that's all."

It was time to back off a bit, so that he could charge in more fully later. "Sorry," he said, "I'll be glad to tell you anything that you believe will help."

The postal inspector smiled. "Well, for example, you said there was no restriction on the number of coupons that can be bought and redeemed."

"You're certainly aware that I'm one hundred percent correct on that."

"Yes," said the inspector. "Unless, of course, the coupons are counterfeit."

So that's it! He isn't even going to ask how I get coupons from countries that no longer issue them. He's worried that I'm printing my own coupons!

"Inspector, how long do you think it would take someone to grow rich by counterfeiting coupons that are worth a two-cent or three-cent stamp each?" He saw the official's knowing nod and shook his head. "Besides, I'm sure your offices would report any counterfeits as soon as they got them in any quantity. Have you had such reports?"

With a shrug, the man answered the question. "You seem to know a whole lot more than I gave you credit for at first," he said, and Ponzi's antennae sensed the intent to put him off.

"Now, don't make be blush, friend. I really don't know enough to get in out of the rain." In the chuckle that followed, Ponzi opened the humidor of cigars on his desk. "Have one, gentlemen, unless you think it constitutes some sort of bribe. In which case—"

The officers were already reaching for the cigars, and in a moment, a thick cloud of smoke hung in the office air. "The thing that bothers me, Ponzi," the postal inspector began, "is that if you're making a profit by speculating in coupons, it must result in a loss for someone else. We're interested in finding out if it's the U.S. government or the government of some other country."

God, it was going to be as easy as he feared! He took a deep puff of his cigar and stared straight into the official's eyes. "Your basic assumption is wrong, I'm afraid. There are no losers. Everyone makes a profit."

"That's absurd!"

"And so is a giraffe. You know the story about the rube who had never heard of a giraffe and said, 'There ain't no such animal,' when he saw one at a circus." As the trio smiled, Ponzi flipped to a fresh page in the large notepad on his desk. "Now, gentlemen, if you don't mind, I'm going to show you a giraffe."

He began his lecture, scribbling along the way:

"Let us assume that France needs fifteen million francs. I borrow in this country one million dollars at fifty percent interest, as I'm doing now on a small scale. The one million, at the current rate of exchange, is equal to fifteen million francs. I send a draft for it to the French government with the understanding that France will issue to me fifty million International Reply Coupons. France can obtain them from the Universal Postal Union on open account. As soon as I receive the coupons, I exchange them here for stamps. Then I sell the stamps at ten percent discount. Let us assume that I also pay a ten percent commission to the agents who have been instrumental in obtaining for me one million dollars from the public.

"Now, the transaction, insofar as I'm concerned, would show the following balance." Looking up, he turned the page toward them.

```
Cash on hand from sale of
50 million U.S. 5¢ stamps
(less 10% discount) . . . . . . . . . . . . . . . . . . . . . . . . . . . .$2,250,000
Principal due to note holders . . . . . .$1,000,000
50% interest. . . . . . . . . . . . . . . . .   500,000
10% commission to agents . . . . . . . .   100,000
Gross profit for Securities
   Exchange Company . . . . . . . . . . .   650,000
                                          _____
                                          $2,250,000
```

The three men were nodding their heads in unison, following each scratch of his pencil with steady gaze, not wanting to halt his lesson with a question.

"Now, gentlemen, on the other hand, the ledger of the Universal Postal Union shows the U.S. government a creditor to the extent of $2,250,000 and the French government a debtor to the extent of $3 million." He saw the postal inspector draw a breath, but asked the question for him. "Why *$3* million? Because the coupons cost the French government fifteen million francs payable in gold, at their gold parity of five francs to the dollar. But they cost me only $1 million, at the current exchange rate of fifteen francs to the dollar. The difference between what France must pay and what the U.S. can collect represents the charges of the Universal Postal Union for the service.

"Let's move on, then. Assume that France is called on to settle its debt. Since it has received only $1 million and owes $3 million, it stands to lose $2 million. The loss can't be avoided so long as the franc remains at the ratio of fifteen to the dollar. If the ratio should decrease, the loss would decrease in proportion, and it would disappear entirely if and when the franc sold at its gold parity of five to the dollar. But, as I'm sure you're all aware, depreciated currencies take a number of years to recover, as a general rule."

Again, the trio nodded their heads.

"Stay with me, now. France can't defer its settlement with the Universal Postal Union. The payment must be effected. The best way to finance it is through a bond issue. Let's say they offer $3 million worth of twenty-year bonds, paying three percent, and payable in dollars. The carrying charges for the bonds will amount to $1.8 million in twenty years.

"But don't forget that France already has on hand some fifteen million francs derived from the sale of the coupons to me. Those francs, if loaned by the government to private or self-liquidating enterprises for a period of twenty years at an annual interest of five percent, would eventually amount to thirty million francs or $6 million. That would be sufficient to retire the bond issue, with interest charges of $1.8 million, and would leave in addition a profit of $1.2 million for the French government."

They were blinking at the numbers now, the two police officers somewhat rapidly and the postal official slowly in deep thought. Ponzi once again turned the pad toward them, tapping the figures slowly with his pencil point.

"As you can see, the public invests a million and makes a profit of $500,000 in six weeks. My agents give their time and service and earn $100,000. The Universal Postal Union collects another $500,000 for its services. The U.S. Post Office sells $2,500,000 worth of stamps and, presumably, makes a profit. The firms or individuals who buy the stamps from me at a discount split a profit of $250,000 among themselves. France comes out ahead by $1,200,000. The holders of the French bonds earn another $1.8 million. The enterprises launched with the fifteen million francs

93

loaned by the French government, presumably, earn a profit of some kind. Not only that, but they provide work for a number of people who also then earn a living. Last, but not least, I make roughly $650,000 on the deal."

He tossed the pencil carelessly onto the pad, winked at Miss Meli who had sat open-mouthed and silent throughout his discourse, and said: "If any of you can show me where the entire transaction produces a loss for anyone, I'll buy him a Stetson hat."

There was a long, long period of silence. The postal inspector raised his head from the page of numbers. "Am I to assume, Mr. Ponzi," he asked, "that you are the unofficial representative in this country of some foreign government?"

"No," he said aloud with obvious amusement, "Ponzi represents no one but himself."

One of the official's hands, moving slowly and almost involuntarily, reached out, ripped the top page off the pad, and stuffed it into a coat pocket. "Uh, you don't mind if I take this?"

Ponzi stretched his grin to its full width. "Not at all. Study it over. You can win the Stetson at any time." He rose to show the visitors to the door. "Just one thing, gentlemen: Please bear in mind that we have been discussing only theories of finance, and not facts. I've explained how I—or you, or anyone, for that matter—could make money with postal reply coupons. For obvious reasons, there are certain techniques, certain facts, which I can't divulge." They were walking now through the outer office, which was beginning to fill with the noontime crowd of investors. Ponzi waved a hand at the people in the lines. "The investments of these good people—why, some of them have brought in their life's savings—must be protected. I'm sure you understand that."

Nodding in uncontested agreement, the postal inspector started down the stairs. But the two policemen hung back, waiting inside the open door for a moment to survey the growing crowd. Several investors who had collected their money stood greedily counting thick stacks of greenbacks.

"Uh, Mr.—er—Ponzi—" one officer began.

There's no need to finish it, Ponzi thought, recognizing the familiar gleam in the man's eyes. "Certainly, your investment would be protected like everyone else's. Step in line right now if you want, or drop back anytime. No rush. We're open from nine to five."

He left the office in good spirits. The morning had provided a warm-up at least for the complex poker games that lay ahead, and he enjoyed the pace. In the shiny and smooth-engined Hudson sedan, he drove carefully out Huntington Avenue, heading for Brookline. A new agent had opened a branch office there in what should have been a rich area for prospects, but no business was coming through the front door. Something smelled funny.

He pulled up in front of the dingy office, where his grey-haired agent was already waiting for him at the curb. As he got out of the car, Ponzi reached for an object that rested on the front seat beside him. It was a slim walnut cane, smooth and lustrous, and topped with a gold handle. Swinging it with an ease that implied he might have been born with it in his hand, Ponzi walked back and forth on the sidewalk to survey the new addition to his spreading office network. On either side, a bakery, a butcher shop, a small hardware store—all had customers. In front of a restaurant on the corner, a dark-skinned man stood with his hands on his hips and watched Ponzi with smiling hostility. Behind him a small group of other men waited.

"Let's get it over with," Ponzi said to his agent, and walked toward the group, swinging the cane lightly.

"I'm Charles Ponzi," he said, gesturing with the cane in lieu of extending his hand.

"Vito Chavonelle. I own the restaurant." The man flicked his eyes toward the building behind him, in a motion that made Ponzi think of a snake's darting tongue.

"I'm always glad to meet another countryman who has also found success in America."

The eyes narrowed, snakelike again. "I'm from Genoa," said the restaurant owner.

Ponzi remembered instantly a saying learned almost in infancy by Italian children: "It takes seven Gentiles to get the best of a Jew and seven Jews to get the best of a Genovese." He knew that the odds were virtually a hundred to one that he would have to give the man whatever he asked. "Why waste time?" he said. "What do you want?"

"These people—our customers—are our friends. We want to protect them. If your business is—uh—closed up, all of a sudden, there ought to be some kind of—uh, insurance. We have nothing at all against you opening an office here among us, but if you're making the money we've heard about—"

"What do you want, friend?"

The man glanced at the handful of merchants with him. "A third of what you take in."

The wheels in Ponzi's head whirred instantly. It was the old protection racket, that was all. *You want your fingers in the pie?* he

95

thought. *All right, I'll let you stick them in up to your knuckles.* He seemed to think the request over, then tapped his cane emphatically on the pavement. "I have an idea," he said. "My agent here will be working alone, and one-third of what he takes in might not amount to much. Suppose I appoint each of you as his subagents? Then, any money you get from your friends to invest in the company would entitle you to a five percent commission. I am sure that you all have enough customers coming in each day to do quite well."

It only took a minute for the merchants to talk it over. Then there was a series of handshakes, and a smiling, satisfied Ponzi moved off down the street. The deal would greatly increase the office's gross, but not cost him a dime.

"Christ, I'm drier than a Methodist conclave," he said to his agent. "Where can we get a beer?"

"Milwaukee is the nearest place I know."

Ponzi shook his head in exasperation. When you outwit a Genovese, it calls for a drink. "Where's the nearest church?" he asked.

Some ten minutes later, they were blithely discussing with the parish priest a donation that the new office would make to solidify its position as a community enterprise. "I believe in contributing to the spiritual—as well as the financial—well-being of my investors," Ponzi said, smiling as the priest poured three glasses of wine from a choice bottle. The church would benefit also, he noted.

"When your parishoners begin collecting their interest, their tithes will increase considerably."

The priest sipped from his own glass. An idea seemed to come to him. "Mr. Ponzi, is there any reason why *I* could not invest with you?"

Startled, Ponzi drained his wine before he answered. "No, no reason at all, Father. We have investors in all walks of life."

The priest had no money of his own, he explained. But the church for some months had been collecting funds for a much-needed repainting. So far, $600 had been amassed. "The contractor won't start work until August anyway. Why should the money lie idle for three months when you can double it for us?" He hesitated. "You understand that I cannot afford to gamble the money, Mr. Ponzi. I can only invest it in a safe thing."

"Of course."

"And if I needed it—for any reason—before maturity of your note, what could you do for me?"

Ponzi spread his hands in an easy gesture. "Why, upon surrender of the note at any of my offices or through a bank, I would return the principal to you. There would be no interest, of course. That is my standing agreement with all of my note-holders."

"Then," said the priest with a thoughtful nod, "there's no problem. I might as well make a check out to you now and save myself a trip to your new office." He looked questioningly at the dapper financier who sat casually, his gold-headed cane across his lap, a glass of red wine in his hand. "I—uh—I'm not making a mistake, am I, Mr. Ponzi?"

"My dear Father," said Ponzi easily, *"errare humanum est."* And he laughed softly.

"Of course. Of course," the priest replied, laughing and signing the check.

PONZI!

THE BOSTON SWINDLER

BY
DONALD DUNN

Sporting a diamond stickpin and a gold-handled cane, Charles Ponzi looked every inch a millionaire in July, 1920.

At thirty-eight, Ponzi radiated
$10 million worth of confidence,
and in her obligatory Bachrach
portrait, twenty-year-old Rose
Ponzi displayed youthful innocence.

(Courtesy Boston University Journalism Library)

On the porch of his newly acquired mansion, the wizard of finance coaxed his wife and mother to pose for newsmen and motion-picture photographers.

(Courtesy Boston University Journalism Library)

The Lexington, Massachusetts, home that was rumored to contain a secret vault filled with Ponzi's fortune.

Ponzi's clerks paid out millions from behind barred windows of the Securities Exchange Company.

(Courtesy Boston University Journalism Library)

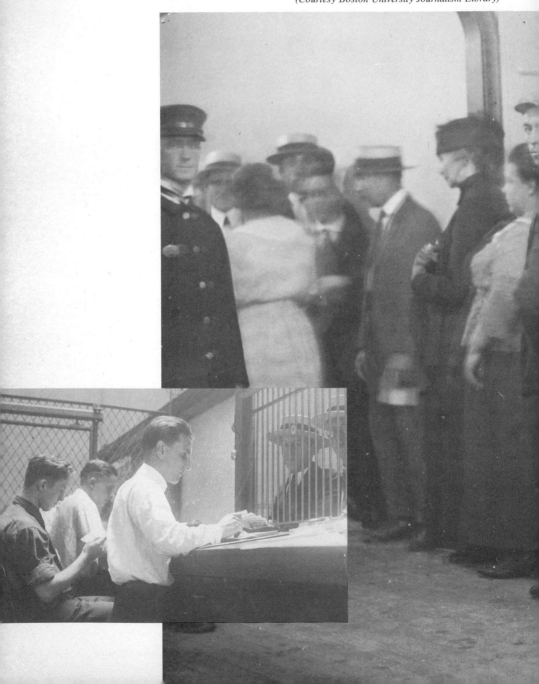

In the corridor of 27 School Street, investors lined up to redeem their notes as the first "run" began.
(Courtesy Boston University Journalism Library)

When the Boston *Post* ran Ponzi's rogues' gallery photos from Montreal, his financial bubble exploded.

(Courtesy Boston University Journalism Library)

While Ponzi scoffed at the exposé, the *Post* kept the pressure on with cartoons.

Filling School Street and Pi Alley, thousands waited long hours to collect their money.

Jaunty as ever, Ponzi strode to court in a crowd of investigators and still faithful fans.

(Courtesy Boston University Journalism Library)

Out of prison, Ponzi in 1925 posed at a cheap hotel in Jacksonville, Florida, where he tried to sell Florida swampland to investors.

(Courtesy Boston University Journalism Library)

Forever faithful, Ponzi made out the first note in the Charpon Florida land scheme to his wife.

(Courtesy Boston University Journalism Library)

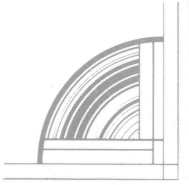

No. 64.

October 24ᵈ

Certificate No. 1

Name Rose M. Pon

187 Strathmore rd.

35 Brighton M

Units of Indeb

$350⁰⁰

Redeemable at $1,050⁰⁰

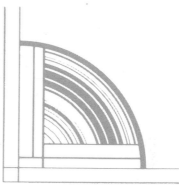

Ponzi's diminutive stature was evident on the witness stand as he pondered an attorney's question during a federal hearing.

(Courtesy Boston University Journalism Library)

CHARPON LAND SYNDICATE

Jacksonville, Florida

Units

192

This is to Certify that

is the owner of   Units of Indebtedness of the Charpon Land Syndicate, of the Par Value of TEN DOLLARS ($10.00) each.

This Certificate is redeemable at three times its par value, or   Dollars ($), in accordance with the terms and conditions printed on the back hereof.

CHARPON LAND SYNDICATE,

Per

Shortly before his death, Ponzi
flashed a confident smile in the
charity ward of a Rio de Janeiro
hospital.

(Wide World Photos)

Immigration inspectors surrounded the aging financier aboard the S.S. *Vulcania* for deportation to Italy in 1934.

(Courtesy Boston University Journalism Library)

It was time to go on to bigger things—time to take on the banks.
Now.

Ponzi sensed that the entire country was caught up in a
strange, unexplainable feeling of excitement. No one was asking
questions. No one was thinking carefully about the future. No one,
except senile and conservative fuddy-duddies, was worrying. At
least, no one was worrying about anything important.

The revelations by that new young author—F. Scott Fitzger-
ald—about the manners and morals of modern youth in *This Side
of Paradise*? The protest marches and demonstrations over inflated
prices on everything from milk and steak to apartment rentals? The
strikes affecting mining and manufacturing? The surprising experi-
ments with something called radio? The easily surmountable
difficulty of getting a good drink of whiskey?

Subjects for dinner party conversation, that was all they were.
Things to talk about while the brain went on clicking away in
private, planning and scheming to build up the bank account.
Calculating how best to gain money, property, power. With America's industrial output soaring to new peaks and with the stock
market climbing to a postwar high, the men who controlled the
nation's wealth were interested only in controlling more of it.

When a man's vision is fixed on one thing, thought Ponzi, *he
might as well be blind.*

There were any number of banks that he could have gone
after, of course. But, as he sorted through the growing collection of
passbooks that he kept locked in his desk, he set two aside. One
was for the Tremont Trust Company, which took pride in placing
large newspaper advertisements that informed prospective deposi-

tors: "Our officers and directors are men of the highest type, men who value their good names more than riches." The ads, Ponzi knew, were designed to appeal to the working class, to the small depositor. The bank spent little effort trying to reach the monied blue-blood levels of Boston. It would have done no good, for the executive who founded and ran it, vice president Simon Swig, was a Jew—a Russian immigrant whose appearance on the social scene only caused the noses of the city's Mayflower descendants to tilt a bit higher.

For Ponzi, at the present time, Swig would be a good partner. The banker had his own axe to grind against certain financial organizations in the state. In addition, he had built up strong political connections as he moved over the years from his beginnings as a peddler of tinware, to junkyard dealer, and then on to ownership of a drygoods store and posts such as city alderman and state representative. But Swig was shrewd, too shrewd not to see immediately what Ponzi was up to.

The other bankbook was from the Hanover Trust Company. Its president was Henry Chmielinski, the Polish newspaper publisher and financier who less than a year earlier had refused Ponzi's request for a $2,000 loan to fund *The Trader's Guide*. The moment of embarrassment came back to Ponzi in a sudden rush of recollection. He knew that it would be sweet revenge to best Chmielinski, and he sensed that the man was both foolish enough and greedy enough to walk into a trap.

There was the sound of commotion in the outer office.

"It's Mr. Cassullo again," said Miss Meli in a disapproving tone. Her employer nodded as he watched his associate move through the crowd of waiting investors, calling their names in a loud voice and slapping several of them heartily on the back.

Ponzi forced a smile to his lips. "Louis! You're back sooner than I thought."

Cassullo brushed past Miss Meli, muttering something beneath his breath that caused her to blush and turn hastily to her work. Then he dropped a large, heavy carton wound with manila rope onto the desktop. "There you are, Charlie. Six fifths of Hennessy Three Star, compliments of the French Line. The docks in New York are crawlin' with cops, but I got the stuff off right in front of their eyes."

"Three Star? Great!" Ponzi said, half-wishing that the police had picked up Cassullo with the bootlegged liquor, and grimacing as his associate helped himself to a fistful of cigars from the humidor on the desk.

"Well, Louis, what's the situation in New York?" he said evenly.

Cassullo inhaled noisily to get a cigar lit and blew a cloud of smoke in his direction. "I decided that Sam Milanese's pals couldn't run a good agency there. But a guy named Powderly wants to buy in as a partner."

Ponzi could imagine what had happened. Cassullo had run into someone in New York who had money, and had probably already collected a sizable fee to suggest that Ponzi sell part of the growing company.

"A partner?" he said, his eyes revealing nothing, "It's something to consider."

Preening, Cassullo flicked cigar ash onto the clean office floor. "Yeh, we ought to think about it."

His advance agent was using that "we" far too often, Ponzi realized. One of these days, Cassullo would have to be dealt with in a serious manner. Right now he was an inconvenience whose presence required Ponzi to continually think up errands to keep the man busy.

The smile returned. "Louis, I've got something important for you to handle. Look at these." He started to spread some slips of paper on the desk, then stopped. "Oh, Miss Meli," he said, "perhaps you'd better go to lunch a bit early." He waited until the unquestioning secretary caught up her pocketbook and closed the door behind her. Then he spread the papers wide. They were withdrawal slips for varying amounts at a dozen different banks.

Ponzi gave his instructions quickly, so that there was no chance of Cassullo asking too many questions. He wanted the money withdrawn from the banks—in the form of drafts made out to his account at the Hanover Trust Company.

"I've written instructions to each bank, it's all here," he said. "Use your car and get the checks personally. When you do, take them to the Hanover and deposit them. Start with this one for $60,000 and put the others in one by one—over the next few weeks. I want the account to grow, a bit at a time. Chmielinski will probably not notice it, but if he does, I want him to think it's a dormant account. He won't worry about any major withdrawals."

Cassullo looked at him suspiciously. "What're you up to, Charlie?"

"You'll hear about it, friend. You just start building up that account, slowly, so the Hanover invests my cash just like everybody else's."

As soon as Cassullo left, Ponzi picked up the telephone to call Charles Pizzi, who managed the Hanover Street branch of the

Hanover bank. Pizzi frequently had grumbled about his unsatisfactory salary. Some weeks earlier Ponzi had presented him with a couple of bottles of wine, and had casually suggested that the bank could be managed more effectively—"better service for the public, better conditions for employees"—if other officers and directors were in charge. Pizzi had agreed wholeheartedly.

"Charlie," Ponzi said into the phone, "I'm going to act on what we talked about. I imagine you know some shareholders who are not happy? Could you contact some of them and buy me some small lots of Hanover stock? Maybe a hundred shares or a little more. What's the price, now? $125 a share? All right, you'll need $12,000 or so. No problem."

He repeated the instructions, then added: "I want *you* to handle the purchases for an important reason. I don't want the stock transferred to my name on the Hanover books. Just have the sellers endorse it over to me, along with their voting proxies."

Pizzi, too, wanted to know what was up.

"We'll have a drink some night and I'll tell you about it. But remember that I've always been a man who takes care of his friends."

He knew Pizzi would have to go along with him and hope for the best. The bank executive had already told him more than he should have. The Hanover, he had revealed, was undercapitalized in these inflationary times, and its officers planned to make a new offering shortly, of two thousand shares of stock. Ponzi had grasped at once that it would save considerable time if he went after that stock, rather than trying to buy shares on the open market—where the price would climb as soon as someone got wind of his intentions.

Putting the receiver back onto its hook, Ponzi studied his finances. At the end of April, another 471 investors would have poured more than $141,000 into his coffers. He had spent large chunks of that amount, however, for the house, car, and furniture—but each new investor was out telling others about the company this very minute. *By the end of next month*, Ponzi thought, *by the end of May, I should be able to walk off with the Hanover.*

He was not sure that he could wait to see Chmielinski's face.

In the following weeks, while the cash in his Hanover Trust account climbed toward the half-million-dollar mark, Ponzi arranged a series of small gatherings at his new home for some of the bank's stockholders. There were six in all, and each controlled a relatively small percentage of the total capitalization through ownership of a hundred shares or so. But each had a kinship with Ponzi: an Italian heritage. And when Messrs. Stabile, Locatelli, Badaracco, Di Pietro, et al., received an invitation to dine with Mr. and Mrs. Charles Ponzi, there was not one refusal.

The men, like everyone else in the Italian community, had heard of the sudden appearance of Ponzi on Boston's financial scene. They were curious about his origins, about the tales of wealth that sprang from everyone's lips. Was there truly a tremendous vault in the basement of the house stocked with gold bullion? Did Ponzi actually have ten private policemen with vicious Dobermans patrolling the grounds? Was it true that at his various offices money came in so quickly that greenbacks were stuffed into wastebaskets and desk drawers and closets until someone could get them to the banks?

At the dinners, while the businessmen's wives chatted about the soaring cost of good beef and whether or not women should smoke cigarettes, Ponzi talked finance with the husbands. When one—disappointed, perhaps, that his host's tour of the estate did not include a private vault—asked a direct question about Ponzi's wealth, it would be turned aside with a smile, a chuckle, an offer of another dollar-cigar or glass of excellent French wine. But by the end of the evening, each guest was positive of one thing: Charles Ponzi had set his mind on gaining control of the Hanover Trust, and it would be both sensible and profitable to go along with him, rather than voice opposition.

One by one, the Italians fell into line. By early May, he had them all. It was agreed that their individual shares would be voted in block on any issue, and voted the way Ponzi wanted.

During the month of May, 1920, exactly 1,525 new investors bought more than $442,000 worth of notes from the Securities Exchange Company, and the stack of bankbooks in Ponzi's desk grew several inches thicker.

Once, looking at his assets, and just for the sheer, terrifying thrill of it, he had computed his indebtedness. He calculated that for each hundred dollars of nearly $900 that he had been given in December, he would owe $2,000 in June. It was proportionally less for each hundred of the $900 more given him in January, the $5,000 in February, the $28,000 in March and so on. But the total came to a staggering sum.

Still, Ponzi had told himself, he had done nothing wrong. Each investor who had put up money in the hope of making 50 percent interest in forty-five days, and who had asked for his money, actually had received both his principal and interest. No one had been turned away. No law had been broken.

Obviously, as the debt mounted daily, his predicament was worsening. But other financiers had been in severe straits previously, and had weathered them. No one is threatening me, Ponzi thought. There is time, plenty of it. Who could say that around the next corner there was not a simple solution? Who could say that when he had found the solution he would not be called a genius, a wizard? A foolhardy one, perhaps, but a man of financial brilliance!

Meanwhile, the outer office had begun to resemble an illegal betting parlor, or a corner of the stock exchange. Always it was filled with a dozen or more people of all ages, sexes, and descriptions who waited to invest, waited to collect, or merely stood discussing the wonderous ease with which money could be made these days if one knew how to do it. Several times a day the crowd would separate to leave a path from the front door to the door of the inner office, and a momentary silence would fall while Ponzi made his entrance or exit and the people stared at him in awe. As the days passed, the crowd grew larger, and the passage of Ponzi was greeted with a smattering of applause.

With a wave of his gold-headed cane or a smart salute against the brim of his new straw skimmer, the diminuitive financier acknowledged the adulation of his subjects. Several times during the month his chauffeur had to brake the shining Locomobile suddenly to avoid hitting investors and spectators who peered into the car to catch a glimpse of the regal figure in the rear seat.

Ponzi was beginning to feel like a king, although he doubted that many kings had their days and their minds occupied with so many petty details.

For example, there was the task of dealing tactfully with F. P. Powderly, Cassullo's New York contact who wanted to open a branch of the Securities Exchange Company. As Ponzi had suspected, Powderly was too small a fish to bother with.

With reference to opening an office in New York on a partnership basis, he dictated to Miss Meli:

> I will say from the start that a partnership is entirely out of the question unless you would be willing to cough up at least one million dollars bonus to me.
>
> Usually, I pay the expenses of all my out-of-town offices and I pay either a salary or a ten percent commission to my managers. I feel, however, that New York is too big a city for me to tackle through agents as the technicalities of my scheme are such as to require my presence when dealing with postal authorities. For the time being, I will let the matter rest, as I propose to visit New York in the near future, then we will have an opportunity to discuss this subject further.

He reread Powderly's letter of the previous week, searching for the passage where the New Yorker had told of another possible partner—a man named Norris—who had backed out at the last moment. Ponzi winked at his secretary:

> With reference to Mr. Norris, you may tell him for me that I will mail him a hot water bottle for the serious case of cold feet that he has developed.
>
> Business here is pretty good. We are making just about one hundred thousand dollars profit per week and we hope to do better in the future.

That should produce a counter-offer from Powderly, he thought. Perhaps a profit of $100,000 weekly was a slight exaggeration, but by the time the New Yorker pulled his team of prospective partners together, profits would be at that level—or above it.

He fired off another letter, this one to Carlton, the agent in Meriden, informing him that an account had been opened at the Hartford Connecticut Trust Company: "After this, instead of making remittances to me, you may simply deposit the money to the credit of our Company in the Hartford bank and mail to me the duplicate deposit slip receipted by the bank. All payments will be made through said bank. With reference to the several prospects you have, you may be sure that if they will come in to see me, I will take care of them."

There were other details to see to, particularly a potentially explosive problem with the office in Manchester, New Hampshire. Joseph Bruno, the agent there, had been forwarding several thousand dollars each week—much of it in Liberty Bonds that he had taken in lieu of cash—but had run into trouble with the state insurance commissioner. Bruno reported that he had been told to close down until he got a license, and he did not know enough about the workings of the Securities Exchange Company to apply for one. "Sit tight," Ponzi had told him over the phone, "until I get there."

He didn't want to head for Manchester, however, until he had a plan of attack. He turned in his chair to stare out the window at City Hall across the way while he pondered the best approach. One thing was growing more certain each day: the details of the business were becoming too much for him to handle alone. More and more he was required to be out of the office, and that could cause trouble—for only his signature on a check could provide money to an investor. There already had been several instances where greedy depositors had been forced to wait a few hours for him to return and release their funds. If one grew angry enough to complain to the police about a delay in payment—well, it wasn't something that a well-run bank would permit. He decided that he would have to let Miss Meli (who could be trusted as much as his beloved Rose or his own mother) file signature cards at various banks, so that she could sign in his absence.

And, although he told himself that it probably was a mistake, he instructed his secretary to get signature cards for Louis Cassullo, too. As Cassullo made the rounds of the offices—there were over thirty-five of them now—he frequently had to pay extra commissions to some of the managers, and always complained that he was short of cash. It was a gamble, Ponzi knew. If he let Cassullo think he trusted him enough to give him the key to certain bank accounts, the man might be lulled into inactivity, into waiting for the moment when he could make the biggest score. Meanwhile, however, it would lessen the danger that a disgruntled agent, worried about collecting his commission, would start spilling the beans about the whole operation.

He spun in his chair as he heard movement behind him, and turned to face two dour-looking men that Miss Meli had gestured into the office. One of them Ponzi recognized: a postal inspector who had visited him some weeks before, and had ended up buying a hundred-dollar note.

"Mr. Ponzi," the inspector said, "good to see you again. I'm afraid that Chief Inspector Mosby wants me to ask you a few more questions. This—uh—gentleman is from Commissioner Curtis' office."

Ponzi rose, smiling, to shake hands. *Police Commissioner Edwin Curtis himself, eh?* he thought. *If he's in with the head of the Post Office Department now, the boys must be onto something.* Aloud, he said, "Of course, of course. You boys are coming in here so often that maybe we should print up a timetable."

There was a moment of polite laughter. Then, the postal inspector said, "We've found that some of your statements can't be—shall we say—reconciled with certain advices that we have received at the department."

Ponzi eased himself onto the edge of his desk. "Which is to say, since you would not dispute the advisers, that I must be a liar."

"No, no, nothing like that. We're just interested in what explanation you have to offer."

"On what subject?"

"Why, your purchases of International Reply Coupons. Where do you buy them?"

Ponzi realized at once that word had finally reached "upstairs" about the European countries that had stopped selling coupons. *Idiots!* he thought. *You probably were notified by some ten-dollar-a-week clerk who has to read all the official papers that come into the department, and you're here preening like you've done more for America than Alvin York!*

"Gentlemen," he said, "you know that I have no intention of telling you that. I will merely say that the coupons can be profitably bought in any country which has a depreciated paper currency."

"For instance?" insisted the postal inspector.

"For instance, Italy, France, Rumania, or Greece, or—"

"Exactly! But we have information that Italy, France, and

Rumania withdrew from the postal agreement, Ponzi. They haven't been selling coupons since the end of March."

Ponzi knew that he could not bat an eyelash. "You're telling me nothing new, friend. That information was sent out some time ago by your department to every post office. I have copies of the bulletin."

The inspector was surprised, but relentless. "Then you admit that coupons can no longer be obtained in those countries?"

"I admit nothing. If it helps you, I will say that it is my understanding that coupons are not available to the general public. But I have every reason to believe that my orders are not being turned down anywhere on this earth."

"Ponzi," said the postal inspector, "if you're still buying coupons in those countries, it's being done without the knowledge of their governments."

"Perhaps, but that is not my concern. All that I'm interested in is getting the coupons."

The man sensed a bluff. "Assuming that you can get them, how do you redeem them?"

"The same as usual. By presenting them at the post office, here or elsewhere."

Now the men smiled in unison. "But all postmasters have been instructed not to redeem coupons issued by those countries after March thirty-first."

Again, Ponzi smiled easily. "Gentlemen," he said, making a short explosive sound with his tongue, "if the coupons are still obtainable in the countries, as I say they are, regardless of all regulations to the contrary, it would be an easy matter to have them stamped with a date prior to the thirty-first of March."

The inspector thought it over, then asked, wondering, "Do you mean to tell me you have connections with some postal officials disloyal to their own governments?"

Ponzi shook his head. "I don't mean to say anything of the kind. I am merely showing you how certain difficulties can be overcome, particularly for the right price. You may draw all the inferences you want."

He sensed that the men were not satisfied. Furthermore, they obviously had no intention of leaving until he had answered their questions more completely. He would have to think faster, have to dazzle them with some fancy footwork. Or find a miracle.

One of his agents, the jeweler Al Ciullo, put his head through the open door. "Charlie," he said, "I got to get back to the shop. Can I just give you something?"

Ponzi ordinarily would have objected to the interruption—but ordinarily by this time he would have been in the middle of a lengthy, convoluted explanation of his enterprises. Now, however—and he knew it was for just a brief instant—his brain had gone blank.

"Certainly, Al, these gentlemen won't mind. What is it?"

"I just got these in and don't know what to do with them. I figured you would." He handed a thick brown envelope to Ponzi. "It's three hundred coupons from my uncle in Italy. He paid for them himself."

"What?" murmured Ponzi, upending the envelope and pouring the scraps of paper onto the desktop.

"I wrote him last February about what you could do with them. When he got word that they were stopping sales, he back-dated these and mailed them over."

Ponzi's smile slid readily into place. "Gentlemen?"

The postal inspector turned angrily toward the jeweler. "You got these from Italy? From your uncle, you say?"

Ciullo did not understand the man's angry interest. "Yes, he's a postmaster in Mantua." Laughing, he added, "Now, I guess he's an investor. Right, Charlie?"

"When did you get these coupons?" snapped the inspector.

"Why, this morning, in the mail."

The inspector caught up the envelope. He looked at the cancellation date. Then he looked at the police officer. "I'll be damned!"

Ponzi fought to keep a sarcastic inflection from his voice. "You see, inspector, it's evidently possible that any number of people besides myself can get coupons abroad, even in countries that supposedly don't sell them anymore. Now, I'm afraid I have some other things to attend to—"

When the men had made their way through the crowd, muttering and whispering to one another on their way down the stairs, Ponzi turned to his friend. "Al," he said, "I don't know what brought you up here this morning, and I'm not asking. But I'll pick you up at your store for lunch. I owe you the biggest lobster we can find."

It was luck. He knew that. It was luck, the kind that comes to a winner when he is going to win big, when he can do no wrong, when everything is in his favor. It was luck. And he had it.

And while he had it, he was going to squeeze every bit of reward out of it that he could.

This afternoon, he would move in on Chmielinski!

☆

At precisely quarter-to-three, he appeared at the office of the Hanover Trust Company to keep his appointment. As the several secretaries showed him into inner office after inner office, until he reached the president's door, he recalled the unprofitable meeting of a year earlier. This one would be different. This time, Chmielinski knew quite well who he was.

The bank president, his short grey hair standing like a stiff-bristled brush atop his head, was flanked by two vice presidents. In unison, they looked up as he entered, then stood to shake his hand.

"Mr. Ponzi," said Chmielinski, "glad to meet you at last. We've all heard much about you lately."

Ponzi slid the band off a cigar and lit the rich tobacco. He did not bother to offer one to the others. "We've met before," he said softly, "but you probably don't remember."

Chmielinski's eyes clouded for an instant. "I—uh—I don't, as a matter of fact. Should I?" He observed Ponzi's shrug. "Well, is there something I can do for you?"

"Yes, I think there is. As a major depositor in this bank, I'm prepared to buy a block of stock that should qualify me as a director as well."

The three bankers glanced at one another, then smiled and nodded simultaneously. "I'm sure we can accommodate you. Would you want as many as one hundred shares? Most of the directors have at least—"

"A hundred shares would not really interest me at all. I would like to buy twenty-five hundred."

The bankers coughed, one after another, in a rapid sequence. "But, Mr. Ponzi, the entire capitalization of the Hanover calls only for two thousand shares," said the portly vice president at the left of the desk.

"The original capitalization, you mean. I have it on excellent authority that you plan to offer two thousand shares of new stock." He saw the glances flick back and forth among the trio once more. "Am I wrong?"

Chmielinski's voice was calm. "We have not offered the stock yet, and had not set a date when we would."

"You could set the date now, the three of you. You could set it for today, and issue all of the stock to me. It would save you considerable trouble."

The thin man on the right said, as if in explanation: "We can't do that, Ponzi. That would be selling you control of the bank."

"That's precisely what I want."

Chmielinski stared into his eyes. "We wouldn't consider

anything like that. Six months ago, Ponzi, no one had heard of you—"

The stout executive saw Ponzi sit up suddenly, seeming to lengthen his tiny frame. "We *are* willing to make you a director," the man offered.

Ponzi's voice was angry now. "What good is that? A minority stockholder in a corporation is like nothing at all. If my deposits are good enough for your bank, I want to have some say as to how the money is invested."

The man on the right was speaking quickly, interrupting him. "Do you think we're going to give up control we've all spent time and money to get?"

"And do you think that the money my investors place in my care is going to be turned over to you, to do whatever you want with it? My millions mean as much to me as your control does to you, if not more. And my financial standing entitles me to an overriding say-so on this bank's activities."

Chmielinski hauled a large silver watch from his pocket and took a quick look at its face. "I'm afraid, Ponzi," he said, "that this will get us nowhere. Why don't we all think about what has been said, and meet again in a few days?"

Ponzi shook his head and took a checkbook from his pocket.

"Gentlemen, I'm not going to have time in the weeks ahead for additional meetings that may prove just as fruitless as this one. You keep your bank. I'll look for another." He opened the checkbook. "Can one of you tell me my balance as of today?" Calmly, he wrote the word *Cash* on the check, signed his name, and waited.

There was a sputtering sound from one of the vice presidents. "Your balance? You're not intending to withdraw your balance?"

"It's somewhere around $500,000, I believe?" said Ponzi easily.

Chmielinski turned over a piece of paper that lay on his desk. "When you asked to come in, I took the trouble of looking into your account," he said. "The exact figure is $473,806.42. But I must ask you not to withdraw it. For such an amount, Ponzi, we must have notice."

"The money is in a checking account. It has been faithfully deposited and accepted whenever I chose to put it in. Is there some reason I should not write checks to the extent of my balance?"

"There is no reason, of course. But this bank does not keep such a large amount of cash on hand. I'm sure you are aware of that."

"Then," said Ponzi, "get it. You have securities to sell—"

The banker angrily snapped the cover of his watch closed. "It's almost closing time! What kind of a loss do you expect us to take if we start selling at this hour?"

"That is not my concern? The amount—$473,8—"

Chmielinski abruptly turned the paper face down, concealing the figures. "Ponzi—" he began.

Ponzi closed the checkbook with a snap. "Do you mean this bank does not have sufficient funds to cash a check for me? I've seen stronger institutions than this one go under when word like that got out."

"Ponzi," the banker repeated, "I'm sure we can compromise."

"What have you got to offer?"

There was a hurried consultation. "We'll sell you half of the new shares. A thousand, at $125 each."

"Nothing doing. That would be like throwing good money after bad. We can't get together on that basis."

"But the three of us do not own that many shares," the other vice president said, almost pleading.

"Perhaps not. But you control more than that."

Another consultation. Chmielinski spoke then, with finality. "We'll sell you as many as we control. An equal number. No more. No less. The independent holders will vote with whatever side they choose."

Ponzi appeared to think it over. "How many shares do you believe you control?"

The three men put their heads together once more. "Not more than fifteen hundred, all told," Chmielinski stated. "You can buy fifteen hundred shares of the new issue."

You're counting on hanging onto my Italian friends, aren't you? Ponzi thought. *Too bad you won't have time to check them.* "All right," he said, "if the directorship goes along with it."

The three bankers nodded. "We'll call a special meeting for tomorrow morning. Director and permanent member of the executive committee—that's what you want, right?"

"Right." He opened the checkbook, tore out the half-finished check, and began to make out a new one. "That's fifteen hundred shares at $125 apiece. There you are, in payment to the Hanover Trust Company." He passed the check across Chmielinski's desk. He chuckled. "It feels funny, gentlemen—to be depositing my money into my own bank."

The Polish banker ran his hand over his bristle of hair in exasperation. "I beg you to remember, Mr. Ponzi, that the bank has a number of owners." He reached for a telephone and gave instructions to prepare the necessary certificates.

It was just past three-thirty in the afternoon when Ponzi stepped outside the gloomy, silent lobby of the bank into the sunlit and traffic-noisy intersection of Water and Washington Streets. In his breast pocket rested the stock certificates that for all practical purposes gave him control of the Hanover Trust Company and its $5 million worth of assets. He could not resist turning—as he stood in the middle of the street with automobiles and wagons passing on either side—to look up the fourteen-floor height of the Journal Building, in which the bank was located. That, too, was practically his now.

For a moment, he felt dizzy. But, he told himself, it was a natural result of staring up into a bright sky.

For some reason, he did not want to tear his gaze away.

With less than a million dollars of his own, and for an outlay of only $187,500, he—Charles Ponzi—had pulled off one of the great bank thefts of all time!

She was there.

A tiny figure, hardly more than an elongated dot of black high up against the railing of the ship—but it was her beyond a doubt.

"There! Rose, there!" He pointed his cane, straight and slender as an arrow, and shouted as loud as he could. "Mother! Mother!"

He did not care that Rose, standing beside him in the throng on the dock, might think him childish or insane. He was fairly leaping up and down, waving the cane frantically to attract his mother's attention. Now he fought his way through the crowd to reach the foot of the first gangway that slammed into place. Rose hung back, understanding. It was as if his mother had returned from the grave.

Ponzi, his eyes searching the faces hurrying down the gangway, found himself trembling with excitement. He glanced back once to where his wife stood, and felt a momentary pang of embarrassment. Rose's own parents—her father first, and then her mother—had died during the past year, and he realized how doubly fortunate he was to have both a devoted wife and a beloved mother. The thought brought his attention once more to the gangway.

She moved down it like a queen. Mrs. Imelda Ponsi. A tiny woman, in a black street-length traveling dress that showed an elegant bit of white lace at the throat. She had made the most of the $565 her son had sent her for a wardrobe and her passage. With her snow white hair, long and piled high at the top of her head like a crown, and her careful, slow step, there was only one word to describe her appearance. Regal, that was it. Regal.

Now Ponzi was pushing his way to her side. The sound of

frantic Italian—of laughter and tears—carried over the roar to Rose as her husband, immaculate, dapper and princely in his deep blue suit with its lapel carnation, practically lifted his mother from her feet in an embrace. Her spindly arms caught at him, accidentally knocking his straw skimmer to the ground, where it was promptly trampled underfoot. Ponzi laughed as his mother's face grew apologetic. He was still laughing as he led her to Rose.

"She's worried, Rose, about the cost of the hat! You'll have to convince her that I can buy hats by the carload. I don't think she believes me."

In the ensuing days, however, Rose's mother-in-law proved to be unquestioning, quite ready to accept the fact that her only son was a millionaire in America. After all, had he not been sent to the land of opportunity to become just that? Had he not written her faithfully over the years to tell her exactly how close he was—and growing closer each day, each year—to his goal?

Once his mother had settled into the large house, Ponzi told himself that everything he had wanted from America was now his. In the morning, before he sat down to the light breakfast prepared by the cook and served on sparkling new china by the young Italian maid, he frequently stepped through the doors of the second-story master bedroom and looked out from the wide sundeck. It was an impressive view. An expanse of lawn, green and smooth as a billiard table. The garage, large enough to house both the Hudson and the Locomobile with room to spare. Oaks and maples so tall that he felt sure if he climbed them, he could see the ships in Boston Harbor a dozen miles away. At times, he smiled down at Rose as she gathered a basket of fresh flowers, or at his mother who sat dozing on the lawn in a wicker chair.

He had everything. But he could not stop reaching for more.

There were bank shares to be added. A few in Simon Swig's Tremont Trust, a few more in the Fidelity Trust, the Lawrence Trust, the Old South Trust. One afternoon, when other tenants complained that Ponzi's line of investors was blocking the stairs, he threatened to buy the Niles Building and dispossess everyone else. The joke gave him the idea to settle an old score with his former employer, J. R. Poole.

At Poole's building, he went striding casually among the rows of desks and cubicles, stopping to chat with several young men and women who had worked alongside him less than two years earlier. A few of the girls touched the expensive fabric of his pin-stripe suit in obvious admiration, and the men grinned as he passed out the ever-present cigars.

"Charlie Ponzi!" said Poole when he reached the private office. "Have a seat. You're looking prosperous."

"I am prosperous, J. R. I've come a long way since you paid me sixteen dollars a week here."

"I heard you've made out well. Something to do with foreign securities of some kind, right?"

The smile. The cigar into the ebony holder. The cloud of smoke. "Something like that. I've come for some advice, as a matter of fact. I have a few dollars to invest."

The old man stuck out his lower lip and nodded. "Why don't you buy a few shares of J. R. Poole preferred? It pays seven percent."

"I'd rather have common, J. R., assuming that it pays more."

"Well, yes, then, I'll give you twenty-five of each."

Ponzi frowned. "That hardly seems worth bothering with."

A puzzled look crossed Poole's face. "How much do you want?"

Indifferently: "I'll take all you have."

Now Poole laughed. "You beat all, Charlie, you know that? One day you're working for me, and the next day you want me working for you. It takes a lot of money to buy this company."

Ponzi looked straight into his eyes. "I figured it would. That's why I waited this long to call on you. I wasn't sure I had enough before this."

The laugh faded, and Poole took a pencil to a pad on his desk. "If you think you can afford it, you can have four hundred and seventy-five shares of preferred—for $47,500—and two hundred common for $35,200." He waited as Ponzi appeared to do some mental figuring.

"Do I get a directorship as well?"

Poole, convinced now that his former employee was joking, nodded in good humor.

"All right," said Ponzi, "make out the certificates." He wrote out a check.

Poole's eyes widened as he studied it. "I didn't think you meant it," he said.

"J. R., I never bluff. I don't have to." He took a half-dozen certified checks from his wallet and fanned them before the old man's eyes. They were for $100,000 each, payable to Charles Ponzi.

"Good Lord, Charlie. That's over a half-million!"

Ponzi slid the checks casually into the billfold. "And there are several more million back of them."

"It will take a few days to prepare the certificates." Poole seemed to be having trouble speaking.

Ponzi got to his feet, held out his hand. "No problem, J. R. Ring me up when you're ready. Deposit my check, of course, right away." He tapped his gold-handled cane on the floor in a gesture of finality and walked out.

When Poole telephoned the following week, Ponzi took his call in his new private office on the second floor above the Hanover Trust. "Yes, J. R., I decided I needed more privacy than I get on School Street. It's like the Curb Exchange over there, so many investors are coming and going. My friend Chmielinski here has set me up here in the old Journal Building with quite a nice layout. You should come see it."

Poole had a new proposal. He was prepared to give Ponzi all of the outstanding stock in his company—750 shares of common—for $205,000, and he wanted to borrow $150,000 more. Some of the loan, he said, would go to settle some debts, and some would be returned to Ponzi in the form of investments in the Securities Exchange Company.

Ponzi was elated when he put down the phone. He agreed to Poole's offer at once. What a story it would make in his autobiography some day! How a sixteen-dollar-a-week clerk bought out his former employer! It was a major purchase—one that gave him control of a sardine factory in Maine, a meat packing plant in Kansas City, and other distant holdings of the J. R. Poole Company.

Business negotiations delighted Ponzi. He enjoyed giving directions to his hesitant, almost frightened lawyers, telling them to draw up this contract and prepare that one, ordering them to stop work on this deal and take up the other. He knew that for other wealthy men—even Rockefeller himself—things would be difficult at times; there was often the problem of making sure that sufficient funds were on hand for each move in a series of investments. No such problem seemed to exist for Charles Ponzi. Money flowed in each day in growing amounts, as steadily as the Charles River flowed into its basin near the harbor.

And there were always surprises, unexpected windfalls—Pizzi, for example. The Hanover Trust employee was doing an excellent job as an agent selling Securities Exchange Company notes to his fellow workers, and wanted to invest a large sum of money himself. But, he told Ponzi, the most cash that he could lay his hands on amounted to a few hundred dollars.

"And that's hardly enough to make me rich, Ponzi," he said.

"'Course, I could always borrow some of the bank's cash, without telling nobody, that is."

Ponzi smiled at the slow-thinking clerk. "There's no sense doing anything illegal, Charlie. You get in trouble that way. I've got a better solution. You go to Chmielinski and to treasurer McNary and tell them you want to borrow $40,000 from the bank, and have each approve a note for $20,000. Bring me the cash and I'll give you my note for $60,000—that's your investment plus fifty percent interest. Then, you take my note and trade it to Chmielinski and McNary for your two notes that say you owe the bank $40,000. Tear them up. Then, in forty-five days, when I pay the $60,000, you and the bank can split the $20,000 profit. I think Chmielinski will go along with that, don't you?"

"And it hasn't cost me a cent!" Pizzi fairly shouted, nodding his head vigorously. "Ponzi, you're a goddamn genius."

The bank officials had gone along with the proposal. After all, the $40,000 loaned to Pizzi and reloaned to Ponzi had come back to the Hanover in the form of a deposit to the account of the Securities Exchange Company. How could anyone lose?

Particularly Charles Ponzi.

There *was* one way—it came to him one afternoon—one way that he could lose. Lose everything.

If Death decided to collect the debt that every man owes him.

If a fast-moving motorcar should run him down in the street, if an irate investor too angry to wait for an explanation should draw a revolver, if a sudden illness ravaged his system, Charles Ponzi knew that his wife, his mother, and his creditors would be left with practically nothing.

He decided that they must be protected. An insurance agent, told that Ponzi wanted to speak to him about a policy, was seated in the financier's office not more than ten minutes later. He listened to Ponzi's request—a policy for a year equal to the total value of his company's outstanding notes, which then amounted to nearly $3 million, payable to the First National Bank.

"And your purpose—"

"Is to see that, in the event of my death, my creditors are paid in full out of the policy. That will leave my entire estate intact to my family."

The agent said that it seemed an eminently sensible action. He agreed to write the policy so that its face value could be increased as the indebtedness of the Securities Exchange Company grew, and the First National Bank agreed to act as beneficiary.

It is one more piece of evidence, Ponzi thought, *that my basic objective is honesty at all times. Has Morgan or Carnegie or anyone else gone out of his way to protect the investors? I doubt it.* He wondered how the various inspectors from the authorities looking into his operations would reconcile the latest move with their suspicion that somehow he was a simple thief. *It will make a good story for the papers. I'll have to start seeing that this kind of thing gets out.*

He had given increasing thought in the last few weeks to spreading word of his company on a wider scale. Advertising, or publicity—something was needed to increase the number of investors more quickly. It was nearly the end of June, and something over seven thousand people this month had brought $2.5 million to Charles Ponzi. But in six weeks, those same people would want almost $4 million in return. He had to figure out where that amount would come from.

It's damn certain that the J. R. Poole profits won't come to that, he thought. *I'll have to stop buying everything in sight and keep my mind on business. Something will turn up.*

It was difficult, though, to concentrate on making more money when other problems were continually demanding his attention.

For example, although he had had the front office outfitted with grilled windows and metal dividers so that it resembled a bank's paying-and-receiving department, certain investors had taken to treating the Securities Exchange Company in a highly unofficial fashion. They had purchased his notes with checks upon their own banks, then stopped payment on their checks. Nevertheless, six weeks later they had brought in their notes for collection. No one knew how many dozens of people actually had done this—Ponzi's clerks were not skilled in the ways of finance, and his records were makeshift to say the least—but in Ponzi's view enough were doing it to add up to a sizable swindle.

He discussed the problem with Cassullo, a man schooled in the art of the swindle. If the company stopped accepting checks, it would seem distrustful, and that might scare off some of the small investors. There was no time to institute a new method of bookkeeping. And if word got out that the great Ponzi was concerned about losing a few hundred dollars, a few thousand dollars—why, that might weaken confidence in his entire operation. After all, if he could make hundreds of thousands of dollars each day, as word had it that he was doing, why should he show great concern over a petty sum?

Ponzi instructed his clerks to study a man's face for honesty before accepting his check—but to accept it. There was nothing else he could do.

It was a minor worry.

A larger one was the circular that had been mailed out by the Post Office Department asking certain questions of Ponzi's agents throughout New England.

In a directive to his agents that he dictated to Angeline Lacarno, a dark-haired young beauty hired by Miss Meli to help out with the growing correspondence, he said, "We feel the questions should not be answered before we are consulted. We kindly ask that you communicate with us by return mail, in the event that you have received such a circular." The new secretary was told to send the instructions to each of the company's forty-five offices.

"You can skip Joe Bruno in Manchester," he amended his order. "Get him on the phone and tell him I'm on the way up."

Leaving the Locomobile behind for the use of Rose and his mother, Ponzi sped in a hired limousine to the small New Hampshire town. He met with the agent in the office of a vice president of the Merchants National Bank. The bank official believed the pressure from the state insurance commissioner—who was insisting that the Manchester office could not operate without a license—was a result of complaints from rival banks.

"It's well known in financial circles," he told Ponzi, "that we have invested certain of our own assets with your company, while you in return carry a large balance with us. Some of our competitors no doubt are jealous, particularly if their own depositors are making withdrawals to give Bruno here."

The banker named a local lawyer who had considerable influence with various political figures in the state capital at Concord. "He's expensive—but worth it, I believe," the officer said tentatively.

"To a man in my position," Ponzi replied simply, "nothing is expensive."

An hour later, he sat with his agent in the attorney's Stutz as it sped along the dusty roads toward Concord. The commissioner proved to be an affable man who seemed genuinely interested in the affairs of the Securities Exchange Company, not so much out of suspicion, but rather in appreciation of the fact that some persons could still find the road to riches in America. It was he himself who had suggested that the conference be held in the lawyer's car instead of his own stuffy office. "That way," he explained, "you gentlemen will be able to see the beauty of our countryside while we talk."

In Manchester again that evening, the lawyer phoned Ponzi at his hotel. "I've just talked to the commissioner on the phone," he said, "and I think he's going to rule that he has no jurisdiction over your office here."

"Then we can go ahead? Fine!"

"He seemed quite impressed with your operation. In fact, I don't think he would mind making a small investment with you himself."

Ponzi sensed what was coming. He had learned enough about politicians to be surprised at nothing. "That sounds too good to be true. I'd be happy to have his name on my books as an investor."

"The problem—uh—is that he has no loose money right now."

Ponzi was glad that the lawyer could not see him grinning into the phone. "Oh? That's no problem. He can have a note of mine without putting up a cent. His name is worth more than money."

Now the lawyer grew cagey. "It would never do to issue him a note without proper consideration. If it got out—why, it would look like you'd bribed him to drop the license matter."

Ponzi fought to suppress a laugh. "Oh, of course! I should have thought of that." He paused. "Have you any ideas on what we could do?"

"Hmm," said the lawyer, "let me see. We want to do the thing right. Say, here's a suggestion: You could arrange it for him to borrow a few thousand at your bank here. He could invest that with you, then pay back the loan when he collects."

"Sure! Others have done that with me frequently. Why didn't I think of it?"

It took only a few minutes the next morning to arrange a $2,000 loan for the commissioner. "When the note comes due," Ponzi told the bank executive, "if he does not pay it, just charge it to Bruno or to my account here."

Two days later, seated in the School Street office to sign some letters churned out alternately by Miss Meli and Miss Lacarno, Ponzi took a phone call from his agent in Manchester. "Ponzi, you won't believe this," Bruno said excitedly, "but I got word from the commissioner's office yesterday that we don't need the license. Then he came by this morning with the lawyer, and had $2,000 to invest. And the lawyer put in $15,000 of his own! They got their notes, and the money's in the bank right now."

"Something funny?" said Miss Meli when Ponzi hung up the phone. She had noticed the familiar smile, wider than ever, on his face.

"Amusing, Miss Meli. Very amusing," he replied. "Anything else on the schedule this afternoon? I promised Mrs. Ponzi I'd try to get home early."

The secretary sorted through some notes. "The senator called again for an answer. I didn't know what to tell him, Mr. Ponzi. I never know how to talk to a senator."

Ponzi laughed easily. "He's a state senator, not one from Washington, in the first place. If he calls again, tell him that his group's offer of a million dollars for my secrets is ridiculous. Why, next month, we should be talking in a million a day! And if he wants to talk further, I'll—"

He stopped in midsentence. The door from the outer office had been thrown open, and a familiar figure—a police inspector—stood there in embarrassment. A large, red-faced woman with him was shaking a rolled umbrella in Ponzi's direction.

"That's him, officer. He took my money."

"Mr. Ponzi," the officer began apologetically, "this lady—Mrs. Campbell, her name is—says you sold her a note last week."

Ponzi did not recognize the woman, but he shrugged. "That's quite likely, Hanlon. We have many investors. Is something wrong?"

"Wrong!" the woman half-shouted, half-sobbed. "I got friends tellin' me you're a crook, and I want my $200 back. That what's wrong."

He rose from behind his desk and walked toward her. "Legally, madam—and the officer here knows it—there's nothing that can force me to redeem my note before it matures. But it has always been my policy to refund to dissatisfied investors upon request. I'll have a clerk prepare a check."

"You will?" The woman's red-rimmed eyes were wide. "You *will* give it back?"

Ponzi spread his hands. "Of course. Your principal was $200? Eddie—" he called to a youth in the outer office.

"Wait, wait a minute," the woman said. "My friends, they said—*I* wasn't worried, Mr. Ponzi, until they started talkin'. Keep the money—"

"Lady," the policeman protested, "you put me to a lot of trouble, comin' over here—"

"I'm glad you're here, Hanlon," Ponzi said softly. "I'm sorry Mrs.—Campbell, is it?—but you must take your money now. I do not want it. I do not care to have as investors persons who have no confidence in me. Go back to your friends. Show them your cash, and thank them for the service they rendered to you."

Bewildered, the woman stepped to a cashier's window to receive her check. "I told her you were on the up-and-up," the police officer said. "If anybody else comes in with a complaint, Mr. Ponzi, you can bet I'll tell them how you do business."

Tell them, Ponzi thought. *Tell them how I refund $200, knowing that the stupid woman's friends will come in with ten times that much when they hear how honestly my investors are treated!*

He was about to reenter the private office when he felt a tug at the back of his coat. Turning, he looked down at a boy about fourteen years old, whose oversize cap almost covered his large brown eyes. Behind the boy, another youngster hung back at the edge of the crowd.

"Yes, son, what is it?"

"I'm Frankie Thomas, Mr. Ponzi, sir. I've been runnin' money in from some of the branches t' here."

Ponzi nodded approvingly. "Oh yes, all you boys are doing great work. Keep it up." He turned away.

"But, Mr. Ponzi, can I ask ya somethin? Is it okay to invest myself? Me and my pal here, we got ten bucks saved up 'n we—"

Ponzi raised his voice for the benefit of the crowd at the cashiers' windows. "And you wonder if it's safe? Sonny, do you think the Securities Exchange Company is so hard up that it would risk the savings of youngsters? If you want to buy one of my notes, you and your friend will get the exact same treatment given to bankers and millionaires. Eddie—" he called to a clerk, "take care of these young gentlemen."

There was a spattering of applause behind him as he closed the door to his inner office.

"You're so patient with everyone," Miss Meli said. "That was so nice, what you told that boy."

"In my book, Miss Meli, everyone deserves equal attention, whether their investment is ten dollars or ten thousand, whether they are young, old, man, woman, or child. People are all the same to me."

"It's wonderful," sighed the secretary. "When you talk that way, I feel so sure I did the right thing, putting my $600 into the company."

Ponzi coughed slightly. "I didn't know you had invested, Miss Meli."

She opened her desk drawer to display one of the familiar yellow notes with *Charles Ponzi* rubber-stamped at the bottom. "Oh, yes, months ago, and I got my $900 yesterday. But I put it all back, Mr. Ponzi. It's so easy!" She turned a page on the large calendar on her side of the desk. "Look, on August twelfth, I'll have $1,350!"

"That's very—encouraging, Miss Meli," he said after a pause. "It shows confidence. I like that. I intended to discuss your salary with you on Friday, but since you've brought the conversation around to money, this might be the proper moment. Beginning next Monday, your wages will be one hundred dollars a week."

"But, I've already had two raises since I've been here," she protested.

He smiled. "If you don't want it—" The young girl's look of dismay widened his grin. "Seriously, you're worth it. How many people do we have working here now—?"

"With the new messengers, thirty-two."

"It's a big responsibility, and I think we're all going to be working longer hours from now on. Take the raise, Miss Meli. It will give you more money to invest with us if you choose."

Although the Fourth of July was yet three days away, the sound of firecrackers made the entire city seem under constant attack from an unseen army. Each morning, the appearance of the sun was greeted with simultaneous explosions from dozens of huge cannon-crackers whose roar echoed from Winthrop on the bay to distant Waltham. During the afternoon, while the sun climbed to set the pavement sizzling, strings of niggertoes and Chinese crackers spattered in the business district to frighten shopgirls and horses. And at night, in the darkness high above the Common, an occasional aerial bomb burst in a shower of sparks and a thunder of noise.

As he rose and prepared to hurry to the School Street office, as he strode the downtown streets on his journeys to banks and branches, and as he lay planning the next day's activities while Rose slept peacefully beside him, Charles Ponzi was reminded by each explosion of the fireworks around him that his own situation was becoming more explosive with each day.

The money was still pouring in, all right. There was no problem about that. But there was the possibility that it might stop at any instant and leave the Securities Exchange Company with an insurmountable mountain of obligations. Ponzi showed no sign of worry—indeed, he did not permit himself to worry—but his feverish mind was kept busy with the need to plug even the slightest chink in his inverted pyramid of money. A pyramid that amounted now to more than $3 million.

He had realized just how precarious the situation was only a few days before when one of his cashiers had come to him with five notes for $150 each. They had been presented by a bank messenger for payment. The notes were poor counterfeits, printed in a bilious yellow on thick and cheap paper. But they had been stamped with Ponzi's rubber-stamp signature and bore the mark of his numbering machine as well. *Cassullo!* Ponzi thought as he fingered the slips of paper. *He's gone into business for himself.* He shook his head.

"Pay them," he said to the clerk.

"But, we can't find any stubs for 'em—"

"They're good," Ponzi snapped. "Pay them." The clerk shrugged and left. Ponzi knew that he had done the right thing, the only thing he could do under the circumstances. If he had refused to pay the notes, the bank which had accepted them in return for a loan would wonder if he was defaulting on his payments. If he protested to the bank that the notes were forgeries, there might have to be an arrest. And a trial, which could place him on the witness stand subject to cross-examination. Better to lose $750 and stay out of the courts.

But Cassullo was becoming more of a threat every day, he realized. He would have to keep him in mind at all times.

He half-expected to see his former prison companion among the group of people in the outer office, and smiled more easily when he saw Cassullo was not in sight. He waved an easy greeting to Uncle John who was chatting animatedly with three of the sub-agents working for Pizzi at the Hanover Trust, and moved through the crowd, wishing the agents good luck with their sales activities and joking with several satisfied investors. Then a familiar face met his gaze. He felt a twinge of uneasiness.

"Daniels! Have you dropped in to see how your furniture holds up in the crush?"

His visitor showed his stained teeth in a grimace of moderate amusement. "It's good strong stuff, Ponzi. You know I only sell the best."

The man was blocking the way to Ponzi's office. When he did not move, Ponzi planted his gold-headed cane firmly on the floor between them. "Then you've come to invest a few dollars, I imagine. Here, let me get one of my boys to take care of you right away. No need for you to stand in line."

Daniels shifted a toothpick in the corner of his mouth. "That's okay, Ponzi," he said. "I ain't putting any money into this company. But I heard plenty of others were. Just thought I'd see if all the stories about you are true."

Ponzi looked at the furniture dealer with suspicion. "Not all of them, Daniels," he said. "Not all of them."

"Yeh. Guess I've seen enough to know what's real and what's lies." He tilted his head and brushed past Ponzi to move down the stairs. "You'll be hearing from me. Good to see you doin' so well."

The sense of uneasiness stayed with Ponzi throughout the day. He sat across from Miss Meli in his customary position and tried to concentrate on the details of the sprawling organization. But it was difficult. Time and again he turned the pages of the three Boston papers he had taken to reading, looking for the opportunity that might produce enough profits to settle his debt in one stunning bit of activity. Once, just a week ago, he nearly had found it, in an item that reported that Poland was trying to negotiate a loan of $10 million with the United States.

"Henry," Ponzi had said excitedly to Chmielinski on the phone a few moments later, "this is your chance of a lifetime to clean up some real dough."

The banker had no idea what Ponzi was talking about. "You know the bigwigs in your country," Ponzi continued. "Get hold of them and fix it so they sell me enough International Reply Coupons to come to $10 million in their money. I'll have the dough in a couple of weeks. And they can deliver the coupons over six months."

"Let me get this straight, Ponzi. You want *what?*" Even after Ponzi had repeated his request, the banker was not sure that he understood.

"It's not important, Henry. I'll get in touch with my lawyers and have them talk to Peter Tague, the congressman. He'll have to get to Burleson—that's the postmaster general—and arrange for the post office to cash my coupons for stamps, maybe a million dollars worth a month. I have it all figured out, and if the exchange rates hold steady, I can make $5 million at least. You get the coupons for me, and a million is yours."

He had actually reached the congressman, meeting with him in the Parker House, and Tague had actually gotten to the postmaster general—who delicately had suggested further discussions on the legality of trafficking in reply coupons. But Chmielinski could only reach some minor Polish officials who seemed to prefer borrowing U.S. government money to getting involved in a scheme that would require approval of the Universal Postal Union and its members.

The fools! Ponzi thought in immediate reaction. But upon reflection, he decided that he was lucky Chmielinski had not been able to uphold his end of the operation. With all the restrictions on reply coupons that had been laid down, the deal would have taken long months to work. And he grew more convinced each day that his solution would be something—had to be something—that turned an immense profit overnight.

He had cut down his spending sharply—and was letting the investors' cash pile up in banks everywhere. His last purchases of major size had been five hundred shares of the C & R Construction Company for $12,000, and about $25,000 worth of preferred and common stock of the Napoli Macaroni Company. ("At least we'll never run out of spaghetti at home, Rose," he had told his wife the evening the deal was made.) He had spent another $14,000 for a small home in Winthrop Highlands, thinking that his mother might like to be on the water during the hot summer months. And his list of property was growing slowly as numerous investors who were short of cash turned their mortgages over to him for security.

Still, he knew that if he had to convert all of his holdings to cash—including the five shares of American Telephone and Telegraph stock he had picked up as a lark at ninety dollars each—and if he cleaned out the bank accounts he'd opened all over the Northeast, the Securities Exchange Company would still be roughly a million dollars short of meeting its obligations. The thought of it was enough to make his head feel light at times. But there was nothing to do except keep on working, holding things on an even keel so that the spiral of investors would grow ever wider.

By increasing his own deposits, Ponzi knew that he was on the verge of crippling a number of banks. He had figured it out on paper time and again after Miss Meli totaled each day's receipts. With banks everywhere offering their depositors 4 percent annually on savings while Charles Ponzi offered 400 percent, there was no way that the banks could hold onto their assets. Some might last longer than others, he mused, but sooner or later they'd all have to close their doors or sell out to him.

One evening he had tried to explain it to Rose: "A closed bank, dearest, is a total loss to its stockholders. Not only do they lose the money they paid for each share originally—say it's $150—but they can be assessed an amount equal to the par value if the bank goes into liquidation. That's another $150!

"Now, when the stockholders see their bank failing, they'll sell out to me for almost anything I want to pay. Maybe fifty dollars a share. And as soon as that happens, I turn around and make the bank solvent again. People have confidence in me, you know that."

He paused, seeing the admiration in her eyes and remembering her surprise and pleasure when strangers waved a greeting to him on the street.

"And they'd rather deposit their money in banks owned by me than banks owned by somebody else, even if I paid ordinary interest. But even without new depositors coming into the bank, I could turn the trick by simply depositing in my account there the money drawn out by the bank's customers to buy my notes."

He realized it was unusual for him to carry on at such length about his business plans. Would it cause Rose to worry that perhaps he was under too much pressure at the office, or that something was troubling him? But he could not restrain his excitement. He added a heavy splash of anisette to his fourth cup of coffee and hurried on. "Then, as soon as the bank is on sound footing again, its shares will skyrocket in value. The public will buy shares in anything I own. Not because it's worth more intrinsically, Rose, but because of my name. My credit. Do you understand?

The next morning, when his head felt less buoyant from the effects of a large meal and innumerable glasses of fine French wine, he realized that Rose had not understood at all. Perhaps it was best that she hadn't—that she had no realization that he was searching for a way to move out of the speculative coupon business into a more conservative line.

Charles Ponzi, Banker. He liked the sound of it. It had a substantial ring to it.

There is a way to achieve it. I know there is!

In the School Street office, he turned the newspaper pages one after another. There was no time to concern himself with Boston's chief topic of conversation, the imminent America's Cup race between the *Resolute* and the *Shamrock IV.* There was no leisure moment in which to analyze the campaign speeches of Cox and his vice presidential nominee, Franklin Roosevelt, who were touring the area. There was scarcely a moment to read about the unsettled situation in Ireland, where three nights of rioting had left a dozen dead, or the crisis in Poland where the Russian army was heavily mobilized and ready to advance. None of these, Ponzi knew immediately upon skimming the headlines, could be turned to profit.

And profit was the only thing on his mind.

Ordinarily he would not have been in the office on Saturday, but in the last month, the weekend seemed to have become the only time when he had a moment free to think. He had sensed Rose's disappointment this morning when he told her he was going downtown. There had been tentative plans to drive with his mother to some secluded spot on the shore—but he had convinced his wife that the holiday crowds would be thick everywhere, and promised that he'd return early in the afternoon for a game of croquet on the lawn before dinner.

"I'll take the Hudson," he had said, "and you and mother can use the chauffeur if you want to go yourselves."

In the stillness of the School Street Office, he remembered the way Rose had shaken her head and said, "No, we'll wait 'til you get home."

Soon, soon, he promised himself as he glanced out at the empty street below, when he found the one big answer he would be able to spend more time with her. This—*searching*—was just a temporary thing, something that would pass and leave him a multimillionaire!

He turned the pages of the morning papers in a steady rhythm, his eyes flicking carefully over each headline, not missing a word.

Then the telephone rang, startling him. Who would try to reach him on the weekend? Perhaps someone had called the house and asked for him. Probably it was somebody looking for money, like that solicitor who showed up at the front door one evening and claimed to have come all the way from Marion, Ohio, to ask a contribution to Senator Harding's campaign. "Senator Harding?" Ponzi had told him. "I can't give money to one senator without giving to the other ninety-five. It would create a bad precedent."

Remembering, he was grinning when he picked up the phone.

It was a friend, a youth who worked as a clerk at the courthouse. He talked softly at the other end of the line, but his words rushed out in a stream broken only by an explosive "Damn!" and "Goddamn!" from Ponzi. When the caller finished, Ponzi sat silently for an instant, feeling the wheels within his mind begin to turn—slowly at first and then suddenly faster, like a locomotive breaking free at the crest of a hill.

"All right, Dominick," he said, "thanks for the dope. Come by the office Monday. A thousand-dollar bill will be waiting for you."

There was a gasp at the other end of the wire. "That's too much, Mr. Ponzi. I never—"

"It's worth it to me. Anything else I should know?"

The young man thought for a long moment. "I don't think so. Oh, yeh, one of the boys from the *Post* knows about it. He goes through the daily actions all the time, and probably picked this up last night."

"Christ, the paper may be trying to find me right now!"

He hung up by pressing the cradle down, then let it up immediately and dialed Chmielinski's private number. Luckily the banker was home.

"Henry, this is important," he said hurriedly. "Daniels! That damn North End furniture dealer! He's slapped a bill of attachment on me. He's suing for a million bucks, claims he's a partner in the company because he loaned me the start-up money."

The heavy voice with its thick Polish accent barked a question.

129

"Goddammit, no!" Ponzi replied. "He doesn't get a cent. I've got enough lawyers working for me to tie him in knots for years. But I've got to get out from under the attachments. Fast, before the papers are served on Monday."

"I can switch your account here. Most of it, anyway. To your wife?"

"No, the bastard would see through that. Put it in a trustee's name."

"Your secretary's?"

"No, don't mix anyone up in it. They might want a piece later and I'd have to fight them in court, too. Here, use this—*Lucy Martelli.*"

"Who's that?"

Nobody, dammit, it's just a name. There's no time to worry about it. Get everything transferred, Henry. Don't fail me."

The banker tried to calm him, saying it would be no problem. "I won't change it all, Ponzi. That would look too damn suspicious. I'll leave $15,000, maybe $20,000 under your name."

"Make it $16,000, an odd number." He hung up, his mind already racing for the next move. Swig's bank, the Tremont, with the next largest account, was listed in the bill of attachment. The Cosmopolitan, with $285,000, was covered, too. If he could get the big deposits out in time, Daniels could have the rest that he was trying to grab—$7,000 in the First State, $14,000 in the Merchants National. He drummed his fingers nervously on the desk as he heard Swig's phone ringing in the distance. "Damn the Jew," Ponzi muttered half-aloud. "It's Saturday! He's probably at *schul!*" Some $340,000 was at stake, and the bank president was out saying prayers!

The phone continued to buzz insistently. Ponzi cursed each time its sound was answered by silence, thinking that he had never wanted to get mixed up with Swig in the first place. But the Tremont, needing all the depositors it could get, had been in no position to question the source of any funds brought to it. In return for Ponzi's money, Swig allowed him to use the bank's name as reference. Listening now to the distant phone ringing, Ponzi wondered if it had been a help or a hindrance. Several times, when he had told a reluctant investor that he had the backing of the Tremont, he had seen the prospect's eyes flash with suspicion.

Now, Swig needed Ponzi more than he needed the banker. All over Boston, people were withdrawing money from their bank accounts—or closing them completely—to invest with the Securities Exchange Company. By staying friendly with Ponzi, Swig at least saw to it that a great many of the dollars taken out by his depositors came right back in the form of additions to Ponzi's account. "But we'll never get along," Ponzi had confided one evening to Cassullo. "Swig thinks a Jew is better than a wop, while I, on the other hand, think the only thing better than a wop is two wops."

The phone was finally picked up by a sleepy maid. Imperiously, Ponzi ordered her to run and locate Swig. "Tell him to call me at once," he commanded. "Just say it's Ponzi!" He pressed the receiver hook, lifted it, and rang the private number of Mitchell, president of the Cosmopolitan. There, a cook told him the entire family had gone to New Hampshire for the holiday weekend. No, she didn't know how they could be reached. With a curse, he slammed down the telephone.

It rang immediately.

"Swig," he almost shouted, "I've been trying to—"

"Ponzi?" said an unfamiliar voice. "Is this Charles Ponzi?"

Instantly, Ponzi wiped the excitement and impatience from his voice. "Yes," he said calmly. "Who is this?"

It was a reporter from the Boston *Post*. "We understand that a chap named Daniels is suing you for a million dollars. That's a lot of money, Mr. Ponzi."

"And where your newspaper is concerned," he said, laughing, "that's a story, right? Well, I'm afraid, Mr.—Martin, is it?—that what Mr. Daniels has filed is merely what you'd call a 'nuisance suit.'" He went on to explain that the furniture dealer had been hanging around the offices of Securities Exchange Company and evidently had noticed how much money was being made there. Perhaps, Ponzi hinted with another laugh, Daniels thought it would be easier to get rich by suing than by investing. "If so, he's making a big mistake. Thousands of my investors are making all they want simply by waiting a few weeks for their interest."

At first, Ponzi talked quickly, hoping to get rid of the interviewer so that the line would be clear for Swig's call. But then an idea hit him. A little publicity in the newspapers might not hurt at all. There were hundreds of thousands of Bostonians who had not yet heard of the Securities Exchange Company. If they read about it, and its manager's wealth, they would come running to invest.

That greedy Daniels might have done him a favor.

He invited the reporter to drop around to his office—"Yes, I'll be here most of the day, in case some investors want to pick up their profits before the holiday"—and hung up the phone again. Swig was on the line a second later.

The banker was not encouraging. "It's Saturday, Ponzi. There's no one I can reach now at the bank. Tomorrow's the

Fourth, and that's worse. Maybe Monday morning something can be done—if the writ doesn't get to us when we open."

"I don't want any *ifs*, Swig! I want that money."

The banker reflected a moment, remembered that Ponzi's last midweek deposit—amounting to $150,000—might not have been entered in the master accounts yet. "I can catch that," he said. "First thing Monday."

"Christ, then Daniels will still tie up $190,000."

Swig said that could not be avoided. "You'll have to get your lawyers on it right away. I don't want that money bottled up any more than you do. Have you thought about talking to this fellow, Daniels? What kind—"

Ponzi snorted angrily. "He's a bastard, I know that. I figured he was up to something the other day when he was hanging around here. Hell, I should have had him tossed out!"

Swig tried again. "But if you talked to him—"

"I'll let the lawyers talk to him. I'll sue him for ten million, and I'll collect. He'll regret it, Swig. He'll regret it."

The banker listened, letting him vent his anger without interrupting. "Ponzi," he said then, "how badly do you need the money?"

It was like a splash of ice water on Ponzi's rage. Suddenly his voice was calm again and his mind was needle-sharp. "Need it?" he asked lightly. "Swig, I don't need it at all, and you know it. With the accounts I have all over New England, the five that Daniels is attaching add up to—oh, maybe a fifth or sixth of the total. It's just the goddamn principle, that's all. I've worked hard for my millions, and no cheap furniture salesman is going to get any of it."

It was the maid who, bringing in the newspaper shortly after breakfast the next morning, first told him his name was in the *Post*.

"Mr. Ponzi," she said with a smile, "the paper has something about you!"

Casually, he said, "Oh?" and looked at the article she pointed to on the front page. "Why, a reporter called on me yesterday afternoon, but he said it might be a few days before anything was printed. Let me see."

Boston Man
Is Sued for
$1,000,000
Defendant Claims Ignorance
As to Action's Cause

It was all there, much as he had related it to the newsman.

Daniels had sued him for $1 million and had moved to tie up his funds in five banks, making an alleged claim to certain profits of the Securities Company.

"Mother, listen," he exclaimed as Rose read over his shoulder. "Listen how they quote me:

> Seen yesterday in his office, Mr. Ponzi said, "I haven't the slightest idea why Mr. Daniels brought the suit. When I opened, I bought furniture from him, but he never left any money with me for investment. The only reason I see is a desire to get some money out of me. If his claim is just, he will have no difficulty because I have $2 million over and above all claims of investors against me in this country. Not included are my funds in foreign banks. The attachment covers only five banks and will not affect more than $100,000. My funds in thirty other banks are not affected."
>
> "Will the suit hurt your business?" Mr. Ponzi was asked. "Not at all. Anyone who thinks so and withdraws his investment will only increase my own profits. At the beginning I needed the public's money, by now my own private fortune is sufficient to meet all demands on the business for ready money."

He tossed the paper onto the stack at the side of his easy chair with a careless gesture, and smiled over his shoulder at Rose. "It's nothing to get excited about, dear. There will be many more stories in the papers about us. I'll wager that the Sunday sections will soon be asking us all—you, mother and me—to pose for their photographers."

"But, Carlo," said his mother from her chair near the window, "this man is suing you! A million dollars!"

He walked across the room to pat her hand. "The man's a swindler, that's all. Remember that people who get sued for a million dollars must *have* a million dollars, and we can easily afford to lose that much. Not that I *will* lose it, of course," he added, turning to Rose. "The finest lawyers in the city are working for me already, and I intend to hire more. In this kind of suit, it is not right or wrong or justice that matters—but, rather, who has the most resources to fight the battle. I can outspend Daniels for legal advice five or ten or twenty to one. Don't either of you worry."

He glanced at his mother who was smiling up at him, her needlework forgotten. "My Carlo," she said. Her eyes were shining.

"Get Dunn in here, will you, Frank?"

The freckle-faced copyboy browsing through the *Post's* sports section jumped to his feet as the assistant editor strode past him. "Yessir," he said, already on his way down the hall to the city editor's office.

"Mr. Dunn," he called over the noise of the typewriters, "Mr. Grozier wants you."

Edward J. Dunn nodded but kept his attention on the galley proof he was reading. Young Grozier could wait a minute, he thought to himself. Just because the old man—Edwin A. Grozier, editor and publisher of the Boston *Post*—had decided to take a summerlong vacation, and leave his kid in charge, that didn't mean the whole staff of the paper had to jump when he snapped his fingers. Dunn made a final correction on the proof and got wearily to his feet.

He went into Richard Grozier's office, half-cursing the managing editor for getting sick enough to land in the hospital. That meant there was nobody else on the staff except himself to deal with this thirty-four-year-old newspaper heir, who single-handedly was now in charge of the editorial, business, and mechanical departments of the *Post*.

"Eddie," said Grozier immediately, "who did this story? The million-dollar lawsuit?"

"Martin. Why, something wrong?" The city editor was ready to protect his reporters almost automatically.

Grozier raised his gaze from the paper, a thoughtful look in his eyes. "No, no problems," he answered. "But what do we know about this Ponzi?"

"Not much more than it says. He started up last Christmas and is getting sued for a million bucks."

Grozier nodded his head. "I don't know," he said.

Dunn studied him. "You don't know what?"

"I don't know how he could have done it so fast. Made so much, I mean. Legitimately."

Of course! Dunn cursed himself for not having noticed it, then tried to tell himself that with the managing editor gone, there was just too much work to keep tabs on everything.

"Mother of God, you may have something. This Ponzi comes out of nowhere and all at once is gettin' sued for a million. Martin had some stuff in there about his offices—said they looked like a shipping room in a warehouse—but I cut it for space."

"A shipping room? For a man with two million? Suppose you turn a couple of boys loose on this—" Grozier glanced at the paper on his desk—"Securities Exchange Company. No immediate story. Just let 'em see what they can find."

At the same time, a similar conversation was taking place at the State House in the office of J. Weston Allen, who had been appointed attorney general of Massachusetts six months earlier.

"Al," said the official to one of his young assistants, "how in hell can this guy be running a business of this size in Boston without *somebody* here having heard of him? What the devil is going on?"

Albert Hurwitz, barely in his thirties, shrugged noncommittally. "You know the newspapers, Mr. Allen. Especially the *Post*. If they don't have a story about a kid getting run over by a truck or some society woman poisoning her husband, they stick in one about a millionaire—whether he has a million or not. This man Ponzi may be no more of a millionaire than you and me."

"That's what I'm thinking, Al, exactly. But it might be more than a case of exaggeration by some reporter."

Hurwitz made a few quick notes on a pad from his breast pocket. "We *should* look into his operations, just for tax information, I guess."

Allen's voice was sharp. "No guesses about it! I've got obligations to the people and industry of this state, and this thing just smells too fishy to pass up. Take what time you need, but let's find out about Mr. Ponzi."

"Mr. Ponzi!"

The excited voice of Lucy Meli reached him even as he was shouldering his small frame through the mass of people in the outer office. The story of Daniels' suit had brought in the crowds, all right, just as he thought it would. The question was whether the men and women were there to withdraw their money, or to bring him more.

"Yes, Miss Meli?" He smiled, waved a greeting to Miss Lacarno and two typists who now shared the inner office. "Quite a gathering out there, isn't it?"

It was the story in the newspaper, his private secretary explained, that must have produced the crowd. "On the front page! It was so exciting. All my girlfriends have been calling to ask if I work for the same Mr. Ponzi. I tell 'em there's only one!"

He waited until she paused for breath, and then asked about the people. Were they in an unfriendly mood? What did they want?

"Oh, the first ones wanted their money back—even without the interest. I told the boys to pay them, like you always say to do. There must have been fifty people in line when I opened this morning, Mr. Ponzi. The stairs were so crowded I could hardly get through. I had to—"

"The ones waiting now, are they withdrawing, too?"

"Oh, heavens, no! From about nine until ten-thirty, we gave back exactly—oh, I've got it here somewhere." She shuffled papers on the desk, then found a note to herself. "Exactly $14,840! But then everybody sort of calmed down, Mr. Ponzi. Some people put it all back again—it just made so much paperwork for us—and then everybody else has just been lining up to buy new notes."

Now the smile on his face was natural once more. He felt almost like calling Daniels and telling him that the million dollars was his. The man *had* done him a favor. Still this was no time for foolish gestures. He reached for the telephone and called Arthur D. Hill. The prominent attorney was retained on the spot to fight Daniels all the way.

"He has no claim on me, Hill, and I won't pay him a damn cent. I've got ten thousand investors who have given me $3 million, and they're the only ones who will benefit from my work! You tell that to Daniels' lawyer!"

Assured by his new attorney that the furniture dealer would have a hard time proving—without any written agreement—that he had contributed to the success of the Securities Exchange Company, Ponzi put the suit out of his mind. But it had started a train of thought in the minds of several of his banking friends.

The president of the First National Bank reached him first. There was a matter he wished to discuss, he said, in the privacy of his office.

"The story in the *Post* yesterday, Mr. Ponzi. Some of the directors are concerned—well, it's awkward when any funds are attached, you know."

"This is strictly a nuisance suit," Ponzi explained calmly. "It's noth—"

"Of course, of course," said the official. "But there's another matter. We understand that you have given our name to some prospective clients as a reference."

"I *do* have a sizable account with you."

"We're not questioning your solvency. It's just that we've had calls about your business, and, frankly, we can't answer them. We know nothing about your business. For our protection, I must suggest that you close your account."

Ponzi returned an unlighted cigar to his pocket and stood up. "It's all right with me. I am now listed with Bradstreet's, and they rate me at $8 million. I don't really need any references from you."

The banker, hearing the ice in Ponzi's voice, struck back. "Bradstreet, as we all know, relies on the information a subscriber gives them to a great degree, Mr. Ponzi. I daresay our reference is every bit as strong as theirs—for any knowledgeable investor, that is."

"May I have my balance?" Ponzi asked edgily.

The banker reached for the phone on his desk. "I'll have a check made out right away."

"Let me have cash if you don't mind."

The hand hung suspended over the receiver. "Cash?"

"Cash."

"You mean that our check is not acceptable? The First National—"

"If Charles Ponzi, worth $8 million, is not good enough for a reference from this bank, I must wonder about the intelligence of some of its officers. And I'm not sure they know how to make out a proper check. Cash, if you please. One-thousand-dollar bills will be satisfactory."

"But," the banker sputtered, "your accounts total $45,000. You could be waylaid on the streets. A check—"

Ponzi flipped open his coat to show the pearl handle of a small nickel-plated Colt automatic in a leather holster. "One of my

137

depositors—a *police inspector* who trusts me—helped me obtain a permit to carry this last month. It's only a twenty-five-caliber, but if any hoodlum tries to make off with Charles Ponzi's money, he'll get a bullet between the eyes. I'm quite used to carrying large sums, friend. Let me have the cash, please."

When he returned to the School Street office, the reporter who had talked to him on Saturday was waiting. "I thought I'd just stop in and see how things ran when your investors were here," the young man said, looking at the lines before the two tellers' windows. "You won't find me investing," he added with a laugh. "I'm afraid the boss wouldn't let me have the day off to wait in the lines."

Ponzi grinned and told him to take a chair, then casually tossed the pack of thousand-dollar bills across the desk to his secretary. "Miss Meli," he said, watching the newsman's eyes widen in surprise, "add this $45,000 to the day's receipts, and deposit everything in the Hanover."

He felt sure that the reporter was impressed.

"Now that you mention it," he said to the newsman, "I'm certain that some of your friends at the paper are investors with us. Quite a few of the printers, I believe. And isn't there a day foreman in the press room named—uh—"

"Harrigan?" the reporter supplied.

"Right. He's put a couple of thousand in, I'm sure. You'll have no trouble finding satisfied clients of the Securities Exchange Company. You won't even have to leave Newspaper Row."

The young man's eyes seemed wider than ever now. "Mr. Ponzi," he said, "would it be all right if I just kind of hung around and asked questions now and then? I don't know much about finance, but I sure think there's a bigger story here than we ran yesterday."

"Stay as long as you like. Ask anyone anything. We have absolutely nothing to hide, just as I told you the other day. This man Daniels is trying to cut in on a good thing, that's all. And, by the way, my attorneys have informed me that he hasn't a chance."

"I guess I should talk to him, anyway. Would you mind?"

Ponzi laughed. "Mind? I don't care if you talk to the devil himself. Oh, I've got enemies—I'm not denying that. A few bankers are after me, but that's understandable. Anytime you deal in high finance, the established money interests are going to resent you. It's a basic law!"

He passed much of the afternoon spinning out his life story for the young reporter—leaving unexplained gaps at some points, and embroidering details on certain events dredged from his memory.

When the newsman's notebook and head both were crowded with facts real and imagined, Ponzi excused himself. "Very important meeting with one of my bankers," he said.

At the Hanover, he went to his own office and phoned Chmielinski's secretary to tell her boss that he wanted to see him. As the bank's chief stockholder, he felt justified in ordering the president around. After all, the man was actually working for him—and from the look on Chmielinski's face when he came into the room, Ponzi knew that the Pole understood quite well where he stood these days.

"It's taken care of, Ponzi," Chmielinski said at once. "All but $16,000. Everything else is in the name of Lucy Martelli."

"Nice work, old man. A damn sight better than Swig did over at the Tremont. He kept $150,000 out from under, but Daniels locked up nearly $200,000. If Swig had wanted to, if he was a friend like you, he could have moved more. I know it."

The banker shrugged his shoulders helplessly. "You'll get the suit dismissed. It may take a few days, but you'll get it thrown out."

"I'm not going to push it. Let Daniels scream his lungs out. I don't need the cash. You should have seen the line of investors at the office this morning. Miss Meli says we'd taken in a quarter of a million by lunchtime."

"And that's money Daniels can't touch."

Through a cloud of cigar smoke, Ponzi nodded, smiled. "His lawyers caught nearly $300,000 at the Cosmopolitan. That damn Max Mitchell took his family out for the day, and I couldn't track him down. But I'll get it when I need it." He paused, deliberately making Chmielinski sit there, wondering why he had been called.

Finally the banker coughed. "Uh—was there something—?"

"Oh, yes. Actually, Chmielinski, I wanted to talk to you about speeding up the way we're increasing the bank's assets. I have an idea."

It was a simple plan. So simple that the president of the Hanover could see nothing wrong with it. Ponzi placed an immediate call to the state commissioner of banking and explained it to him, while Chmielinksi listened in on an extension.

"I think I understand, Ponzi," the commissioner said. "You want to run a contest with a monthly prize of a thousand dollars to the man who brings the most new depositors into the Hanover?"

"That's right. My personal contest. I know the bank can't do it. And I'm not going to use its money. I won't even promote it as a Hanover proposition."

"How are you going to work it out?"

Ponzi explained that he would have a printer run off thousands of cards. "People can pick up stacks of them at my office on School Street and pass them out to their friends. There'll be a place for the signatures of the people who give them out and for the people who get them. When somebody who gets one opens an account at the Hanover, he turns in the card along with his first deposit. At the end of the month the bank turns all the cards over to me, and the person who has passed out the most gets the thousand."

There was a silence at the commissioner's end. "Well," he said, finally, "I don't see how I have any say-so over what a private citizen wants to do with his money. You can give it out as you see fit."

When the call was completed, Ponzi's dark eyes gleamed with pleasure as he studied Chmielinski's face. "You know what's going to happen, don't you, Henry?"

"I can imagine." He also was smiling.

"All over town, people are going to pull more of their money out of the Cosmopolitan, and the Tremont, and the Franklin, the Federal—all the banks. They'll bring it to us. And the others will grow weaker as we get stronger. When they're weak enough, I can go to them and suggest propping them up with a big deposit if they sell me the stock at the right price. They won't be able to do anything else!"

He dismissed Chmielinski with a wave of his hand, and sat soberly in the late afternoon sunlight. It had been a profitable day all around. The publicity from the Daniels suit actually had brought in more investors than his busy clerks could handle in eight hours. Tomorrow there would be half-again as many, and twice as many the next day. The *Post* was going to do a longer story that would bring in even more. And the contest would swell the Hanover's vaults.

He had another idea to increase the bank's assets, too—an idea that he did not bother to clear with Chmielinski. There were certain things that financial circles whispered about the state treasurer, Frederick J. Burrell. It was said that as a sideline Burrell ran a sizable advertising agency, one that specialized in placing ads for banks and financial institutions. The agency collected large commissions for its services, and the institutions in turn frequently were the beneficiaries of state funds placed in their safekeeping by Burrell. Ponzi telephoned the official and guardedly explained what he had heard.

"Of course, it all may just be a rumor, Mr. Burrell."

The treasurer coughed. "Well, Ponzi, it is true that I do own an advertising agency. I have never denied that. And it is true that I place quite a lot of newspaper advertising space for any number of banks and trust companies. But as to the other thing—why, that amounts to slander."

"Of course," Ponzi said. "As an interested resident of this state, and as the major stockholder in the Hanover Trust Company," he said, "I merely wanted to hear a denial from your lips. It's always gratifying to know that we can believe in our officials."

The treasurer gratefully thanked him for his support. Then, as the conversation was about to end, he seemed to think of something.

"As long as you've called me, Mr. Ponzi, I'd be a pretty bad businessman if I didn't ask who handles the Hanover's advertising now? If you're thinking of a change, I must say that my little agency provides pretty good service."

The rumor was fact, just as Ponzi had suspected. And Burrell was not going to let him get away.

"I'm not sure, Mr. Burrell," he said. "Mr. Chmielinski handles that kind of thing personally."

"Well, as the major shareholder, you could bring some weight to bear, I imagine. My rates are the same as everyone else's, of course. But some banks have found that it never hurts to have a friend looking out for them."

Ponzi promised to suggest a change of agencies to the bank president and the board at the first opportunity. "You'll hear from someone at the bank very shortly, Mr. Burrell. And I think I can say that we look forward to doing business with you."

After the call, he rang up the School Street office, catching Miss Meli just before she left with two of the clerks as guards to make the day's deposit.

"It's almost $450,000, Mr. Ponzi," she gasped. "Not all of it from here, but with the checks from all the branches over the weekend—!"

He kept his voice perfectly neutral, advising her to take an extra two or three men along to the bank. "Give each one fifty dollars, and don't let anyone know how much you're carrying." He paused, picturing the thick packs of bills stuffed inside the satchel he had ordered Cassullo to buy for the daily "take."

"Mr. Ponzi, a letter came today. It's kind of official looking. Wait just a minute." He could hear her leafing through the papers on her desk. "It's from the state income tax office, and it wants to know what kind of a 'corporation, association or organization' the company is. 'So as to determine your tax liabilities under Chapter 437 of the Acts of 1903.' I guess it can wait until you get in tomorrow."

"No, before you leave, just drop them a note. Say the

Securities Exchange Company is not a corporation, association, or organization, and therefore we're not covered by—whatever those Acts are. Do you have that? Just say we're not covered."

Taxes, Ponzi thought after he replaced the receiver. *Tax me? Certainly the state can tax its citizens if it chooses to.*

But, he thought wryly, *I'm not a citizen!*

Every morning now, the line of people stretched from his office, down the steps and a half-block along School Street. At first it had only reached from his second-floor door to the sidewalk. The next day it had grown past the jeweler's. A day later it had passed the pharmacy. Then, the barbershop. If it continued to grow at this rate, it would soon turn the corner on Province Street, and begin to meander all over Boston.

As his car rounded the corner off Tremont Street, Ponzi almost laughed at the size of the line. Catching sight of a waiting photographer before the driver touched the brakes, he fluffed up the bright handkerchief in his breast pocket. He stepped out lightly and posed with one foot on the running board to add a bit of height. The cameraman clicked off a picture, reversed his plates, and took another quickly.

"What's the *Post* going to do with all these photographs?" Ponzi asked good-naturedly. "Start its own Sears, Roebuck catalogue?"

He grinned as the men and women waiting in line—waiting to give their dollars to the Securities Exchange Company—laughed and applauded. Like Senator Harding on the campaign trail, he waved at the people as he strode past them, the gold-headed cane swinging jauntily on his arm, a thick cigarette in a five-inch holder pointing upward from the corner of his mouth.

Miss Meli noticed the heavy smell of the Turkish tobacco almost as soon as he reached the inner office. "It's because of my mother," he said. "Cigar smoke in the house has been bothering her. Not just mine, of course. We've had so many bankers over for dinner the place looks like a gents' smoker at times. And mother isn't as young as you girls are."

Miss Meli and Miss Lacarno beamed at their jovial employer. It was swell, each was thinking, to work for a man who never got upset, who never worried about his business—whose business always seemed to be doing well.

Things *had* been going well since the *Post* story brought on the brief run. Going too well, in fact. The influx of money was running $250,000 a day, $300,000, $400,000, and there obviously was no end in sight. Even with the new deposits that the contest was bringing into the Hanover, and with the thousands of dollars of state money that Burrell had already transferred to the trust company, Ponzi's ability to cover his debts was lagging further behind with each day's passing.

On the drive downtown this morning, he had thought of yet another way to plug the dollar drain. A minor way, but still—

"Miss Meli, get a letter out to all the agents. Tell them that next Monday—that's the nineteenth—we'll pay their commissions once a week by check. They should forward the full amount of any investor's money to us."

"Without taking their commission out first?"

"Exactly. Nobody deducts anything. I want all the money in here, and then we'll figure the ten percent and send them a check. It's much more businesslike."

Miss Lacarno gestured at a stack of correspondence on her desk. "But we're getting behind on so much of this, Mr. Ponzi."

"Have one of the men help out if you need him." He motioned to one of the senior clerks. "Masellis, pitch in with the ladies on this, will you." Another thought occurred to him. "In the letter, Miss Meli, tell the agents not to accept checks from anyone unless they're certified. Too many people are putting bum checks over on us."

There wouldn't be much of a saving, but every dollar—*every penny!*—might help delay things until he came up with the big solution. Cassullo had returned from another trip to New York with word of a new prospect, a man calling himself Joseph Herman. Claiming important financial connections, Herman was trying to get some associates together and said he would shortly make an offer for a large piece of the Securities Exchange Company. Cassullo swore that Herman could be trusted. But what did that mean when Cassullo couldn't be trusted himself?

He had to have an alternative. Maybe the shipping company scheme was the answer.

It was something that he had worked out on paper in a frenzied all-night period a few days earlier. Twice, while he sat on the cool

144

veranda behind the house, working by the light of an old kerosene lamp, Rose had wakened and asked him to come to bed. But he could not stop his pencil moving across the lined, legal-size pad, nor the succession of thoughts racing through his brain. In the light of morning, he had studied his figures. It worked—on paper, it worked. But was there time to carry it out?

Well, nothing ventured, nothing gained, he thought. He ordered Miss Meli to phone his primary bankers—Swig at the Tremont, Chmielinski at the Hanover, and Mitchell at the Cosmopolitan—and have them meet him in his private office at the Hanover Trust Building.

"No, wait, there's no telling when a reporter or some snoop from the post office will show up there. We'll meet in the C and R office, on the tenth floor."

He was ready for them when they arrived. The looks of consternation on their faces, however, surprised him, until he realized what they were probably thinking.

"Gentlemen, gentlemen," he said soothingly, "while some financiers only call their bankers together in time of trouble, Charles Ponzi operates quite differently. I've asked you here to give me some advice. I am prepared to make one of the greatest business deals of all time. As my bankers, your opinions are valuable."

Swig had skepticism in his eyes. "What are you up to, Ponzi?"

He took a deep breath and placed a newspaper advertisement from the Boston *Traveler* on the desk, turning it so they could read it. The ad had run in all the important papers in Boston and every other large city in the country.

"You saw this, I'm sure," he said, and the others nodded.

The ad was an offer of the U. S. government to sell the entire Shipping Board fleet, some three thousand vessels which had been built during the war for troop and supply transport. It had cost some $3 billion to create the fleet, and the asking price was twenty dollars per ton, per vessel.

"Gentlemen, I'm interested in buying the entire fleet—some ten million tons of shipping power—for $200 million!"

No one gasped. No one smiled. The three bankers merely looked at him.

"I can have one of my men on his way to Washington in a few minutes with a check for $1 million—no, $2 million—as a down payment."

It was Mitchell, ordinarily slow-thinking and taciturn, who spoke. "You'll only need $198 million more."

145

Ponzi saw the flicker of a smile on Swig's lips. He plunged ahead. "The government is prepared to wait ten years for full payment. I'll offer cash, in thirty days. And I'll deliver it."

He paused, waiting for the question. "How?" Swig said, on cue.

The Securities Exchange Company is now taking in nearly a million dollars a day. You all know that. And I'm operating only in New England. Once the government acclaims me a patriot willing to take this mess of ships off its hands, I'll open everywhere in the forty-eight states!"

"How long would it take you to set up additional offices?" asked Chmielinski.

Ponzi stared straight at him. "Inside of forty-eight hours, I could cover the country coast to coast. I've got requests from every city already, from men who want in on my present operation. Look here—"

He pulled a thick and tattered bundle of letters and cables from a pocket. "Every state in the Union! Here's one from an Indian maharajah who wants to know how many millions of rupees I'll take as an investment. This one's from a mandarin in China who has a half-million taels to give me. These two, they're from mining interests in South Africa and Australia—I haven't even figured out their offers of pounds sterling in dollars."

He started shoving the papers back into his jacket pockets. "Cables from South America, offering pesos, milreis, bolivianos, sucres, sols! A telegram from a bank in Canada saying that a Mr. Leyture—someone I've never heard of!—has deposited $7 million with them to my credit! I can raise $200 million in thirty days, gentlemen! I'm sure of it!"

There was a simultaneous clearing of throats. Swig dug a crumpled handkerchief from his rear pocket and coughed wetly into it. Mitchell started to say something, then halted, frowning.

"You probably can, Charlie," said Chmielinski. "But what in hell are you going to do with the fleet when you get it? There's hundreds of freighters and tankers. The *Leviathan* alone—"

Ponzi had lain awake for hours working out the answer to that question, he explained. The fleet would actually cost him $320 million. That's $200 million borrowed from my investors at fifty percent, and $20 million in commissions to my agents." He brought two crude hand-lettered organizational charts from beneath the desk, laid them out for the bankers to study. One was for the Charles Ponzi Steamship Company, which would own the fleet.

"And this one," he said easily, "is for the International Shipping and Mercantile Company, which will lease and operate the vessels. Now, the Ponzi company will be capitalized at $1 million—we'll issue one thousand shares of common at $1,000 each. And it will issue $350 million worth of ten-year bonds paying twelve percent.

"The IS and M will be capitalized at $350 million, with three hundred and fifty million shares of eight percent ten-year preferred stock and seven million shares of no-par-value common. The leasing company—the IS and M—will exchange half the shares of its common for half the shares of the CPSS common. And it will underwrite the entire bond issue at ninety-three, or, for $325,500,000, paying for it with demand notes. That way, it can offer to the public at large one one-hundred-dollar bond, one one-hundred-dollar share of preferred, and one share of no-par-value common, all for $200."

Now there was absolute silence in the room. Ponzi felt perspiration on his face. He waited for the next question, deliberately neglecting to tell the bankers that his plan involved letting the public purchase the shipping shares by presenting their Securities Exchange Company notes upon maturity. Sale of the shipping companies' stock, whether for cash or against his notes, would wipe out the liabilities of the Securities Exchange Company, which he would promptly phase out of existence.

Swig had been studying the figures that Ponzi had jotted so quickly on the legal pad. Now he looked up. "What I see here is a man who owns a great many useless ships, and who owes a great deal of money."

The Jew, the damn fool Jew! Ponzi thought. But his voice was soft and unemotional. "Let's go on from that point, Swig. First we clear up the debt. The IS and M Company leases the entire fleet from the CPSS for $80 million a year for ten years. The CPSS applies the money to the payment of interest on the bond issue and to the amortization of the principal. The interest comes to $420 million over ten years. That leaves $38 million each year for amortization, and that money, banked at three percent, will bring in at least $12 million. So, we're left with $42 million after payment of the principal to be distributed as dividend to the common stock. That's something like $42,000 per share, I believe—and I can't see any investor in his right mind turning that down!"

"No one's questioning your appeal to the common man, Ponzi—" Swig began.

"Wait a minute, now" Ponzi said swiftly. "Let me get through this, so you understand it all. The IS and M will sublease the vessels to a number of subsidiary companies. They'll pay $150 million a year for ten years. That leaves $70 million a year to pay the interest on the preferred stock and to amortize the principal. The interest comes to $280 million in ten years. We set aside $42 million a year for amortization, and it earns at least $15 million in ten years, at three percent. If we get higher interest, we come out that much more ahead. After payment of the principal, there's still $85 million to be distributed as dividend to the common stock. That's twelve dollars a share."

The bankers were coughing more obviously now, and were daring to smile at one another. But Ponzi, his eyes on the pad that rapidly was becoming covered with figures, did not notice.

"Of course, I'll have to organize and control the subsidiaries—the companies that will actually use the ships. They'll be set up with preferred stock and no-par-value common, and the IS and M will hang onto fifty-one percent of the common. The rest will be offered to manufacturers, exporters and importers, and the public. Each subsidiary will pay the IS and M a rental price of fifteen dollars per ton per year on each ship it leases.

"The whole fleet consists of ten million tons. The Charles Ponzi Steamship Company leases it to the IS and M for eight dollars a ton per year, and the IS and M subleases it to the subsidiary companies for fifteen dollars a ton per year. Now, do you gentlemen know what shippers are paying these days to move their goods?"

He looked up at the three bankers who were sitting uncomfortably in their chairs.

When no one answered him, Ponzi plunged on. "They're paying anywhere from twenty dollars and up per ton, that's what they're paying. Now, if a subsidiary of mine leases a ten-thousand-ton vessel, it pays $150,000 a year. It can easily make four round trips a year—that's eighty thousand tons of cargo. I'm not sure on operating expenses—let's say they're eight dollars per ton. That means the total cost is only about ten dollars a ton for freight, or about half what shippers are used to paying. Do you mean to tell me we'll lack any business at those rates?"

"I don't mean to tell you anything, Ponzi. It sounds eminently practical." Swig was standing up now, slipping the watch he had taken out back into his pocket and adjusting the loop of heavy gold chain across his stomach. "But I'm afraid you'll have to excuse me. I promised Mrs. Swig that I'd get home early. It's a fine idea—"

"Wait just a minute, friend. You haven't heard my plan for the passenger ships. They'll be floating sample rooms for American products! I'll send them from port to port, all over the world. Oh, tourists can ride along, but the bulk of the passenger list will be American salesmen and buyers. The salesmen will carry goods that can be delivered right on the spot to buyers overseas. And on the return trip, the cargo holds will be filled with imports picked up at bargain prices because the merchants abroad will want to grab an immediate sale. Naturally, I'll get a commission on all sales and purchases."

They were all on their feet, the three of them, swaying back and forth in impatience. Swig had the door open.

"It sounds practical," he said, "Very practical."

Mitchell nodded in agreement as he moved toward the doorway. "You won't have any trouble finding support, Ponzi. It's an excellent opportunity for investors, and there's the whole patriotic aspect—"

"Exactly! I wanted to talk about that. My papers are not due yet, but you all know that I'm one hundred percent American! More so than a lot of the natives! And that includes a lot of people in Washington." He tried to catch them before they were in the hallway. "Then you think it will work? All of you?"

The trio nodded in unison. "You'll only have the problem of the British shipping interests," Swig volunteered. "There are a lot of people who don't want to see the Union Jack replaced by the Stars and Stripes. But I think you can find a way around that—the way you have found a way around all the other obstacles in your plan."

He turned his back and started toward the elevator. Then he glanced back at Ponzi who stood silently, holding the yellow pad and pencil. "Really, Ponzi," he said, "you're quite a remarkable person. Quite remarkable."

At home that evening, Rose could tell by the absence of her husband's usual jesting mood that the day had not gone well for him. He put off her questions with the explanation that the business was growing so quickly that he had not taken time for lunch.

"Do you know, I had Miss Meli go over the books today, and I have one hundred and eighty agents and subagents working now? No wonder the office is so crowded all the time. About fifty of them are in the city alone, and they're in and out all day long. I've hired ten policemen, a dozen, to keep order, and still there's a jam like the trolley on a rainy day."

"You should have more help, Carlo. Surely you can afford it," his mother said.

Afford it! he wanted to say. *With nearly $5 million in the bank, I can hardly afford anything!* Every penny had to be saved now, hoarded, hung onto until the time when he could invest it in something gigantic. Something big enough to let him pay off the widows, the wounded veterans, the laborers, and all the others who had trusted him. Perhaps the shipping deal had been *too* big; certainly it had frightened off the bankers who could provide needed references for him if and when he contacted the U.S. government. But something else would turn up. There was still time, despite the notices from a half-dozen agents in various states that unfamiliar faces had appeared in their neighborhood to ask questions about the company.

He went directly the next day to the new office in the Hanover Trust Building. There was no time to make a casual appearance on School Street for the crowd's accolades. He had a proposal to lay before Chmielinski, and it would have to be acted on at once. He ordered the secretary to summon the banker, then turned his attention to three men who were lounging about the waiting room.

"You remember us, Mr. Ponzi. From last week? I'm Charley Brightwell, and this is Ray Meyers and his brother Fred." The man paused, standing silent and tall.

Ponzi looked up at him. "I remember you," he said. "The three of you. And I told you that I don't need any help. If you want to bring in money, the way the other agents do, you'll get the same commission. Now, I've got a lot of work to do—"

Brightwell gestured to one of the others, who took a slip of paper from his pocket. "You ought to look at this, I think," the tall man said. He handed the paper across the desk.

It was a note from the Securities Exchange Company—except that it wasn't. Identical in every respect—paper, ink, fancy border—the note bore a different heading. *Old Colony Foreign Exchange Company.* And the address, *54 Devonshire.*

"Across the street, eh?" murmured Ponzi.

"Just about," Brightwell said, "Naturally, we'd rather work with you. But if our offer of $10,000 for a half-share in the future profits doesn't suit you—well, you don't leave us much choice. We didn't want to start in business, though, without giving you a chance to change your mind."

"Change my mind? What the hell do you cheap crooks think you're doing? I wouldn't have you working for me if you offered $10 million!"

Brightwell folded the note and carefully tucked it into a pocket. "I kind of thought you'd feel that way." He turned to his associates. "Okay, boys, I guess we open shop. Ponzi, you—er—wouldn't know if there's any vacant office space in your building, would you?"

The glint in his eye was signal enough. Ponzi knew that Brightwell and he were kindred souls. From the moment that the tall, well-dressed figure had first approached him several weeks earlier, Ponzi knew the man meant trouble. He had asked a friend on the police force to run a routine check, and had found out only that Brightwell was said to have once been in the oil or mining business, that he had lived for a year in the Hotel Bellevue, and that he recently had taken furnished rooms on Bay State Road. But he evidently had no record—at least he had none under the name of Charles M. Brightwell.

"I'll bet he has a record, and I'll bet he has a list of aliases a mile long!" Ponzi had snapped into the telephone after getting the report. But there was nothing he could do about it—then or now.

"You open up," he said, putting a cold edge in his voice, "and I'll have the police close you up so fast your head will spin. I can charge you with a dozen different things, you know."

Brightwell's face twisted into a sneer. "Such as?"

"Trying to deceive the public, for one! Trying to make them think that you're part of my company! Practically counterfeiting my notes! You don't seem to realize that you're talking to Charles Ponzi, and I swing a lot of weight around this part of the country."

One of the Meyers brothers shifted his feet nervously. "Maybe we—" he said, but Brightwell turned him off with a gesture.

"You're bluffing, Ponzi," he said simply.

Ponzi studied the man's face. It was there, in his eyes, the glint of knowledge. The other man *knew*, that was it. Somebody had talked to him, had given him background that was unknown to anyone. But who—

Of course.

It had to be Cassullo. Several times in recent weeks, Cassullo had complained about his salary in relation to the money that he knew was coming through the tellers' windows. Ponzi had raised him to $5,000 a month, even while continuing to overlook the petty thefts he was obviously committing. Twice Cassullo had asked him for signature cards at the primary banks where the largest deposits were made, and had been put off on the grounds that he would only have to make withdrawals at the out-of-town banks in case of an emergency. "Miss Meli or my wife could get anything I need here in Boston, if I took sick," Ponzi had told him. "And, of course, I have a half-dozen attorneys who could see to my affairs." Cassullo had sulked, and started drinking himself into an angry, fitful stupor—until Ponzi, fearing his loose tongue, offered an inducement.

"I'll put the house in Winthrop in your name, Louis. Then, if anything happens to me—I guess I could get run over by a milkwagon—you'll have a good, solid piece of property."

The offer had been greedily accepted. But now, looking at Brightwell, Ponzi understood that it had only delayed things a bit. Cassullo was not satisfied, and he evidently had been talking. There was no other explanation for Brightwell's confidence.

"If you think I'm bluffing, Brightwell, go on and open your Old Foreign whatever-you-call-it! You'll see how fast the cops close it. I have more than $5 million in the banks of Boston, and I'll spend every nickel to make sure that you don't cheat the people of this town. They are *my* friends, *my* investors, and I'll protect them if it costs me every cent! Now get the hell out of here!"

Long minutes after the three men had left he sat fuming at his desk. There was a difference, he told himself. Brightwell and his confederates were out to fleece the public. There was no doubt about that. It was easy to see that none of them knew anything about foreign exchange.

But his own position—critical as it was, and growing more so day by day—was at least built on a premise of honesty. It was that kind of thinking, that kind of honesty that encouraged men and women to cheer his automobile in the street. To wait on corners to see him stroll by. No one would do that for Brightwell and his crowd. The people would recognize thieves and swindlers when they saw them. Perhaps he—Charles Ponzi, the millionaire with the people's welfare at heart—should tip off the police before the Old Colony operation got off the ground.

He reached for the telephone, and then moved his hand away. Of course that was impossible. How could he explain his certainty that this new company could not pay the same high interest rates that the Securities Exchange Company was paying? At least, that it could not pay them honestly. And bringing the police into it would only make them intensify their investigations into his own business. At the first accusation, Brightwell would make an equal one against him—and they both would go down together under a stampede of investors fighting to get their money back.

There was nothing that he could do, except play for time. Let the rival open shop if it wanted to. People would continue to invest with the man they could trust, with the man who had paid back every investor who presented a mature note. It would take the Old Colony days, perhaps weeks, before its assets amounted to anything. Hadn't it taken the Securities Exchange Company six months to get $5 million in the banks?

There really was nothing to worry about.

Particularly now that he had the solution to his primary problem.

He began explaining it to Chmielinski over lunch. It involved gaining control of a great many more banks by turning their own depositors against them. Quickly.

"Suppose the Hanover comes out in favor of a plan I've devised—a plan that gives depositors more for their money than just four percent interest?"

"We can't pay more," the banker said quickly. "The state won't—"

Ponzi cut him off. "Of course not. I know that. But I don't think the depositors get adequate returns for the millions they give us. I propose that they be allowed to elect a certain number of directors. We'll work out how many later. But the depositors should have somebody on the board who looks after their interests. They have a right to know what goes on at our meetings, at any bank's meetings."

Chmielinski was frowning, but he nodded patiently. He stopped agreeing when Ponzi offered his second idea: That stockholders in the bank be paid a definite annual dividend—"If the depositors get four percent on their money, the shareholders should get, say, seven percent"—and any earnings in excess of the dividend should be prorated equally between the two groups.

"You're advocating some kind of profit sharing in banking?" said the surprised Hanover Trust president. "I've never—"

"Heard of such a thing? Of course not, because anyone who proposed it would be called a Bolshevik. But it sounds equitable and fair, doesn't it? And if we came out for it, it would bring millions of dollars from all over Massachusetts into this bank!"

Chmielinski was forced to admit that it probably would, especially if other banks opposed the idea. *That*, Ponzi explained, was the whole point. Other banks would have to go on record as being against profit sharing and their depositors would promptly withdraw their savings to put them into the Hanover, a bank that obviously had the interests of the "little guy" at heart.

"There will be boycotts! There will be runs! There will be frantic bank presidents all over the state! And inside of forty-eight hours, banks will be begging us to take them over before they go under. I tell you, Henry, we can do it!"

The banker looked into Ponzi's shining dark eyes and knew that he was perfectly serious. That same intent look had been there the afternoon he had showed up to buy control of the Hanover.

"We could call in the editors of the financial papers and give them the story," Chmielinski volunteered.

Ponzi twisted a cigarette into place excitedly. "They won't run it, Henry. Not when they live off advertising from the Boston banks."

"Then how do we tell anybody about it?"

"We spend money. *I* spend it, rather. I get a good publicity man to write up a circular for every depositor in New England. All at one time. Then, we just sit back and wait forty-eight hours!"

Chmielinski shrugged. "It's your money." He suggested that William McMasters be put on a retainer for publicity purposes, and Ponzi was on the telephone with the noted promoter a moment later. Chmielinski listened to the flow of words for several minutes, then decided to leave the office quietly. He was at the door when a shout made him turn.

"Hey, Henry," Ponzi said, his hand over the mouthpiece of the phone, "any preference as to which bank we help out of its troubles first? I kind of like the Tremont!"

Chmielinski heard the little financier's laughter behind him as he stepped into the hall.

He dressed especially for the occasion. He asked Rose, her eyes glowing with admiration, to assist him that morning—first, by agreeing with him that the white trousers and blue blazer, summery as they looked, were much too informal to wear to a meeting with the bank commissioner of Massachusetts. And, then, by helping him smooth his freshly pressed deep blue pin-stripe jacket across his narrow shoulders with an affectionate gesture.

"My son always was a handsome man," his mother said when she saw the results.

He looked into the mirror, surveying the figure that stood there with such confidence. His blue and grey striped club tie, sparked with the diamond stickpin, was precisely right. Although he, like most young men, had taken to wearing soft shirts with their own collars in the fashionable pointed style, today he had decided to wear a rounded, detachable stiff collar above a delicately striped and starched shirt. A trifle more formal, a bit more prosperous looking.

He plucked a fresh white carnation from one of Rose's plants at the side of the house and pinned it carefully to his left lapel. Then he kissed his wife quickly on the cheek, sensing her shy concern that one of the men working on the lawn might see them.

An hour later Ponzi stepped into the office of Joseph G. Allen at the State House. His eyes swiftly took in the group of men gathered there to meet him.

The young, gangly fellow coming across the room toward him, hand outstretched—that must be Hurwitz, the assistant to the state's attorney general, J. Weston Allen. It was Hurwitz who had phoned his office and invited him to this "conference." The rotund, red-faced man with the dour expression—obviously Bank Commissioner Allen. There was another youthful chap, probably just an assistant. And a man with a pencil mustache, who had a foreign look about him—could he be a financial expert of some sort? Probably.

All in all, not an imposing looking bunch, he thought.

"Mr. Ponzi," Hurwitz said amiably, "thanks for coming, and right on time, too." The young lawyer's hand, Ponzi noticed, was damp with perspiration. "Let me make the introductions—"

Ponzi shook hands all around, marveling to himself how precisely his instincts had guided him. The man with the mustache was a vice president at one of the city's most prestigious banks—and an expert in foreign exchange. And the overweight, unhappy looking man was the bank commissioner himself.

"Well, Ponzi," he boomed, "I must say it's an honor to have you with us this morning. The whole city is starting to talk about you. I understand that my friend, Bill McNary, said some wonderful things about you Saturday night. Called you 'one of our most knowledgeable financial men,' wasn't it?"

"Something like that, Mr. Allen. I think his exact words were 'one of the greatest financiers that America has ever produced.' If you heard, however, that there was great applause when he said it, I have to admit that the occasion was a dinner for the Hanover Trust employees. Well, I'm a director there, so I had a lot of friends present."

The others smiled readily. Allen chuckled without changing his glum expression. "From what I've heard, you get applause all over town, Ponzi. In fact, when Hurwitz here suggested this meeting, I asked around and found that a half-dozen people in this department have invested with you. They gave such glowing reports, I don't really see the need to have you here—other than to make your acquaintance, that is."

The commissioner was greeting him with an excess of enthusiasm. Ponzi recognized the tactic. *The way a cannibal greets a missionary*, he thought.

"Nonsense," he said, "Nonsense. I appreciate the compliments, Commissioner, but you've asked me here to learn about my business. Why be bashful about it?"

Again, without changing his face, the official laughed. "Very well, Ponzi, I like a man who puts his cards on the table. This shouldn't take long."

"I hope not. My office is taking in nearly a million dollars a week, and I have to be on hand to keep an eye on things."

He saw the foreign exchange expert lift his eyebrows, and the two lawyers exchange glances. *This*, he thought, *will be a cinch*.

In actuality, it was not difficult at all. Within forty-five minutes, the bank's vice president had lived fully up to Ponzi's definition of the word "expert"—that is, someone who expressed what he did not know in language that no one understood. Hurwitz and his associate had admitted that their office had received no complaints about the Securities Exchange Commission, and that it did not appear to be in violation of any state laws. And the bank commissioner had noted that Ponzi had neither used the word "bank" in his advertising or correspondence, nor offered any traditional banking services such as checking or savings accounts. "Therefore," he said, with an apologetic glance at the two assistant attorneys general, "I don't see that your company comes under my jurisdiction."

"But I don't see how it's possible, Mr. Ponzi—despite everything you've told us about dealing in reply coupons—for you to pay investors fifty percent." It was Hurwitz speaking, and Ponzi sensed—if not a superior intelligence—the kind of dogged persistence that frequently meant trouble.

"I really don't have time to go through it again," he said, plucking several sample reply coupons from the desk, along with the page from the *United States Official Postal Guide* that he had used for his demonstration. "Why don't you save us both trouble by speaking to some of the post office inspectors, or some of the men from the police department? They've all been in to see me several times."

"And from what I've heard," chuckled Allen, "they've ended up buying some of your notes! That's pretty good evidence, Hurwitz."

Ponzi looked at the young lawyer, almost feeling sorry for him. "After you've talked to them," he said, "you might want to get in on my offer, too."

There was no levity on Hurwitz's face. "I'm investigating, Mr. Ponzi," he replied evenly, "not investing. There's a difference."

Despite the late July heat, Charles Ponzi felt a faint and sudden chill. "Gentlemen," he said, "if you'll excuse me—"

The men in the office were silent for a few moments after the dapper financier strode down the marble-floored corridor. Then Hurwitz polled the others. Politically wise, the bank commissioner offered no opinion as to Ponzi's honesty, but stressed the point that he had no authority over the Securities Exchange Company.

"He certainly has a magnificent grasp of the intricacies of

157

foreign exchange" the exchange specialist remarked. "I must say, there were times when he was going on about the advantages of moving coupons from countries where the currency has fallen below gold parity—well, he nearly lost me. And I pride myself on—"

"Then you think he's legitimate?" Hurwitz insisted.

"Well, if you want a yes or no, I'd have to say yes. He knows more about depreciation—"

"Al," said the other youthful lawyer, "we're not going to make a name for ourselves with this one. Have you ever seen a cooler duck? Only a man sure he can hang onto his millions would be that cocky."

Hurwitz pressed his lips together in agreement. "I guess so. But I've still got this feeling—" He folded his briefcase, stuffing a few errant papers into it angrily. "I think I'm going to ask him to bring his books, all his records, over to our office. Mr. Allen can have an accountant look them over."

"How're you going to make him do that? There's no crime charged. You can't make anybody give evidence against himself."

"I know. But I think if I ask him to bring his stuff in, he'll do it. As you say, he's got nothing to be afraid of, has he?"

☆

Dressed as immaculately as he was, and aware of it, Ponzi left the State House and walked the few blocks to the School Street office. The thousands who had invested their money and their confidence in him deserved the chance to see him. He was slightly disappointed to find only a dozen people lingering in the outer room, and wished that he had strolled in later, during lunch hour, when the clerks and shopgirls from the surrounding buildings would be on the streets.

His smile broadened when he saw that Martin, the reporter from the *Post*, was waiting for him, along with Bill McMasters.

"You two know each other?" he asked jovially. "Mr. Martin, I don't want you to listen to any lies from McMasters here. Publicity agents tend to elaborate sometimes, you know—and this company is doing well enough without any exaggeration."

The newspaperman laughed, as McMasters—a gruff and corpulent figure in a rumpled Panama suit—waved his hands helplessly. "When you've got a client who's doin' as well as you are, Ponzi," he said, "it's hard enough to get these newspapers guys to believe the truth, much less try puttin' anything over on 'em."

The reporter had dropped in to check a few last facts for a

158

major story that the *Post* might run in a few days. "How come you've added a publicity man? With the money coming in the way I've seen it, you shouldn't be worried about getting your name in the paper."

"He isn't paid to get my name in the papers, young fellow. Mr. McMasters is working up a special program that will be of immense benefit, I might say, to thousands of bank depositors in the state. I've given him $7,000 to set up a separate agency—but until it's operating, I'm afraid I can't talk about it in detail."

When the reporter was ready to leave a half-hour later, the outer office again was filled with investors. Ponzi watched the newsman shake his head in awe at the sight of the bundles of money in the hands of some of the men and women as he pushed through the crowd toward the door.

"That's funny, McMasters," he remarked. "That reporter thinks I'm paying to get into print. I've paid off a half-dozen people in my time to keep my name *out* of the papers!"

McMasters pulled deeply on his cigar, measuring his employer with a steady gaze. "You don't mind spending, do you?" he asked.

"Not if I get something for it. Nothing greases the wheels, nothing gets things moving like money, Bill. I'm telling you, I want those bank depositors scaring the living daylights out of every bank president in the state. I want it done fast. And I don't care what it costs!"

McMasters nodded quickly. "I'm your man, Ponzi. You know it. The circulars are at the printers now, and I'll pick up the mailing lists this week."

"By the way, Bill, I just came from the bank commissioner's office, and he said he wants to invest a few thousand. The attorney general is supposed to come in, too. And Pelletier, the district attorney. I guess Mayor Peters will be around any day now—"

"Is he in with you, too? The mayor?"

Ponzi hesitated, wondering for just a second if he had gone too far. "No, not yet, but he's interested. You know he and I are the only people who can park next to City Hall? If you ever talk to some of the reporters about me, you might tell them that." *But don't tell them*, he thought, *that I'm paying the police on the block a hundred dollars a week for the privilege!*

McMasters' face had a skeptical look on it. "It's a good story," he said. "I'll try to work it in someplace."

There was something about the man that Ponzi did not like. He knew that McMasters was reasonably honest—as honest, that is, as any publicity man can be. The profession, such as it was, had never appealed to him.

"Bill, let me ask you something," he said. "You've worked with a lot of the politicians in town. Have they been talking about me?"

"You mean, out of the ordinary? No, they're plenty curious about where you're going to put all this dough, which party you're going to be backing in November, that's all."

Ponzi relaxed slightly. The meeting that morning with the bank commissioner must have tightened his nerves more than he had thought. But McMasters hobnobbed with plenty of wardheelers, and if he had not heard of any all-out investigations, things might not be too bad. Not too bad at all.

By the time the last investor had pushed his money through a teller's window—the man, a smiling Miss Meli told Ponzi, was a war veteran who had been gassed and hoped to profit enough to head for Arizona—Ponzi once more felt completely at ease. There was no reason to worry, he decided. The office was taking in a quarter of a million dollars daily, and the area's banks were beginning to show the first signs of trouble. He sensed the banks' desperation in a front-page announcement that the wily Swig placed in the afternoon papers:

REAL DOLLARS

are still made in the old-fashioned way—working and saving. A real dollar cannot be made from bubbles.

Our last monthly interest dividend was $5^{1}/_{2}\%$ and was paid from our earned and collected income as are all our monthly dividends.

Ponzi grinned when he read it, grinned because he knew that Swig was directing the ad at Securities Exchange Company investors. But how could the Tremont—or any other bank—hope to draw the public's dollars with an interest rate one-fortieth the size of his? In the next few days, Ponzi felt certain that similar messages would be placed by dozens of banks all over the state, as they tried to talk sensibly to their fleeing depositors. *It won't do any good*, he thought. *Money talks. Not newspaper ads.*

Miss Meli and her accompanying quartet of security guards had already left with the nightly deposit. He was alone now, waiting for Cassullo. The street outside was silent except for the faint rumble of several fruitcarts being trundled along the pavement. From his window, Ponzi could see the white façade of City

160

Hall glowing pink in the light of the slowly setting sun. He found it extremely pleasant to sit in the old office, once the clerks and secretaries and the constantly clamoring crowds had departed. There were letters for him to sign—brief notes to a few of the agents: MacIntosh in Worcester, Schultz in Lowell, Illingworth in Fitchburg—but he did not feel like tending to them just now.

He looked around the office, cluttered with furniture, thick with desks and chairs and typewriters. Just a few months ago, just six short months ago, the place had been almost empty. *As empty as my head had been of ideas*, he thought.

"Let's get down to business, Louis," he said as soon as Cassullo walked in, "I don't like to keep Rose waiting dinner. What's the word on our New York friends?"

Herman and his partners, said Cassullo, claimed to have raised half the money to take over the Securities Exchange Company, and thought they could come up with $5 million more in the next two weeks. "But, Charlie, I think we oughta make sure we know what we're doin' before we go for the deal."

"You know I wouldn't let anyone in on this unless I was sure they had the money. All of it."

Cassullo leaned closer in his chair. "I ain't afraid they can't come up with the money, Charlie. That's just the trouble."

Ponzi shot him a questioning look.

"It's where I think they're going to get it from. These guys ain't bankers, Charlie. They've got connections, but I don't think they're legit. If they cough up $10 million for something that looks like a solid business, and they find out it ain't—we're both goin' to be in big trouble. And I got the feeling that these people know how to take care o' things like that."

So Cassullo had blundered into negotiations with some big-shot gangsters! The Black Hand. The Mafia. One of the gangs organizing to control the liquor business. It didn't matter. Leave it to Cassullo to get mixed up with the wrong people. Not that he was much to blame. The rapid growth of the Securities Exchange Company had to attract attention from honest and dishonest businessmen alike.

Ponzi sighed. "It's all right, Louis. If they make a firm offer, I'll turn it down. I can always say that I'm worried about what new management might do to my investors."

"There's somethin' else we could do, you know. Get the money and clear out. Head for South America—"

We! More and more Cassullo was cutting himself into the operation.

Patiently, Ponzi explained that there was nothing to worry about—a half-dozen investigations into his business had produced no evidence of chicanery, and he had not failed to pay off a single note presented to him.

Besides, he insisted, he had a master plan in the works—a plan that would assure the solvency of the Securities Exchange Company beyond all doubt.

Cassullo's eyes were skeptical.

"I can't go into details yet, Louis, but in a nutshell it involves making a public offering of stock in the company, at one hundred dollars per share. People will buy it—they'll buy anything that has my name on it—and I'll use the proceeds to wind up the note business."

Dimly, a light began to glow behind the small dark pupils of Cassullo's eyes. "Jesus Christ!" he said. "You really know how to get out of this? Maybe I should o' talked to you before—"

"Before what?" Ponzi asked, sensing a blow.

"Well, Christ, I know that the attorney general, this guy Allen, has been sniffin' all over Boston 'bout you."

"Yes?"

"When I was in New York last week, I saw a guy about gettin' him killed."

Ponzi sat for a split second in stunned silence, then jumped to his feet. "You stupid bastard!" he shouted.

"I thought I was doin' you a favor! Doin' us a favor!" Cassullo roared back at him.

"Us! We! Dammit, this is my company. You're in because of old times, that's all. And you've done all right. But it's mine, and you keep that in your head! Now, tell me that you're lying."

Cassullo, six inches taller and thirty pounds heavier than Ponzi, stared up from his chair at the frenzied figure standing over him. Grimly, he shook his head. "I promised the guy fifteen thousand."

"Oh, Christ!" Ponzi turned away in fury. He stared out the window at the darkening streets. "Fifteen thousand," he repeated. "For a politician! None of them are worth that much. And Allen's not even worth the gunpowder." He spun around and glared into Cassullo's eyes.

"Listen to me, friend. I've had my fingers in a lot of messy pies over the years, but I'm no murderer! Do you think I'd stand for anything like that? You go ahead with it, Louis, and I'll deliver you to the cops myself."

Cassullo was whining now. "But I gave him $500 already. He's goin' to be comin' all the way up here."

"That's your problem. Get rid of him."

"Charlie, I thought I was doin' you a favor."

Ponzi's voice dropped to a whisper. "I don't want that kind of favor!" he hissed. "If any official is an obstacle to me, I can take care of him. I don't have to have him killed. I can spend half a million—a million if it takes that—to discredit him, to make him look like a fool. Now, you get rid of this guy, and fast!"

"But if he gets up here, he's not goin' t' turn around and go back—'less I pay him."

"Well, you tell him—." Ponzi stopped in midsentence. Was it possible that Cassullo was pulling a con on him? On Ponzi, who had pulled the greatest con of all time? What if there was no paid assassin? What if his old friend from prison was trying to lay his greedy hands on $15,000 in one quick grab?

But, the damn trouble was that Cassullo was just stupid enough to have done what he said he had done.

"Louis," he said, "I'll give you $4,500—in cash, so there are no receipts and checks to turn up later—and you turn your friend around. With the $500 you say you gave him, he's getting a third of his price. Without doing anything for it. He should be satisfied with that."

Cassullo nodded. "Let me have the dough. I'll try 'n get him off it."

For the first time in his life, it seemed, Charles Ponzi felt tired. He sat in his office, in the hard wooden chair behind the large, inexpensive wooden desk, for long, long minutes after Cassullo had gone out into the hot July evening. Ordinarily—on any other night—he would have been eager to get home to the huge house in Lexington with its unaccustomed comforts, and the warm greeting that waited for him from Rose and his mother.

But this evening he felt physically and emotionally exhausted. It had been a long day. And what had he accomplished? He had managed to save more than $5 million and the life of a human being.

He smiled, then put his straw skimmer into place, carefully tipping it back so that the front of the brim just touched his hairline. Suddenly, he was rejuvenated.

Five million dollars and a human life. *Not a bad day's work.*

This workday, like so many recent others, did not end with his arrival at home. The young maid handed him a half-dozen notes that meant telephone calls had to be returned. And between each call he made, the phone rang as someone else called him. He barely had time to finish dinner, finally telling the girl to serve his coffee in the study where he could complete his business.

Two of the calls were from the presidents of banks—quite substantial banks—that were soliciting his investments. Outwardly, the officials were calm, but he heard a hint of nervousness in their voices. One almost pleaded with him to open an account at his institution.

"I'll be glad to talk to you about it later in the week," Ponzi said. He heard a sigh of relief at the other end of the wire, and he smiled. By the middle of the week, Ponzi knew, the man's bank might be near collapse.

He took a call from Hurwitz, the assistant to the attorney general. "I saved your boss' life this evening," Ponzi was tempted to say to him casually, but instead listened quietly as he laid out his requests.

"Mr. Hurwitz, I have no objection to letting Mr. Allen or anyone else look over my books, and I'll be glad to bring them in to you. I must ask though, that you wait until the end of the week. I'm sure you understand that the volume of business I'm doing is such that my staff must make daily entries, and I can't let the books out of the office for even an hour. If you can wait until the weekend—"

"That would be fine, sir. Then Mr. Allen could go over them at his leisure."

It was so easy, Ponzi thought, *to put off these lawyers who insisted on doing everything politely and according to regulations.* He could close his eyes and visualize the attorney general trying to make sense out of his "books"—a pile of thousands of index cards and a single ledger! Even with them, it would be virtually impossible for anyone else to determine how much money the company had taken in, how much it had put out, and what it still owed.

He took two more calls before retiring. One was from a police inspector who used an assumed name when he identified himself to the maid. Ponzi recognized the gruff voice immediately and asked for a report.

"I can tell you that this guy Brightwell was in your building today, talkin' to the super' 'bout renting space. Nothing was signed, but it looks like the Old Colony bunch wants to get as close to your customers as they can."

"Of course they do! They can't draw flies on Devonshire Street. Can I keep them out of the building some way?"

"I don't see how. They haven't broke any laws that I know of.

164

You move against 'em, and the newspaper boys'll jump all over you."

"Yes, this is the land of the free, isn't it?" He thought the news over. "You couldn't find anything on them in the records, right?"

"Not a thing. 'Least not under the names they're using. Brightwell claims he's got a guy workin' overseas by the name of Carl Lindbled, but, hell, I can't check that out from headquarters. Somebody'll get suspicious if I start sending cables."

"Don't get yourself in trouble. I've got the Pinkertons making a full investigation anyway. They'll turn up something. And I'll pass it on to you so your boys can make the arrest. Meanwhile, keep your eyes and ears open, but don't say anything."

The policeman agreed that seemed to be the best approach to the problem. "One thing, Ponzi, I don't know how you're so sure this Brightwell is a crook. If you can trade post office coupons, why can't he?"

Ponzi was glad that the officer could not see his weary grin. "Because I've met him, and I'm positive he does not have the intelligence to do what I've done. He's just trying to sell worthless pieces of paper by cashing in on my success. Believe me, I know it to be a fact. And when I can prove it, I want him closed up fast—without a lot of publicity—to protect my name and my investors."

"All right, don't get excited. If I hear anythin' else, I'll let you know Thursday at the office."

"Thursday?"

"Sure, I've got a thousand-dollar note that's due. You think I'm goin' to miss a chance to pick up fifteen hundred dollars?" The policeman laughed heartily. "I'll tell ya, this sure beats bettin' on baseball, Ponzi."

The final call of the night was from Dunn, the city editor of the *Post*.

"Frankly, Mr. Ponzi, this is somethin' I've never done before," he said with obvious embarrassment. "A couple of my boys have put together a story on you that we're goin' to run in a few days. That is, if you can convince the boss here that what the reporters say is so."

"You mean, that my company is doing as well as your men say it is?"

"That's right, sir. Now, I got to tell you that I checked around, and there's at least fifty or sixty men in our press room here who have invested with you. And they swear by you. But my boss—well, we've got the boss' son runnin' things for a few months—and he's not knowledgeable, you might say, in how big business works. He's the one who's—well, suspicious, I guess, about your company. And I can't run the story 'less he's convinced."

"I understand," Ponzi said thoughtfully. "Suppose I came in and talked to him one day this week?"

"That might help, sir. Listen, understand that this isn't my idea. Mr. Grozier just doesn't want any problems while his dad is away. You know how it is, Mr. Ponzi—"

"Certainly, Mr. Dunn. No problem at all. You tell Mr. Grozier I'll be in to see him on Wednesday. With all the proof he needs."

Dunn's tone became apologetic. "It's not that he wants proof, sir. It's just that he—"

"No need to apologize for him. I've met plenty of skeptics in my time, and I know how to deal with them. Tell him to expect me Wednesday morning."

In the office of the *Post*'s acting publisher, Grozier waited until Dunn had hung up before he put his own extension down. He looked at the city editor with a thoughtful expression.

"So that was Ponzi," he said. "He sounds pretty damn sure of himself."

"That's what all the boys tell me. There's not a question he doesn't answer."

Grozier nodded. "The important thing now is that he thinks our story is locked up. But you keep the boys digging anyway. It's a hunch, Eddie—and I know that's all it is—but this guy's impossible. We'll come up with something."

"Oh, that reminds me," Dunn said, "I want Evans to cover the police beat for a while."

Grozier shrugged. "Any special reason?"

"No, but if the cops come up with anything on Ponzi, I have a hunch that Evans would pick it up before Harry."

"How come? Harry's been doing a great job."

"Yeh, he has. But he's got a couple hundred bucks tied up in Ponzi's company. And I don't think he'd want him closed down until he got his money out."

"For God's sake," Grozier sighed with a shake of his head, "everybody in Boston must be giving Ponzi their cash!"

"Not everybody," Dunn replied. "Just the smart people. Not the dumb ones like me—and you, if I'm not steppin' out o' line."

Grozier grinned. "Eddie, you may be right. We might turn out to be the dumbest of all, if Mr. Ponzi is straight."

On Saturday morning, July 24, 1920, Charles Ponzi—impeccably dressed in a dark brown dressing gown over his soft shirt and white trousers—sat at breakfast with his wife and mother. He began to tell them about the police chief of a small Massachusetts town who had brazenly asked that Ponzi lend him $500 to invest with the company, and promised to repay the loan when he cashed in his note.

"'Chief,' I said, 'I won't argue with you because I can put my time to better advantage, but if you have nerve enough to come in here and take me for a sucker, I'll pay for the laugh you've given me.'"

"Carlo," his mother said, "you gave him the money?"

"Of course. But then some hellcat of a woman reporter came in a few days later, saying I had swindled her boyfriend. He turned out to be the chief. He had told her about his investment, and she was convinced he'd never see his money. She threatened to expose me. Isn't that rich!"

Basking in the light of the two women's smiles, he laughed aloud. "I told her that she was about to bite the hand that fed her friend in the first place. I practically threw her out of the office!"

He was thoroughly relaxed, thoroughly enjoying himself as he reached for the fresh copy of the morning *Post* brought in by the maid.

"Well, now," he said softly, studying the front page. "Well, now, here we are."

He had not expected a front-page story. But there it was, just under the banner about *Resolute*'s victory over *Shamrock IV* in the America's Cup race, a two-column headline that said exactly what Charles Ponzi wanted it to say.

DOUBLES THE
MONEY WITHIN
THREE MONTHS

I couldn't have written it better myself, he thought. He turned the page so that Rose could read with him. "Look, dear, it's all about the company."

50 Per Cent Interest Paid in 45
Days by Ponzi—Has
Thousands of Investors

Deals in International Coupons
Taking Advantage of Low
Rates of Exchange
A proposition fathered by Charles Ponzi as head of the Securities Exchange Company at 27 School Street, where one may get 50 per cent interest in 45 days, 100 per cent in 90 days, on any amount invested, is causing interest throughout Boston.

Yesterday his offices were crowded with people trying to loan him money on his personal note.

The proposition has been in operation for nine or ten months, rolling up great wealth for the man behind it and rolling up much money for the thousands of men and women who are tumbling over themselves to entrust him with their money on no other security than his personal note, and the authorities have not been able to discover a single illegal thing about it.

He turned the page hurriedly, looking for the continuation of the article. It was not hard to find. There were nearly three full columns that repeated almost word for word what he had told the *Post* reporters.

"Well, well," he said, "it says I'm worth $8,500,000. 'Purchaser of business blocks, trust companies, estates, and motor cars!' That's what it says, mother!"

It was almost too good to be true. There was a paragraph that told how his investors "rich, poor, prominent, and unknown, have seen their money doubled, trebled, quadrupled." Another line told of skeptics who had checked with federal, state, and city authorities before they invested, and had been informed that nothing illegal had been found in his operation. Several paragraphs were devoted to his explanation of his transactions in International Reply Coupons. Several more noted that he himself had voluntarily gone to the authorities to discuss his business, rather than wait for a probe to begin. As a result, numerous officials had invested with him, "as they can see nothing illegal in my business."

He began to read the lengthy biography he had dictated to the newsman. "Here's your name, Rose," he said with pride. "'In February, 1918, I was married to Rose—*Guecco!*' Oh, damn, they spelled it wrong." He grinned at his wife, "I'll have them correct it, I guarantee. There will be plenty of other stories for them to get it right."

He skimmed over the columns of type. "Here, listen what it says about our home. 'It is newly built and furnished with the best. It does not give the impression of nouveau riche either, for the fine Italian taste of the owner fixed that.'"

Elated, his face flushed, he pointed out the paragraph to Rose, then pulled the paper from her hand and went on reading aloud: "'I don't live miserly, neither do I live extravagantly. I have no desire to lavish money on this and that just for the sake and fun of spending money. I get no pleasure out of spending money on myself, but a great deal in doing some good with it. Always I have said to myself that if I can get $1,000,000, I can live with all the comfort I want for the rest of my life. If I get more than $1,000,000 I will spend all over and above trying to do good in this world. Now I have the million, and I have put it aside.'"

There were a few closing paragraphs, but he brushed over them quickly. The newspaper noted that any scheme that paid 50 percent in forty-five days would attract the attention of bankers and authorities, and that a number of investigations were under way. Attorney General Allen was quoted as saying that one of his men had been working on the case, but was currently in New Hampshire and unavailable for a statement. "No, I have not found that there is anything illegal," Allen had told the *Post*. The chief post office inspector noted that under the direction of U.S. District Attorney Daniel Gallagher he had been looking into Ponzi's activities for months, but could not make any statement "at this time." Boston police headquarters also had nothing to say.

"Oh ho," Ponzi said, "they're scouring around trying to get a list of my investors. Listen—" He read aloud that the paper "learned yesterday that some of the most prominent businessmen of the city . . . may have invested sums as high as $25,000."

The telephone rang before he finished the sentence, and rang again with an apparent urgency. "It's Miss Meli, sir," the maid said, scurrying into the room. "She says to please hurry."

He laid the newspaper aside, grinning at his name in the headline. At the upper left corner of the front page was the *Post*'s current advertising slogan: "The Great Breakfast Table Paper of New England." *This morning*, he thought, *that line is right on the button.*

"Yes, Miss Meli?" he said, half-knowing what she was going to tell him.

"Mr. Ponzi, you'd better come in quick! There must be thousands of people here. I've never seen anything like it! You can't walk in the streets, and there's all kind of shouting—"

"Calm down," he said soothingly. "It's Saturday, and you can close at noon like always—"

"I don't think we'll be able to. There are too many people, and the phone keeps ringing. Wait a minute, Mr. Cassullo wants you."

"Charlie, you'd better get down here. The goddamn Old Colony has opened up right down the hall and they've got a guy in a Stetson hat yellin' to our people to come on in. Honest to Christ! And there's a crowd outside like it's Armistice Day all over again."

"All right, hold your horses. I'll be there." He thought to tell Cassullo to call police headquarters and hire some extra men to keep order, but then decided to do it himself. The further Cassullo kept from the cops, the better. He called Inspector Joseph Cavagnaro at headquarters and gave his orders. "And, listen," he said, "the Old Colony gang has opened up next to me with a barker doing a spiel. That should amount to disturbance of the peace, right? Can we get a warrant for that?"

In the bedroom, a Palm Beach suit had already been laid out for him. "Thank you, dear," he said to Rose. "If the paper's right, it's going to be in the 80's today." Her silence let him know she was displeased. He reached for her hand. "I'm sorry about this," he said. "I haven't forgotten that we were going to visit your brother, but I can't very well tell the newspapers when to run their stories."

She did not answer him, and he thought he knew what was on her mind. The statement in the *Post*. That foolishness about getting a million dollars and living comfortably for the rest of his life. Well, he had the million, but there seemed to be no end to his business dealings.

"Soon, dear," he promised. "There'll be an end soon."

When his car made the turn onto School Street, he nearly cried out in excitement.

The sidewalks and the street itself were thick with people, hundreds of them. Men in suits, men in workmen's overalls, boys in knickers and caps, women in long dresses and huge beribboned hats. And all of them clutching rolled and folded copies of the morning *Post*. In the morning heat, a team of twenty uniformed policemen loudly urged the crowd back on the sidewalk, back against the building so that pedestrians could pass and a few horn-tooting drivers could get their vehicles through.

One of the officers recognized the blue limousine immediately, and touched the visor of his cap in a salute. Ponzi grinned as another, like a hotel doorman, reached to open the door of the car. Then, adjusting his boutonniere and swinging his cane, he stepped to the street.

"There's Ponzi!" someone shouted in the crowd. Heads turned, and instantly he was surrounded by a dozen men, two dozen, reaching to pat him on the back. There were cheers, and cries of "Mr. Ponzi! Mr. Ponzi!" from all sides. Through the roar of sound, a derisive voice reached his ears:

"I'd like to see the man who can make a million in six months!"

Ponzi glanced at a doorway where a sweating and evidently angry man was addressing a small knot of apparent skeptics. "Hey!" he called. "You want to see him? I'm the man! I'm doing it!"

A surge of laughter from the people close to him greeted the remark.

"You tell 'em, Ponzi!" a boy shouted, and the laughter grew.

He moved through the crowd, his small figure repeatedly lost to the newsmen and photographers who were out in force. As he hurried up the stairs to the office, shaking hands with people in the line along the way, he could hear the cries of the ballyhoo man on the second floor.

"Right this way," the big man in the Stetson hat was calling. "Right this way! A new million-dollar company! Fifty percent in forty-five days! Just like Ponzi! Absolutely on the level!"

When Ponzi appeared on the landing, he could see a thick line of people winding into the Securities Exchange Company office, but a handful of others—impatient to invest their money—were filtering through a door newly painted with the words, *Old Colony Foreign Exchange Co.*

"Christ, what took you so long?" Cassullo snapped. "These guys must have siphoned off $10,000 already!"

Ponzi stepped quickly into the office, fixing his smile into place and cheerily waving to the investors waiting there. "Don't worry," he whispered. "Cavagnaro's on the way over to see about a warrant." He looked about, saw a woman waiting in line with a baby in her arms, and moved to her side. "My dear," he said, "you look exhausted. Can I help you?"

The woman began speaking in rapid Italian. She had come to collect her money, she said. She was owed $150 for her note of one hundred dollars. She had not expected such a huge crowd. Her baby was hot and cranky.

"Here, give me the note," Ponzi said, and took the scrap of paper from her sticky hand. He pushed through the mob into the inner office, then reappeared with several bills in his hand. "Take your money, and good luck." The woman mumbled a fervent "Bless you, Mr. Ponzi!" She made her way down the steps and out to the street, but the story of the millionaire's kindness raced along the line of investors ahead of her. When she reached the sidewalk, she was surrounded by a group of reporters.

Ponzi started for his office, throwing a baleful glance at the man in the Stetson who stood silently outside the Old Colony door. The barker took up his challenge.

"Ah, Mr. Ponzi, want to put in a few thousand?"

"If you've got a few thousand, mister, you better hang onto it for bail. There's a couple of policemen on their way to see you."

There was more laughter and a few scattered cheers from the crowd. He pushed his way back into the inner office, where Miss Meli and Miss Lacarno were making entries in the ledger and filling out deposit slips with quick, repetitive gestures. The phone was jangling incessantly, and the jabber of people waiting to leave their cash with the Securities Exchange Company added to the din.

"Did you ever, Mr. Ponzi!" exclaimed Miss Meli. "Look at this—and we've only been open two hours." The grin returned to his face as he looked at the surface of the huge desk, which was covered with greenbacks. "There's $50,000 here already."

"Looks like it'll be a good day. We'd better not close until five, or we'll have a riot outside." He caught sight of McMasters shaking his head in disbelief at the crowd. "Bill," he called, "get out some sort of word to those people in line—a poster or something—letting them know we'll stay open until everyone has had a chance to get his note." He wanted to add that he'd be willing to come in on Sunday for anyone with cash, but knew the city's Catholic fathers would never stand for it.

"One thing more, Bill, get the space in all the Sunday papers for a front-page ad saying I'm not connected with any other business but this one. If I can't get my friend Cavagnaro to close the Old Colony up, I sure as hell can let people know that I think they're crooks. That should slow 'em down!"

Chmielinski was on the phone. "Ponzi," he barked, "I've had calls from the *Post* and the bank commissioner's office. Allen says he didn't know you had so much stock in the Hanover. You just told him you were a director. He's plenty curious about the connection."

"I'll see you first thing Monday, Henry. Don't get excited. There's no problem."

"No problem? With the paper saying you're being investigated from top to bottom? You're cra—"

Ponzi cut him off. "I'm telling you there's no problem. Take it easy, and don't be afraid to talk to anyone. I have nothing to hide, you know that."

Simon Swig was not so easy to convince. The newspaper story had upset him. "I'm tired of answering questions about you, Ponzi. I'm tired of having our depositors pull their money out of here and give it to you, so you can put it back in. There's something fishy going on, and I don't want any part of it. This is notice that the Tremont wants your account closed first thing on Monday."

"It's your loss, Swig," Ponzi said with more than a trace of irritation.

"As of now, your balance is $565,000. The attachment covers $190,000, but I'll have a check for the rest ready for you at nine."

"Like hell you will! I wouldn't trust one of your checks, Swig. Not with people drawing on you the way they are. I want ten-thousand-dollar bills, thirty-seven of them, and a five-thousand-dollar one to top it off."

"Goddamn you, Ponzi. It'll be ready."

He slammed down the telephone. It rang immediately. Rose was on the line, talking excitedly about reporters and photographers all over the front yard, wanting to photograph her, his mother, the house. And, he was told, a caller had said that some men from the Fox movie company would come by on Sunday to take his picture for the newsreels!

Rose's ebullience did not dispel the bitter taste in his mouth left by the conversation with Swig.

The incredible thing was—he told himself as he looked at the busy clerks taking fistfuls of dollars from eager citizens—that there was no sign of trouble at all. As long as money was coming in in amounts far larger—thousands of times larger—than those going out, there was no reason to worry. Let the newspapermen run all over the city and ask questions of politicians, bankers, the police.

They would find nothing, for the Securities Exchange Company saw to it that investors from such elite ranks got their interest and principal promptly—and sometimes at 100 percent rather than 50 percent. Several minor city officials, for that matter, had shown up at the tellers' windows on occasion, pleading that they needed cash and seeking to get back their principal before their notes had matured. Ponzi had given it, along with the interest.

No, he had plenty of real friends, he realized. Friends who would stand with him. Against the newspapers. Against the two Allens, Gallagher, Pelletier, and any other investigators.

Let them question and study and probe. Charles Ponzi was doing precisely what he promised to do. He was borrowing money and paying it back with 50 percent interest, and what was wrong with that?

The automobiles moving in a slow and steady stream past the house woke him early on Sunday. He pulled on his dressing gown and came downstairs to find Rose and his mother, fully dressed, standing at the front door.

"What is it? What's happening out there?"

The two women looked at him, their eyes gleaming. "So many people, Carlo, so many people!" his mother said proudly. "They've come to look at the house. They want to see you."

He reached for the morning paper. A two-column photograph of his mother, posed daintily in a rocking chair with Rose standing tall and proud behind her, drew attention in the middle of the front page. A huge headline five columns wide noted that "Ponzi Has a Rival Next Door to Him," but a smaller one noted that a great crowd once more had come out "to Loan Ponzi Money at a High Interest Rate."

"It's marvelous, isn't it?" he said to his wife, thinking, *that should double the crowds on Monday!*

There were four more pictures inside, and a lengthy story detailing his wildly cheered appearance at the office on Saturday. He grinned with satisfaction at the *Post*'s account of his attack on the Old Colony crew that was so obviously out to fleece the public, and he grinned still more when Chmielinski was quoted as verifying that Ponzi held a large interest in the Hanover Trust and was a director there.

"The investigations, Carlo—" said his mother when he looked up from the paper. "Rose says they ask all over Europe for information—"

"It's nothing, dearest. Nothing. I've made so many bankers angry that they are making all sorts of wild charges. And the officials have to say they're looking into it." He gave her a warm smile, and turned back to the picture on the front page. "You look lovely. And you, too, Rose. Both of you."

His eye caught the sizable advertisement at the bottom of the page, and he grinned once more.

It was a good ad, simple in its meaning. But the edge was taken off it by the larger ad placed immediately adjacent by the Tremont Trust Company. "Our advertisements speak frankly," it read. "We do not mislead for the purpose of getting depositors. Gold bricks are not offered, but a just and reasonable interest is paid, such as belongs to the people."

So Swig is not going to let up, Ponzi thought. *Even after I agreed to get out of his bank! When I take over there, he'll be out so fast that—*

The doorbell. And the telephone, almost simultaneously. McMasters was outside with two reporters from the *American* and the *Globe.* Cassullo was on the phone, reporting that Herman in New York had seen the *Post*'s Saturday story and was more interested than ever in making a deal to buy the company.

"Tell him he'll have to come up here and talk to me. Stall him until next week. Set up a session at the Parker House. I'll know in a minute whether or not he's got $10,000,000."

He turned from the phone to face McMasters.

"Ponzi," the publicity man said with a sharpness in his voice, "have you been leveling with me? I've got every reporter in the Northeast on my tail, wantin' to talk to you—and, by God, if this thing turns out to be some kind of hoax—"

Ponzi leveled his gaze at him. "Look around you, Bill. Look at this house. Look at the furniture. Look at my wife and mother— don't their faces tell you how straight this is? Here, look at these—" He dug into his pocket for the certified checks that he never let out of his possession. "There's over a million here! Doesn't that prove something to you?"

McMasters' eyes signified neither agreement nor dissent. "It's just that I got into this thing awfully late, and it's getting bigger every day. If I handle it right for you, Ponzi, if I get the right stories in the right papers, your idea of takin' over banks may come off in days instead of weeks."

"And you want to be paid more, right? Bill, you'll be taken care of. Everybody who works with me will come out all right."

The maid suddenly was in the room. "Mr. Ponzi, they're here. The movie cameramen! They're outside now. They want you and Mrs. Ponzi to walk back and forth in front of the house."

He nodded and hurried upstairs to dress. Behind him, McMasters began ordering the growing group of reporters about, moving them into various rooms of the house in twos and threes, informing them—according to the importance of their newspapers—just how long they'd have to wait before they could have an interview with the wizard of finance. Two newsmen from the *Post* were having a whispered consultation with the publicist when Ponzi came back down the steps, all smiles and carefully adjusting the handkerchief in the breast pocket of his blue pin-stripe suit. There was something in McMasters' face—a hint of suspicion, perhaps, of distaste—that Ponzi tried to ignore.

There was no time to find out precisely what it was. The ladies and gentlemen of the press were everywhere, ready to take down his every word. And outside, cruising in cars or strolling up and down Slocum Road, were hundreds of curious citizens of the area waiting for a glimpse of Charles Ponzi.

Like a king brandishing his scepter, Ponzi raised his gold-headed cane and moved down the staircase, slowly, toward the crowd below, whose envy and curiosity shone in their upturned faces.

It was late that evening before the crowd thinned out. In addition to the newsmen, the house had been full of visitors throughout the day. Uncle John and a half-dozen local agents, Rose's brothers, several bank officers, Miss Meli and a few others from the office, and a number of people who identified themselves only as "from the attorney general's staff" or "from the district attorney's office" had appeared at the front door. Ponzi and his wife had greeted everyone cordially, supervised the pouring of drinks and the making of sandwiches, and soon found themselves hosting what seemed to be a grand and unending party.

Following the departure of the last of the relatives, Ponzi caught sight of McMasters slumped in a parlor chair with a half-finished drink in his hand, his tenth or eleventh of the day. He was obviously waiting for something. Ponzi kissed Rose lightly on the cheek and sent her up to bed. "I'll be along in a few minutes," he said.

He strolled into the parlor and closed the door behind him.

"Ponzi," McMasters began, "how the hell many lawyers do you have working for you?"

"Nine or ten. Why?"

"Because I kept bumping into another one every time I turned around all day long. I didn't know you had Leveroni on a retainer, but here he was!"

Ponzi disliked the prying tone McMasters had adopted. "What's wrong with Leveroni?" he asked.

"Nothing, nothing at all. Just 'cause he's a judge in juvenile court doesn't mean he can't be on the payroll. But some of the reporters found it a little suspicious. Almost like you're expecting trouble."

"Frank Leveroni has $5,400 invested in the company, and he volunteered to help out with any legal matters I might need him on. That's all there is to it, McMasters. And I must say that I don't like your attitude. You're working for me, and I insist—"

The publicity man stood up suddenly, looking down on him. "You insist?" he said, laughing. "You're in no position to insist on anything."

Ponzi watched McMasters swallow the last of the gin in his glass. He could think of nothing to say, nothing at all. He was very tired. Too many people, too many questions all day long, too much talking, too much thinking . . .

"I'm no financier, Ponzi, and I don't know much about banking. But I know newspaper people, and I know when they're onto something. The boys from the *Post*—some of 'em are old friends o' mine—they're hot on the story. I can tell it. I can tell from the questions they ask, and the look in their eyes when you give 'em an answer."

"They'll find nothing wrong!" he protested. "My company is solid as Gibraltar!"

"I'm not sayin' it isn't. But, dammit, a lot of people are asking a lot of questions. I'm on your side, but—"

Ponzi poured himself a glass of white wine from a crystal

decanter. The wine was unpleasantly warm, but he drank it quickly in several gulps. "What do they suspect, Bill?"

"What do you think? They're convinced that you're using the cash from today's investors to pay yesterday's. It's that simple."

"Well, they're goddamn wrong! I'll tell it to you straight, Bill. Even if I had started that way—and I know they're trotting out memories of old Willie Miller and the others—I've gotten into so many legitimate things—banks, shipping companies, real estate, everything—that there's absolutely no danger, absolutely no problem of paying off every investor just the way I say I will!"

"Then all we have to do, Ponzi, old man, is prove it." He carefully placed his empty glass on the table. "You know how we can slow down the investigations like *that*?" he said with a snap of his fingers. "Tomorrow morning you go to the D.A. and offer to stop taking in any more dough until he's convinced you're on the level."

It was not a bad idea. Ponzi realized that immediately. In the past, how many times had he slowed up the authorities by volunteering to help in any investigation? McMasters' suggestion would throw the Boston officials off balance for a bit. Also, it would keep his indebtedness from growing at the fantastic rate of the last few weeks. After the *Post*'s stories on Saturday and Sunday, and with a dozen other papers in New England sure to run something in the next day or two, thousands upon thousands of new investors would be flocking to his offices—and every dollar he took in would put him that much further behind.

"Bill," he said levelly, "ordinarily I wouldn't bother to try to prove anything to anybody, and you know it—"

"Sure," said McMasters without emotion.

"But I'm paying for your advice, and if you think this is what I should do, well, then, let's try it."

McMasters waved a hand in agreement. "First thing in the morning."

"Fine," said Ponzi. He reached into his jacket pocket for a small packet of yellow tablets and popped two into his mouth, gesturing apologetically toward his right side. "Sour stomach," he said with a grin. "Too much wine today, I guess." He held out the package to McMasters.

"No thanks. Those things do any good?" he asked.

Ponzi turned the small tin box over in his hand. "I don't know," he said. "It's a new kind. *Goldenglo*. There's a free offer in the papers. Send in six cents in stamps and they give you the box free. I had Miss Meli send for them." He smiled weakly, and moved up the stairs toward his bedroom.

McMasters watched the small figure climb with uncharacteristic slowness, then he let himself out into the cool night. His mind could not shake the thought of a multimillionaire pridefully reporting that he had saved fifteen cents on a pack of mints.

The *Post* uncorked a surprise in its Monday morning edition.

Ponzi cursed in the rear seat of the Locomobile when he unfolded the paper and saw the headline:

QUESTIONS THE MOTIVE
BEHIND PONZI SCHEME

Three columns wide and in letters two inches tall, it was not likely to be missed by any reader. An enterprising reporter had reached Clarence W. Barron, "recognized internationally as among the foremost financial authorities of the world" and the publisher of a financial news service. Barron, interviewed at length, stopped barely short of saying he considered the Securities Exchange Company a fraudulent operation.

"No man of wide financial or investment experience," Ponzi read, "would look twice at a proposition to take his money upon a simple promise to pay it back at interest of 200% annually . . . If Mr. Rockefeller, the richest man in the world, should offer even 50% for money and be found putting his own money into 5% bonds, there would not be much money offered to him by financial people."

There was more, considerably more, and even Ponzi had to admire the logic that had led Barron to his conclusions. The publisher had gone so far as to check the Boston post office, and had learned that an average of only eight dollars worth of International Reply Coupons had been redeemed each day over the last few months. "In brief," the article concluded, "why don't the postal operations reflect Ponzi's, if he truly is dealing in millions of coupons? And why does he keep such large amounts of money—several millions in Boston banks and $5 million abroad, he claims—in institutions and holdings that only pay him 5% while he claims to send his investors' funds overseas to earn 400%?"

I'll hit him with a million-dollar libel suit, Ponzi thought. He made a mental note to contact his lawyers as soon as he reached the office, then skimmed the rest of the article.

It wasn't all bad. After the first paragraphs, which pointed out that European authorities and half of Massachusetts and Washington seemed to be investigating him, there were lengthy and favorable quotes from Judge Leveroni, who had been asked a potentially dangerous question. "As a judge of the juvenile court," the *Post* reporter had phrased it, "do you think it a proper thing for a concern of that kind to accept loans from a 14-year-old boy?"

"Mr. Ponzi has given me assurance that his promises to pay are good," the judge had answered. "I believe him, and on that score I consider it perfectly proper for him to accept loans tendered by anyone."

The paper even played up the judge's response in a small headline on the front page. "Attorney Leveroni is Certain Scheme is Legitimate," it said. *If only that headline had been the big one.*

His thoughts were interrupted by a flood of sound, and he leaned forward to peer through the windshield at the disturbance in the street ahead. The car was a block away from School Street. It could go no farther, a policeman indicated with impatient gestures. Behind him, the narrow thoroughfare was choked with a roiling mass of humanity.

Shaking his head in amusement, in amazement, Ponzi stepped from the car. On one side of the street, a line of investors stretched four abreast from the City Hall annex through City Hall Avenue and School Street, all the way to the entrance of the Niles Building, up the stairs, and into the outer office. Across the street, hundreds of spectators milled around in idle curiosity, waiting, watching for the Great Ponzi himself. Six mounted policemen nudged their horses along the street, keeping the crowds in check and occasionally clearing the way for an official car.

Ponzi strode along the center of the street as if he led a parade. He had thought, after the demonstration on Saturday, that he would be used to it, but he suddenly realized that he would never be less than thrilled. By the time he reached the rear office—having seen the crowd part in roaring deference to him the way the waters parted for Moses—he could not contain his excitement.

"Miss Meli!" he shouted. "Look at the hope and greed on those faces! It's madness! I'm practically the master of their lives!"

He caught sight of McMasters, who had a cynical smile on his lips. "How about 'their idol' or 'their hero' as well?" said the publicist. "I could use something like that in the bank circulars if you want."

The sneer in McMasters' voice brought him only partway to earth. He tried to concentrate on business. Miss Meli reported that

181

a letter had arrived from Swig at the Tremont, confirming the bank's intention to close his account.

"If you bring the Tremont balance here, Mr. Ponzi, I can deposit it in the Hanover at noon with the investors' money," she said. "The way things have gone this morning, I'd say we'll take in nearly a million dollars by then!"

A million! More than all of the Boston banks put together would take in on a Monday morning. He turned to the waiting McMasters.

"Bill, you've got to say I'm giving the Yankees and Puritans the best show ever staged in these parts since the first Thanksgiving! And it's a show that isn't going to stop. You just wait and see."

"Mr. Pelletier," Ponzi said, extending his hand. "Nice to meet you at last. The newspapers have printed your name so often in the last few days that I feel I know you."

"The things they've printed don't make me happy," the district attorney snapped. But he extended a cold hand to Ponzi.

"I don't blame you. Any time the papers start calling public officials lax in their duties—well, it's a ticklish situation. Frankly, it frightens me. I mean, if you start feeling pressured to respond, you might take a rash action of some sort."

Pelletier's eyes went wide. "Like closing you down?"

"Exactly. Without evidence of wrongdoing, without any legitimate charges. And that would be a great injustice, not only to me, but to thousands of holders of my notes who might never see their money again."

"According to the papers, *I* hold one of your notes for $20,000," said Pelletier with a smile. "I don't remember visiting your offices—"

Ponzi returned the grin. "I can't help what rumors get into print. But you're interested in facts, I believe. Specifically, whether or not I have enough money to meet all of my outstanding notes."

The district attorney agreed that the question seemed simple enough.

"Then, all I have to really do is list my assets and my liabilities for you, and let an auditor check things over. Right?"

Pelletier agreed again. The investigation was proceeding according to plan. "Now," Ponzi said, "just one thing is important to me. I'm extremely busy, and I don't want a dozen different departments tearing up my books and disrupting things. Can you get together with Allen and the others and agree on a single auditor suitable to all of you?"

It was an excellent ploy, Ponzi knew. With city, state, and federal authorities all striving to corner him, it might be days or weeks before they got together on a joint effort. And it would be easier to sidetrack one investigation than many.

Pelletier thought it over for a moment. "All right, Ponzi. You'll hear from us on that."

The smile broadened. "I'll make it easy. I'll turn over everything your man needs to figure my liabilities. Then, when he's finished, I'll exhibit my assets. I think you'll find that I'm somewhere in the neighborhood of $2 million ahead." His mind was racing now. "But your auditor will have a problem pinning down my liabilities if I go on issuing notes, so I'm prepared to stop taking investments while he works."

"That's why we're here," McMasters chimed in, and Pelletier nodded.

"Yes," Ponzi said, "I'll announce that after this Saturday, I'll only pay out money, and not issue any more notes."

"Saturday?" said the surprised McMasters.

It was a bold move, and for an instant Ponzi thought he had gotten away with it. An announcement that the public had only one more week to bring their money in for 50 percent interest, he knew, would produce a tidal wave of greenbacks that would give him many, many millions at the same time that it drained the banks of New England. At the end of the week, if all went well, he could be one of the richest men on earth! He would have untold power!

"Saturday?" repeated the district attorney. "No, Mr. Ponzi, I don't think so. If your scheme is crooked, and there are things about it that have a strange odor, you could take in $10,000,000 in a week's time. Then you'd owe the public $15,000,000. For the protection of the people of Suffolk County, you'd better prepare to close tomorrow evening."

"Why not at noon today?" asked McMasters. "It seems to me the sooner the better."

Ponzi started to glare at his press agent, then changed his mind. One day more or less would make no difference if he could not operate for the whole week. What good would a million more do? No, if he had to adopt the second plan, it was best to stop taking in money immediately.

"All right," he said, "noon today it is." He picked up the district attorney's phone. "Miss Meli," he ordered, "from noon on, we shall cease taking money for investment. Until further orders. Post a couple of notices around the office, and you and Miss Lacarno get on the phone or wire to all the agents. Tell them we'll continue to redeem notes as usual. With interest at maturity, or without it before maturity."

His secretary was surprised, but asked no questions. Instead, she passed on the news that Bruno of the Manchester office had called to say the local police chief had closed him up. "He says it's just temporary, Mr. Ponzi, while they investigate him. He said to tell you he's not going back into his fruit business yet. He has confidence in you. We all have."

The exuberance in her voice almost but not quite drowned the sounds of bedlam in the two small rooms on School Street. What would happen, Ponzi wondered, when the notices went up and the lines of waiting people learned they could no longer pour their money into his hands?

There was no time to think about it, now. McMasters had him in tow, and was steering him toward the Devonshire Street offices of U.S. Attorney General Daniel Gallagher. There, he outlined the offer that he had made to the district attorney. The jovial Gallagher readily agreed to a joint audit—it would save time for his overworked staff—and then spent the next two hours listening to Ponzi explain his coupon dealings. Two postal inspectors who sat in on the interview grew as confused as the male secretary whose shorthand failed to keep pace with the financier's verbal transactions.

When Ponzi left the office, the old grin was back in place. "Come on, Bill," he said to McMasters, "I'll buy your lunch!" The discussions of his phantom manipulations, of moving coupons from here to there, of conversations with bankers and international moneymen had acted like a tonic. "Wait a minute, we'd better stop by the office and see what's up," he said, anxious to let the crowds get another look at him.

In School Street, things were quieter than in the morning. Hundreds of people still stood in line to get into the office, and hundreds more milled about, but Ponzi's appearance was greeted by as many jeers as cheers. At the front door to the building, he surveyed the notice scrawled by one of the clerks in black ink:

Beginning tomorrow, payments will be made as usual, but investments will no longer be accepted until further notice. Those desiring to withdraw their principal not matured may do so.

"I'll fix up the wording and get it on the front page of

the papers tomorrow," McMasters said. "Probably 'll cost a few hundred."

The angry and puzzled faces of some people in the crowd had dispelled Ponzi's euphoria. He dug into his pocket, pulled out a thick sheaf of bills, and handed a dozen of them to the publicist. "Here, this should cover it," he said. For a long moment, he looked at the money in his hand, then stuffed it back into his trousers. "Where do we go next?"

When they reached the office of J. Weston Allen a few moments later, the tiredness had returned to Ponzi's face. His white trousers for the first time showed a trace of dust from the city's streets, and his silk shirt was damp with perspiration. He looked at Allen, waiting with Hurwitz, another young assistant, and three stenographers—and knew that he was in for a long session.

Three hours later, he came out of the State House, invigorated once more with the excitement of the combat. Like a skilled fencer, he had parried each thrust of the officials, reminding them time and again that they had made no charges against him, that he was not compelled to provide the names of his foreign agents, and that he had asked his own publicity man to set up the interview. "Remember, gentlemen, I came here voluntarily and I can leave at any time," he had told them. "I am your guest."

They had been bewildered. They had been amused. They had been almost apologetic. And, best of all, Allen had played into his hands by refusing to agree to accept an auditor appointed by anyone else.

"Mr. Allen," he had said in clear, loud tones, "I'm afraid that you will have to wait your turn at my books. For I believe that Mr. Pelletier and Mr. Gallagher are already at work."

A knot of reporters waited for him on the street, but McMasters pulled him away. "Tell them you're too busy," the publicist whispered. "You've talked enough. Let Allen and the others make their statements first."

"Sorry, boys, I'm too hungry to talk. You'll have to excuse me." He followed McMasters through the crowd. Once, he held back a step for a photographer, but hurried on when the publicity man gave a quick shake of his head.

From a window, Hurwitz stared down at the scene. "Look at him go," he said to the others in the office. "Swinging that cane, preening like a rooster!" He turned to the attorney general. "Do you think we have anything on him?"

Allen sat without moving, saying nothing. Finally, he spoke in a soft voice. "He's very good. Damn good. There's one thing, though. It took nearly three hours before he came up with the name of the bank that sends his millions to Europe."

"Banca Commerciale Italiana in New York," Hurwitz offered.

"Right. He didn't want to tell it at first, remember? Said it would open up a secret part of his operation to competitors. Why in hell would it?"

"And he didn't know the address in New York," Allen's other assistant noted. "Funny, if he's been sending all that money—secretly—he must have written a lot of transfers and mailed them somewhere. We know he hasn't been running back and forth to New York."

"Suppose I go down there and check him out?" Hurwitz suggested.

Allen nodded. "Suppose you do just that. And while you're there, check out the other Italian banks. We don't want him saying that he made a slip of the tongue and gave us the wrong name."

As the day progressed, Ponzi found that he could not decide whether it was a good one or a bad one.

The front-page notice in the papers—combined with the *Post*'s stark headline, "Ponzi Closes; Not Likely to Resume"—produced the run that he knew it would.

The streets around the Niles Building office were jammed at 6:30 in the morning. Jammed with frightened Italian laborers, Irish policemen, Chinese cooks, German butchers, and men and women from every walk of life. Many, unable to read or speak English, knew only that the money they had entrusted to the Securities Exchange Company might never be seen again. Squeezed against the buildings on School Street, cramped in the narrow stairway, packed into the tellers' area, the crowd fought to present the notes that would let them get back their investments.

"Pay them! Pay them all!" Ponzi shouted at Miss Meli and the clerks as he pushed his way into the office promptly at 8 A.M. The crowd, he had noticed immediately, was wild and unruly—and he looked about for the uniforms that meant the police were on hand to keep things under control. This morning, there were no officers anywhere in sight.

He got on the phone to headquarters and tried to make himself heard over the noise.

"What do you mean this is a private company? Goddamn it, Crowley, when I'm taking people's money in here, you have your men all over the place. When I'm giving it out, you tell me I'm not entitled to protection! What if somebody gets hurt out there?" He listened impatiently for a few seconds, then snapped a reply. "All right, then, you tell the commissioner I'll get along without his police force. I'll get one of my own."

He ordered Miss Meli to hire a dozen Pinkerton men. "No, I

don't care what it costs. Give 'em a hundred dollars a day if they want!"

"Christ, Charlie, there's riots out there. They're gonna bust through the door downstairs if it gets any worse!" Cassullo, pale as ever despite the exertion of having forced his way through the mob, was shouting at him. "What the hell's goin' on?"

"I'm giving out money, that's all. I'm giving it out as fast as I can!" Ponzi's eyes were bright with excitement, his smile as wide as ever.

"Jesus!" Cassullo said explosively. "What's the point o' that? I read they closed you up—"

Ponzi held a hand up to cut him off. "I'm not closed, Louis. I agreed to stop taking money in, that's all."

Cassullo pulled him aside, away from the desks where the busy clerks were making out checks for the mob outside. "It's the same thing, Charlie. You're closed down. Why give anything back? Let 'em take it away if they can, but why the hell give it back? How stupid can—"

"Stupid? You just watch, friend. I'll come out of this with millions!"

There was disbelief on Cassullo's face. "Charlie, you know how these things go. Once the run starts, the law moves in 'n it's all over."

"Not this time. I'll bet some of the bankers and politicians got to the police and pulled them off the street. They want a riot, they want somebody hurt. Then the coppers can move in and shut me up as a public danger. I'm not letting them get away with it!"

The phone rang, and he gave a hurried statement to a local correspondent for *The New York Times.* Somehow, McMasters had squeezed into the office with a sheaf of out-of-town newspapers and he passed them, one by one, before Ponzi's eyes even as the little financier was answering the newsman's questions. "Wait a minute, Mr. *Times*," Ponzi said with a laugh, "your competition at the *World* calls me 'a modern King Midas.' Maybe you'd like to use that in your story?"

"Charlie, let's talk—" Cassullo said.

"Wait a minute, wait a minute," he said, "let me look at these." His name was there, in dozens of papers, and he gloried in looking at it. "'The American people,'" he read aloud, not caring that no one was listening, "'will have to take their hats off to a man as clever as he is.' That's the Rochester paper! Listen, 'Ponzi makes everybody rich quick!' And, the Utica *Press* says, 'He began in a small way, but he can make $40 million before Thanksgiving'! Louis, isn't it fantastic!"

McMasters piled the papers on a desk. "There's enough good stuff here, Ponzi, t' maybe balance the *Post*'s implications. We may come out of this okay. I tell you, if all the investigations don't show anything, business will grow so fast that the crowd outside 'll look like a few close friends at a weddin'."

Miss Meli hurried over with a handful of messages. Swig, wondering why he had not picked up the money on Monday. Chmielinski, wanting him to stop by the Hanover at once. More reporters with questions.

"Bill, take care of the newspapermen," he ordered. "Tell them I'm giving back money to anyone who wants it to prove my love for the public. Tell them I might run for office someday and will need their votes. You know the kind of stuff they want to hear."

Cassullo followed him to the car and climbed in the rear seat. "Charlie," he said, "we got t' talk."

Ponzi knew what was on his mind. "You think I ought to cut and run, don't you, Louis?"

"Goddamn right. Right now. Today!"

"But I haven't done anything. If I skipped with the money I have, I would be committing a crime, and I could be jailed for it. Listen, I have a way out. A dozen ways, if need be."

The other's narrow eyes focused on him. "Damned if I see how, Charlie."

Ponzi took a deep breath. He hadn't intended to tell anyone about the card he had up his sleeve. He hadn't told Rose. He hadn't told his mother. McMasters didn't know. Nor Chmielinski.

But, Christ, the plan was so brilliant that he had to let someone know about it! And even Cassullo, as ignorant as he was, would appreciate it.

"Now, the way I figure," Ponzi said softly as the chauffeur nosed the Locomobile through the crowded street toward the Tremont Trust, "I've got about $8 million in the banks right now. And I owe maybe $15 million. This run that's started has people bringing in their notes before they're due, so I'll save the fifty percent interest on every one I get back. Then, McMasters is putting out some warnings about speculators buying up notes at a discount. The speculators are working for me, Louis, and a lot of people will sell to them at a loss rather than stand in line with a chance of getting nothing back."

"Charlie, I don't see what you're driving at. If you give back every cent, you're still way behind."

"But I'm not finished. If I use my $8 million, I clear up about $12 million worth of debt. But I'm still $3 million short, right? This is where I pop the deuce out of my sleeve." Ponzi was visibly

189

excited. "I'm a director at the Hanover. It's a half-block away from the courthouse. We stage the showdown in Gallagher's office, and when his auditor is ready to announce the total of my liabilities, I show up with all my canceled notes, bankbooks, stocks, and anything else on the assets side. But, on my way over, I drop by the Hanover and grab enough cash and securities to make up the difference! There's easily $5 million in negotiable stuff and cash in the vault."

Cassullo's eyes opened in sheer surprise at the audacity of the plan.

"And after the showdown—"

"I stroll down to the Hanover and put it all back. Chmielinski will never even know his bank's a few million short for an hour or so. Then, McMasters lets the papers learn the auditor's verdict— 'absolutely solvent!'—and I sit back and watch the investors come rushing in again."

"With the blessing of the federal government! Charlie, you're a goddamned genius."

The car had pulled up in front of the Tremont Trust, but Ponzi did not get out. The new respect in Cassullo's eyes warmed him.

"There are a few things to take care of, Louis, and I'll need your help. The crowds have to be handled, or someone's going to get hurt. Behind the office, in Pi Alley, there's that old saloon—"

Cassullo nodded. He knew the Bell-in-Hand. "Where the newspapermen used to hang out."

"It's been closed since the start of Prohibition. Find out who owns it, and rent it. We'll have the crowds line up in the alley, go into the saloon—we'll put a couple of men there to check their notes—and then up the back stairs to the office. After they get paid, they'll go down the front steps and out to School Street. A couple of Pinkertons should be able to keep things moving, and the mayor won't be rushing in to lock the doors. I know damn well some of these bankers are so scared at what's happening to them, they got Peters to order the cops off the street. They *have* to close me up, or their banks will go under."

He peeled five fifty-dollar-bills from the roll in his pocket, and dropped them into Cassullo's waiting hand. "This should get the Bell-in-Hand for a month."

"A month? You're not going to be paying out for a month, not at the rate things are going!"

Ponzi stepped out of the car. "We'll need it when the crowds come back, Louis," he said casually. "In fact, we'll probably have to rent the whole Niles Building." He waved the chauffeur on into traffic. As the Locomobile moved away, he grinned at Cassullo's face framed in the rear window, with its grudging look of admiration and the slightest flicker of incredulity.

There was no sign of admiration in Simon Swig's glum expression. The banker barely acknowledged Ponzi's presence. He gestured to a male secretary who stepped forward with a thick envelope.

Ponzi took it and placed it in his pocket. "I won't bother to count it, Swig," he said. "When you get to where I am, what difference would it make if you'd neglected to put a bill or two in here?"

"I heard you've stopped taking money in, Ponzi."

"Only temporarily, friend. Don't think you and your money-hungry pals are out of trouble. I've got plans for the banks of Massachusetts that—" He stopped suddenly, shaking his head. "Well, why go into it? You'll see, Swig."

The banker was silent as Ponzi whirled and walked out of the office. Then he handed a piece of paper to the secretary. "This is the copy for our ad in Friday's papers," he said. "Make sure it gets on the front page."

On his way to his desk, the young man grinned at Swig's latest composition, so obviously another slap at Ponzi. "Hey," he called to one of the tellers, "here's another one." Together they studied the ad:

Men With Good Names Have
Something to be Jealous of
and something to protect. In their administration of a public trust they strive to deserve the public confidence. The members of our executive board stand for something in the state, and they have made this bank stand for integrity and sound financial principles. We are a business company, not a philanthropic institution.

"I'd say the old man is out after Mr. Ponzi's hide," the teller said with a low whistle. "Here's hopin' he knows what he's doin'. The papers say Ponzi has $8.5 million—and that's a hell of a lot more than this bank has."

☆

At the Hanover Trust, Ponzi went to his second-floor office and summoned Chmielinski. In seconds, the bank president was pacing the floor in front of his desk.

"Dammit, Ponzi, I called you to come to *my* office! How does it look, me running up here when you snap your fingers? There's reporters all over the place, and they're laughing up their sleeves."

Ponzi spread his hands. "Henry, they know I'm the bank's major shareholder."

"But, dammit, they know I'm the president!" He paced a few steps, obviously trying to calm himself, then turned in a sudden movement. "Now, what's going on at your place? You're giving money out, right? Not taking any in?"

Ponzi nodded, and explained his agreement with the officials. "It's just a temporary thing, Henry. Nothing to worry about." The telephone interrupted him. Ponzi caught it up and heard an excited Miss Meli at the other end.

Listening to one side of the conversation, the bank president understood what had happened. Several women in the sweltering heat of the School Street line had fainted. Then, a "regular flying wedge" of angry and impatient investors had stormed the stairway, shattering the glass panels of the downstairs door and causing a half-dozen people to be cut by flying glass. Two doctors had offered to stay on duty to assist the sick and injured, but they wanted one hundred dollars a day.

"Fine," Ponzi barked. "Hire them. Whatever they want. And tell the Pinkertons to add more men, too." He outlined the instructions he had given Cassullo to keep the crowd in check on Wednesday, asked a question, and then turned to Chmielinski.

"Miss Meli says at the rate things are going, the office will pay back between three-quarters of a million and a million today, Henry. That should prove our legitimacy, don't you think?"

The banker's voice had an edge to it. "Maybe to the district attorney, but it's me I'm thinking about, Ponzi. Where in hell is the money coming from? The money you're paying back? Out of this bank, right?" It was not a question. It was an accusation.

Ponzi reached into his inside pocket and flipped the envelope of bills onto the desk. "There's $375,000 there, Henry. Credit it to my account."

For a moment, Chmielinski seemed satisfied. But then he raised his voice again. "What kind of game is it? You put this in, and you take that out. A minute ago, your girl says you're giving out a million dollars. How much goes out tomorrow, and the next day? Christ, I know what you've got in here—with those certified checks you carry around, it's maybe—what—two-and-a-half million? Three?"

"I've got that much in other banks, too, Henry. You know it."

The banker stared at him. "Maybe I do, and maybe I don't. But I know, goddammit, if you keep on paying back dough the way you're doing, you're going to need a lot of cash."

"So?"

Chmielinski drew a breath. "Don't you understand? You're not dealing with Chase National or the House of Morgan. You start pulling hundreds of thousands out of one bank here, another bank there, and you're going to pull the banks down with you."

"I thought you had more guts than Swig has, Henry. You surprise me."

"I heard about Swig ordering your account closed. And the bank that has enough reserves to handle you, First National, didn't want any part of you." Chmielinski paused, breathing hard. When he spoke again, his voice was frightened. "Dammit, Ponzi, what have you gotten me into?"

Ponzi almost laughed. *I've gotten you into a goldmine*, he wanted to say. *I've put more money in your bank in a few months than the whole city of Boston has in the past four years! Now, shut up, and let me handle things!* But he could not afford to browbeat the banker—not while the Hanover's vaults held the millions that he would need to prove his solvency.

He fought down his anger. "Believe me, Henry, it's nothing to get excited about." Quickly, his mind sought a solution, an appeasement. "I'll tell you what I'll do. I'll pull most of the balances in my other banks out and put everything in here. You won't have to worry that you'll be caught short." He watched Chmielinski begin pacing once more.

"Another thing," he added, "if I issue the investors checks that are drawn on this bank only, they'll have to come in here to cash them. And a lot of people will open accounts, because they closed out their accounts elsewhere to give me the money in the first place. What it means, Henry, is that the money you pay out of one pocket will come right back into the other. The bank's assets will stay stable." He drew a quick sketch on a notepad before him, showing a laboratory scale with a dollar sign in each pan. "Everything will balance out perfectly, like this," he said.

Chmielinski glanced at the crude drawing. "You'll put the certified checks back into your account, too?" he asked. "You wouldn't cash them all of a sudden and leave—"

"Leave?" Ponzi shot back. "I'm on the verge of becoming the

193

most powerful banking man in the state, and you think I'd clear out? You think I've sweated for thirty-eight years to get where I am, and I'm going to walk away from it? You know what the papers all over the country are saying about me! 'Midas!' That's what they call me. 'The Wizard of Wall Street!' Rose started a scrapbook and it's already half-full! For God's sake, Henry, you—"

In the stillness of the office, he suddenly realized how loud his voice had grown. He drew the bright handkerchief from his breast pocket and wiped the perspiration that glistened on his forehead.

Chmielinski was saying something now, apologizing, claiming to have never mistrusted him. Ponzi strained to make sense out of his words.

"And it's not just me personally who's worried, Ponzi. There are a lot of other stockholders to think about. Now, McNary says that we're not going to get our clearings done unless you take out a certificate of deposit."

"A certificate?" He knew what that meant. A time deposit, one that would lock up his account for a definite period. "What are they complaining about?"

"Christ, look at it from their angle, Ponzi. Suppose you write a check on us for a couple of million and cash it at our drawing bank. They give it to you and then find out there's not enough in here to cover—"

"But I told you I'll put everything I have in here!"

"I'm not saying you won't have the money. I'm just saying *suppose*? They're threatening to stop our clearings, and we can't operate for *anybody* if they do that. Hell, we're not a big federal bank!"

"Henry," Ponzi said evenly, "you're asking me to tie up my balance. I've already got over a half-million tied up in Daniels' suit. I can't lock up any more. I may need money at any time. There are some big deals coming up that will take—"

Chmielinski's eyes were pleading. "It doesn't *all* have to be tied up. A part will do. Half? Maybe a little less. Let's say one-and-a-half million?"

One-and-a-half million! If the run on the office continued, when would it be needed? Next week? Two weeks? It all depended on how many investors poured in for their money, and how fast they got it out. If he used all his other reserves first, he might not need the last million-and-a-half for some time.

"How long, Henry? What kind of a certificate?"

The banker spread his hands. "They'd like it to be for six months at least—"

"Impossible!"

"But they haven't given us any choice! If they stop our clearings, the only investors you can pay off are the ones who come in here with their checks. Nobody else will cash them. Then what?"

It was a plot of some kind, Ponzi felt certain. The damn bankers had somehow decided to get him. But he would not let them get away with it. He would fight.

"I'll take a certificate of deposit for one month. No longer." He glanced at the calender. "A month from today, I might want to withdraw one-and-a-half million dollars, Henry. August twenty-seventh. Now, get me the certificate." His tone held a command, and the banker obligingly moved to the door.

The whole damn banking crowd is going to pay for this, Ponzi thought when he was alone. But revenge could wait. First, he knew that he might have to slow down the pace of the money going out to the worried Securities Exchange Company investors. He felt more exhilarated than nervous. It was just that each move he made, or wanted to make, seemed offset by the next move. His plan to return as much of the investors' money as possible, as fast as possible, to avoid paying 50 percent interest, made sense. But if the money was expended too quickly, so that he had to reach for the $1.5 million held back by the Hanover—and if the Hanover would not release it—he would have to ask an investor to wait for his payment. And that simple request would bring on a run that would make the present one seem like a mere line of people waiting for the trolley to Brookline.

He was suddenly aware that the phone had rung three times. It was Sam Bailen, Judge Leveroni's law partner.

"Ponzi," he said in agitation, "thank God I caught up with you. You know a man named Parker? Alton Parker?"

The name rang no bell. "No, not at all."

"He's got one of your notes for $500. Says he stood in line all afternoon yesterday, without getting his money. So his lawyer showed up in superior court this morning and asked a bill of receivership for the company."

"Well, hell, Sam, he can't do that! He'll get his money like everybody else. The clerks can't work any faster—"

"Hang on, the judge said the same thing. He denied the petition. If you ask me, this guy's got a Philadelphia lawyer who wants to put a scare into you. You don't want it in the papers that one of your investors thinks you're broke."

"Of course not! You follow up this thing, and oppose anything he does." He shook his head angrily, trying to clear it. "Sam, should I try to track him down—Parker, I mean—and buy his note back? Maybe coat it with a bonus of some kind? Just to stave off any more trouble?"

"I don't know. If he talks, if he has friends with notes of their own—well, you're liable to have a whole mob copying him and threatening to haul you into court. Sit tight, until I find out how much his lawyer is looking for. Listen, by the way, the judge is going to put out an official statement on your honesty. That should quiet things down."

Ponzi hung up the receiver slowly, shaking his head in disbelief. *It's only right*, he thought, *that money should buy friends, because it certainly brings you enough enemies.*

At that moment, two of his enemies were whispering in the dim confines of a cheap hotel room a block away. Cassullo leaned close to a man known even to him only as Chiaramonte, and outlined the escape plan that Ponzi had in mind. The idea that the hard-pressed financier could give his millions back to the investors, and then take the money in again, made both men laugh. Quickly they worked out a scheme of their own. Cassullo began to fill in blank notes in his possession, and altered the figures on others bought back from disenchanted investors at a fraction of their value. During the next week, Chiaramonte would easily be able to cash them, shoving them past Ponzi's harried clerks who were working ten-hour days to deal with the impatient crowds.

"We ought to be able to grab $50,000," Cassullo said. "Then we beat it."

Nodding, Chiaramonte agreed. "But what if Ponzi comes out okay, and sends the cops after us?"

Cassullo grinned wickedly. "He won't," he said. "When we're ready to pull up stakes, we drop a hint to the law that maybe they should look into Mr. Ponzi's little 'vacations' in Montreal and Atlanta. After that, he'll be so busy answerin' questions he won't have time to think about us."

It had been a long, long working day and night. So long, in fact, that he could not recall having slept at all. Yet the morning sun was struggling to enter the bedroom windows by slanting beneath the striped awnings, and someone had put the Wednesday *Post*, unfolded and looking strangely unthreatening, at the foot of the bed.

He remembered returning to the office the previous afternoon, to stare in continued amazement at the never-ending line of investors waiting for their money. When closing time had come, there had been shouts of anger and protest, but the crowd had eventually edged away down Tremont and Washington streets. A few dozen people were still on hand a half-hour later when, surrounded by reporters, he had emerged to be driven home. Miss Meli had accompanied him, her arms filled with bundles of investors' file cards, and a photographer had snapped a picture of the two of them getting into the limousine.

"They'll probably hint in the papers that we're having a romance," he had joked to his secretary, and he had smiled at her blush in response.

How disappointed the gossips would be, he had thought later that evening, *if they could see this domestic scene*. His secretary, poring over her records on the sofa. His mother, nodding as she worked on a bit of Irish-point lace in an upholstered armchair. His beloved wife, aimlessly leafing through one of the new motion picture magazines. And he, himself, mired in conferences with McMasters and a half-dozen callers.

The publicity man was proud of the work he had done during the day. He had hired a signpainter to letter a notice that would be tacked up in the Bell-in-Hand first thing in the morning:

Beware of speculators. A syndicate of Money Sharks is buying up notes of the Securities Exchange Company at a small premium for the purpose of holding them and collecting 50% interest. They know all my notes will be paid. I warn the public against disposing of their notes at a loss. I shall pay everything in full.

"And your signature—very big—will go at the bottom," McMasters said. "But that's not all. One of your clerks, Morelli, used to write songs. He's goin' to turn out some handbills with things like this on 'em—

If they should ask you to sell your notes,
Step forward and exclaim,
"No, indeed, I'm sorry, lad,
'Cause my notes bear Ponzi's name."
Just step in line, and wait with ease,
And avoid all sorts of commotion
For Ponzi has as many dollars
As there are ripples on the ocean.

The poem was enough to make Rose laugh and applaud. Her youthful and natural exuberance had reminded him that the pressures of business had kept them apart the last few weeks, and he had promised on the spot to take her to the annual outing of the Hanover Trust employees.

Now, as he reached for the paper, he remembered the promise—and the fact that the picnic would take place this afternoon. He would have to hurry to squeeze a full day's work into the morning hours. Already, the maid told him Miss Meli had dressed in her guest room and was waiting downstairs for the car.

He skimmed the news in the Locomobile. "Million Is Paid Back by Ponzi," the main headline read. In the lengthy article that followed, there was not a word about the series of investigations that were under way.

"Something funny, Mr. Ponzi?" Miss Meli asked.

"It's these reporters," he said. "The way they gobble up anything you tell them. McMasters must have done some of this. I haven't had time to make all these statements."

He pointed out to her the paragraphs that told the public that Charles Ponzi would use his millions to establish a charitable organization called The Ponzi Foundation, that he would finance an Italian hospital, that he had pledged $100,000 to an Italian orphanage. Then, there was a full report on his meeting with U.S. District Attorney Gallagher, after which the official had given his recollection of Ponzi's explanation of his postal exchange operations. Gallagher had hinted to the reporters that Ponzi had told him the Securities Exchange Company was only a preliminary to a bigger plan, one involving a new kind of bank that would share its profits with depositors.

"Miss Meli," Ponzi said happily, "would you send a box of cigars to Mr. Gallagher with my compliments."

The mob was there at the office once more, as he had expected it to be, but his idea of feeding the traffic in a one-way line from Pi Alley to School Street had reduced the congestion. His automobile made it nearly to the front door before the crowd blocked further passage. A circle of reporters was waiting for him. Calling the newsmen by name and shaking hands continuously, he moved toward the office door.

A roughly dressed workman stepped out onto the sidewalk just as he approached. In his hand was a thick sheaf of ten-dollar bills. "Mr. Ponzi!" he said in excited, heavily-accented English. "I got my money!"

Ponzi stopped to grasp the man's hand, turning him around so that the photographers could get their picture. "Of course you did!" he exclaimed. "Everyone gets his money."

"I gave t'ree hundred, 'n I got 'most five back! Mr. Ponzi, you the greates' 'talian of anybody!"

"No, there's Columbus and Marconi!" Ponzi said loudly. "Columbus discovered America. Marconi discovered the wire-less!"

"You discovered money!" someone in the crowd shouted, and the whole street laughed.

McMasters was waiting for him when he reached his desk. Grimly, he handed him two typed sheets of paper. It was a copy of an article that Barron of the Boston News Bureau had wired to his subscribing newspapers the previous evening. The financial editor had amplified his earlier questions to a considerable degree.

Why, he asked again, did Ponzi keep millions in banks in Boston and overseas when he could be sending the money out to buy postal coupons that returned 400 percent? Why did postal records of the U.S. and other countries show no large transactions in coupons? And, Barron wrote, "bank officials gossip about the relationship of the note and coupon business to the recent purchase of virtual control of a local trust company, the election of new faces to the board, and the expansion of its capital to make it much stronger in the eyes of state supervising authorities." While nothing illegitimate had yet surfaced, concluded the financier, "Is it a case of washing this week's business with last week's?"

A reporter from the Boston *American* was on the phone for a statement before Ponzi finished the article. "You can tell your readers," Ponzi said calmly, "that I have seen Mr. Barron's article, and I am instructing my attorneys to file suit against him for $5 million. I will immediately attach everything he owns. The whole article is offensive, and the last paragraph is especially so."

He turned to McMasters. "It's nothing to concern yourself about, Bill. Barron's got no more evidence than anyone else, and they won't come up with anything. Did you see the *Post* this morning? Not a word about any problems!"

"They might be catchin' their breath," the publicity man replied. "I'm afraid to pick up the phone or open the paper all of a sudden. I've never been mixed up in something like this, where questions are coming from all sides."

Ponzi's manner remained relaxed. "They won't be so high-and-mighty once I attach Barron's property. He owns a dairy farm at the edge of town, doesn't he? I'll tie him up so tight his cows won't be able to give milk!"

McMasters looked at him coldly. "It's the stuff that's not gettin' into print that bothers me. It's what the hell is goin' on in the district attorney's office, or down in Washington!"

Ponzi made a careless gesture with the gold-headed cane. "I've got informants all over town. If anything important happens, I'll hear about it."

"But in time to do something about it?"

Ponzi smiled and rose easily from his chair. "Bill, I must take Rose to an outing—she's been a very patient wife these past months—so if you'll excuse me—" He waved the cane in dismissal. "You know what to tell the reporters, Bill. Things are fine and we'll be back in business soon."

He left the anxious publicity man and strolled to his car, acknowledging each cheer and cry of "Hey, Ponzi!" with a wave. A reporter caught up with him as he placed a foot on the running board. The young man identified himself—he was with Barron's news service—and Ponzi turned on him angrily.

"Tell your boss," he barked, "that I would have cleaned up $3,500,000 this week if the authorities had not asked me to suspend operations. No, they didn't order me to close up. I've stopped taking money while they're investigating, that's all. And I intend to open up again bigger than before."

"But the government is looking into you, too—" the reporter began.

"The United States is butting in where it has no concern. Why

200

should it care what my operations are so long as they are legal and I have twice the money I need to pay off investors?"

"But if you're exchanging coupons here—doesn't that entitle the federal authorities to—"

Ponzi stepped into the car, then leaned out to continue the debate through the open window. "It doesn't entitle them to anything. I never said I exchanged any coupons in this country, and I do not intend to!"

The newsman was scribbling furiously, walking alongside the car as it slowly edged through the crowds. "Is your business ethical? Can you answer that?" he shouted.

Ponzi's smile returned. "I am in business to make money. Ethics do not interest me any more than they interest the bankers. They're all in the game to make it pay, and I'm going to show them all up."

Through his open window in the offices of the *Post*, the noise of the crowd carried easily to Eddie Dunn. At least twice a day, he heard the sound, and recognized it as the signal that Charles Ponzi was coming or going, waving to the crowd, throwing cigars, kissing a child like a politician running for office.

Suddenly there was a roar, louder than any Dunn had heard during the days the mob had been there, and an instant later a reporter from the city desk burst into the office.

"Holy Mother of God, did you hear what he's done? Ponzi!"

"Got shot?" Dunn suggested, hopefully. After a week of investigating, his men had turned up nothing, and he was growing exasperated.

The reporter shook his head. "He came out and drove away a couple minutes ago, but he said something about the crowd in line not gettin' a chance to eat lunch. So now—so help me, Eddie!— he's got some guys and girls out there, and they're passin' out free coffee and hot dogs."

Dunn narrowed one eye to look at his reporter. "Come on—" he began.

"Honest to God! Look at this—" He tossed a doughnut onto the papers covering Dunn's desk. "Doughnuts, too! All you want. The mob out there's gobbling them up like pigs."

Dunn took a bite out of the doughnut. "Like pigs, huh? And I bet they're goin' to be slaughtered, too. Jack," he said, "get the hell out of my office and come back when you've got something better than that."

The newsman backed out the door. "All right, Eddie, okay. I thought you'd be interested, that's all."

"Go have another chat with Bill McMasters," Dunn called after him. "I think he's plenty worried."

"What they doing to my Carlo?"

Lucy Meli, surrounded by file cards strewn across the sofa and on the floor of the Ponzi living room, smiled at the sixty-eight-year-old white-haired woman who sat opposite her. Weak and bewildered, Ponzi's mother guessed from the frantic ringing of the telephone, and the increasing numbers of visitors at the front door, that something was wrong. For long hours she would sit quietly, working on her needlework, and then—in faint and confused tones—she would ask, over and over, the same question.

"What they doing to my Carlo?"

"It's all right, Mrs. Ponzi," the secretary said. "Everything is going to be all right. Your son is a good man."

She was glad that her employer burst into the room just then, hurrying to his startled mother with several new newspaper photographs. In one, Ponzi was leaning casually on his cane, alongside a caption that read, "Smiling, debonair and apparently serenely confident, this erstwhile dishwasher and present millionaire today posed for this photograph, unamazed and undisturbed by the storm he has created. He fairly exudes good will and a seeming love for his fellow beings."

The elder Mrs. Ponzi raised the eyeglasses she wore on a long ribbon from her lap and studied the picture as Ponzi explained the English words to her. A knowing smile crept over her lips.

"They say that about my Carlo," she exclaimed. "They say the right thing."

He moved about the room excitedly, his face glowing from the effects of several glasses of costly wine and a rich meal.

"Mother, you're precisely right!" he shouted, kissing her on the cheek. "They say the right thing! I love my fellow beings! And I am undisturbed by the 'storm' I've created. Oh, you should have heard me speak at the picnic this afternoon. I was a match for J. P. Morgan himself." He turned to McMasters, standing silent and watchful behind him. "Bill, can we arrange for mother to hear me when I talk to the Kiwanis next month?"

202

"If you think she'd like to listen to a speech on finance, sure."

"Well, why not? Oh, no, it might be too much for her. Not my speech, of course, just the travel. Rose can come, Mother, and she'll tell you all about it."

Miss Meli had begun to gather her cards. "I'll be ready to go in a minute, Mr. Ponzi, if the car—?"

"Of course. It's waiting for you. Have a pleasant ride home." He gestured toward the paper in her hand. "How much went out today?" He waited until she checked the bottom figure on a long list. It was less than a half-million dollars.

It was not enough. And yet, it might be too much. Alone in his study, he wrestled with the problem. In three days, the hungry crowd had sucked nearly $2 million out of the Securities Exchange Company. He had to give back more before the district attorney's auditor—who would be named any moment now—completed his work. And yet he could not give back so much that he would need the $1.5 million tied up in the time deposit.

He looked at the telephone. It would be a simple matter, he knew, to call this fellow Herman in New York and sell him the company—lock, stock, and empty barrel—for $10 million. But there was something funny about Herman. The man claimed to be backed by one of the largest banking houses in the country, but Swig and Chmielinski had never heard his name mentioned in financial circles. No, it would be best to keep Herman dangling—as a last resort. Once his offer was accepted, it might be necessary for the Ponzi family to leave Boston quickly—for parts unknown.

He would not call Herman yet. But he decided to recruit another ally for his battle against the banks, the newspapers, and the law. He clicked the receiver hook of the telephone several times and gave the operator a number.

"Mr. Coakley?" he asked when the ringing at the far end was interrupted by a gruff acknowledgment. "This is Charles Ponzi."

"Ponzi?" Instantly, the well-known criminal lawyer, Daniel J. Coakley, was wide awake. "I wondered when I'd be hearing from you."

"I don't want to talk on the phone. I'm pretty sure that someone listens in, both here and at the office. Suppose we meet tomorrow at your office to discuss a business matter?"

The attorney laughed. "You sure you know what you're doing, Ponzi?"

"I'm always sure I know what I'm doing. You're the best in the state, if I'm not mistaken."

"You're not mistaken, friend. But you understand that I've got a lot of enemies of my own? Political enemies. Hell, you can't go up against the State House crowd time and again without makin' enemies. You know that, Ponzi."

"Damn right. But I'm not going down to State Street and pick out one of those lawyers with a *Mayflower* pedigree. They've all got appetites like a Great Dane, or a Saint Bernard, and I'll end up with nothing."

"I don't come cheap myself, Ponzi. And from what I hear, you can pay."

"We'll start with $25,000 as a retainer. More, if your services are needed."

Coakley agreed to the figure. "Don't let me scare you," he said before he hung up, "but I have a feeling I'll be getting more, Ponzi."

Swiftly, swiftly, the days seemed to run into each other. The conferences with reporters and lawyers and investigators were endless. The string of phone calls began at six or seven in the morning at home, followed him throughout the day at whatever office he hurried to, and caught up with him at night in Lexington again, interrupting not only his dinner, but, frequently, his sleep. The concern in Rose's eyes, the questions on his mother's lips, seemed unending also—and he found he could no longer banish them with a ready joke or a promise of a drive to the shore.

Only one thing grew less noticeable: the crowds at the School Street office. By the time the weekend neared, the lines had shrunk until only a dozen people waited patiently for their money. Public confidence had been restored, Ponzi proudly told McMasters, despite the *Post*'s barrage of skeptical articles.

"I've given back more than $2 million, Bill, but people still trust me! There are thousands out there who know I keep my promises, who are hanging on to millions of dollars in notes! That should convince the politicians. They have to listen to the people, don't they!"

McMasters sensed that it was more of a question that a statement. He heard an unusual note in Ponzi's voice and remembered it. The words, as always, were positive, but they had to be weighed against the mounting tide of criticism and investigation.

On Thursday, the *Post* had rushed an extra onto the streets. "Coupon Plan is Exploded," the headline screamed. "New York Postmaster Says Not Enough in Whole World to Make Fortune Ponzi Claims." Rival reporters poured into the office within minutes, demanding that Ponzi comment on the postmaster's charge that the Securities Exchange Company would have had to buy and sell one hundred sixty million reply coupons to make $8 million in profits—and that only a few thousand were kept on hand at one time in New York, one of the busiest post offices in the world.

McMasters, by way of reply, handed out copies of a dispatch from New York that had already appeared in several newspapers across the country:

> New York bankers, brokers and merchants who are well-informed about foreign exchange matters are not at all mystified by Charles Ponzi's "discovery" of a royal road to wealth. Ponzi, they say, doubtless has blazed the trail in spectacular fashion.
>
> The key to the situation, according to E. H. Newfield, of the importing and exporting firm of E. Luca Manoussa, Inc., is the simple fact that in some countries, France, for instance, postage stamps are legal tender. Mr. Newfield in an interview illustrated the simplicity of the process and how it is that Ponzi avoids disposing of his International Reply Coupons in America, where they are redeemable only in limited numbers.

When he had first seen the newspaper article, Ponzi had laughed out loud. But then he had read it through twice, more carefully each time. Newfield, whoever he was, had painstakingly described how it would be possible to send money from the U.S. to a Bucharest bank, where it could be used to purchase reply coupons. Those coupons, carried to France, would buy postage stamps which, in turn, could be used at a French bank to transmit money to New York. The profit would be 300 percent. Thus, the "expert" concluded: "This will illustrate how Mr. Ponzi had no difficulty in disposing of his coupons in America—because he never sold them here! This will likewise explain how his operations are absolutely legal!"

His grin jack-o'-lantern wide, Ponzi looked at McMasters. "This Newfield," he said. "Do you know him? Think he wants to start working for me?"

"I think he already is," McMasters said softly.

It was encouraging to know that men like Newfield were around to lend a helping hand. Ponzi was certain that others in various cities, for various reasons of their own, would also rush to his defense. They would have their own varying explanations of how he had done it—but all would swear that people could make huge profits without trusting their money to banks or the stock market. Even Charlie Brightwell, now that he had moved his Old

Colony Foreign Exchange out of the Niles Building, could be considered an aide. Brightwell had been grilled by Pelletier, the district attorney, and had explained that he too dealt in postal coupons—but only in a small way. His chief business, he had told Pelletier, was in "foreign goods," the exact nature of which could not be divulged, but which returned more than enough for the company to pay 50 percent interest to investors. The district attorney, obviously a man who could be easily manipulated, had given the Old Colony a go-ahead to operate after hearing the explanation. When Ponzi received a report from one of his agents on Brightwell's good fortune, he had almost felt like sending a congratulatory wire to his rival.

His feeling of well-being faded shortly afterward, however, when he received a call from the newest addition to his legal team.

"If you hired me to help with my friend, Pelletier," Dan Coakley said, "you're going to be disappointed. He's just notified me that he's been asked to step out of the case."

"What? But he's supposed to be naming an auditor—"

"He doesn't have much choice. The attorney general, Allen, practically ordered him to get out of the picture. It looks like Governor Coolidge wants to get some headlines, too. He's told Allen to look into your operations all over the state."

"Let him. He won't find anything wrong."

Coakley's voice was flat, serious. "He's going to try hard enough. His assistant Hurwitz had a vacation scheduled for this week, but Allen canceled it and sent him down to New York for something. Any idea what he's looking for there? You don't have an agency—"

"No, not in New York." He remembered telling a reporter for the *Times* that he planned to open branches in New York City immediately. "I said something about there not being enough money in all of New England to let me get thirty or forty million by Thanksgiving—but I haven't opened anything there." He thought for a moment, then said, "Maybe they're checking out this Herman who wants to buy me out for ten million? I hope they find something about the man. I sure can't."

He looked up from the telephone to find a familiar figure waiting for him. Instantly his manner became one of complete assurance. "Well, Mr. Santosousso!" he said. "And how are all my friends at the *Post*?"

"Fine, fine, Ponzi," the reporter replied. He glanced around the cluttered office, nodding to Miss Meli and Miss Lacarno, taking

207

in the fact that several clerks were lounging casually in their chairs or smoking cigarettes. "Things seem to have quieted down since I was up Monday," he said.

"Of course they have!" Ponzi said expansively. "Once the public saw that I can keep my promise to pay off notes as they come due—or *before* they come due—there was no panic. Now my investors are sitting back and waiting for their profits." He looked across the desk at his secretary. "Miss Meli, how many people are in line now? Twenty? Thirty?"

"Not more, Mr. Ponzi. And a lot of them are trying to give us money. They don't believe we're not accepting any."

"Put that in the *Post*, my friend. Just tell your readers that in spite of all your insinuations, in spite of everything that Grozier and Dunn have published, the public is still on my side. And point out that if I were running a dishonest operation here, I'd sure as hell be taking in all the money I could!"

Santosousso obediently noted his words. "We're just reporting what people tell us—like I'm doing now. Nobody at the *Post* has taken a stand on your operation." His tone was almost apologetic.

Ponzi shoved a gooseneck lamp on the desk out of the way so that he could reach the carafe of ice water behind it, and poured himself a tall, cold glassful. The temperature in the office had climbed these last few days, as if the mobs had carried the heat of the streets in with them, and he suddenly found it oppressive. The water did not help. When he turned to the reporter, his tongue felt thick. "Sorry," he said softly. "I'm a little tired, I guess. I didn't mean to put you people in the same league with Barron."

Now the newsman coughed. "That's—uh—why I'm here again, Ponzi. We got a statement from Barron—in reply to your suit against him. And I'm supposed to get your answer. I got a copy here—"

"He's worried, huh? Probably never had a $5 million libel action thrown at him before." Ponzi laughed softly. "It doesn't happen every day."

Santosousso waited patiently, then asked, "Do you want me to read it, or just give you an idea what he says?"

"I *have* an idea what he says, but let's hear it." He lit a cigarette as the reporter studied the paper.

"Well, basically, he says that you're taking advantage of Italian immigrants—that they're 'children in finance,' he calls it, and they're entitled to protection from the federal and state government."

"Protection provided by Clarence W. Barron!" Ponzi's face was flushed with growing anger. "He's on the side of the bankers, of course! He has to protect *them*!"

Santosousso shrugged. "He says he's not out to protect anybody 'cept his subscribing papers, Ponzi. Here, at the end he says, 'I shall continue to respond and Ponzi or anyone else in his class may pile their attachments on me as high as Bunker Hill Monument and I shall still be found answering to the best of my ability the mathematical problems that are put to me.'"

"'Mathematical problems!' That's what they're all mad about—that it took somebody outside the charmed circle of moneymen to show them up! If Barron knew anything about mathematics, he could have done the same thing I've done." He was puffing angrily on the cigarette, wrapping his words in a cloud of smoke. The office, he noticed all of a sudden, was extremely quiet, and his own words sounded like miniature explosions, one after another.

The reporter was staring at him, pencil poised in midair. "Is that your statement, Ponzi? Is that what you want me to say?"

He stubbed the butt out, and tried to concentrate. There just seemed to be so much to think about, so many questions to answer. What was it the newsman had told him? What was the man waiting to hear?

"Oh, yes," he said, half-aloud. "Barron. A statement, right? Put this down. I think he's openly hostile to me—has been so all along. I think he's pigheaded about his own qualifications as an expert in international finance, and I think he's prejudiced against the Italian people. He's evidenced a decided contempt toward the Italian race, and I resent it. His attacks on my success were expected, for I anticipated considerable opposition from traditional banking circles. But when Barron makes an issue of nationality, he has forgotten the most elementary rules of politeness."

He paused to let the reporter's pencil catch up with the flow of words. "You're Italian, Santosousso," he said, "what do you think?"

"I'm not paid to think, Ponzi. I print what I hear. But, I guess after all the things I've been called, 'children in finance' don't seem too bad."

Ponzi laughed along with him. "*What* he calls anybody isn't the point. It's the whole business of accusing me of preying on anyone, on any class, in particular. You've been up here and seen the crowds. I ask you, is everyone Italian? My god, there isn't a race on earth that's excluded from my list of investors—Chinese,

Irish, German, Polish, Greek—no, no, don't write that all down. It's not important. Just point this out to Mr. Smart Aleck Barron. Banking had its origins in Italy, and the bill of exchange was devised by Italians. He probably doesn't even know that. Tell him that it's not surprising that I—an Italian by birth and educated in Italy—should have come here with perhaps a deeper and far superior knowledge of foreign exchange, foreign customers, and foreign commerce than Mr. Barron has, ever did have, or ever will have."

He glanced across the desk at Miss Meli who was looking at him with sheer delight in her eyes.

"If you win this libel case, Ponzi," the newsman asked, "what would you do with $5 million more? You don't need it—"

"Of course not! I'll give it all, every cent of it, to charity! Make sure that gets into the story, friend. Ponzi doesn't need a dime, much less $5 million! You got that? Ponzi doesn't need a dime, much less $5 million! Get those words exact."

He felt the blood rushing through his body once more, the words starting to flow easily again. He thought to launch into a brief speech—the one he had delivered several times recently, about entering politics as soon as he became a citizen—but there was a flurry of activity in the outer office, and a handful of grey-suited men looked curiously through the inner door.

"Mr. Ponzi?" one said with some hesitation. "We're from Pride and Company. Mr. Pride's been named by the attorney general to go over your books. He's downstairs with a car, and would like you to go over to Mr. Gallagher's office and sign some papers—"

"Giving authorization! Of course. Delighted to help out." From the corner of his eye, he observed the *Post* reporter taking quick notes. He rose from the desk and caught up his hat, then tipped it rakishly into place. "Miss Meli," he said, "these gentlemen will need the stubs and the book. If you'd help them—"

"But, Mr. Ponzi, people are still coming in for their money. If we don't have the stubs—?"

He paused, thinking. "We'll have to use the file cards. Don't worry about it." He turned solicitously toward the team of accountants who stared in amazement at the dingy, cramped offices. "Don't you gentlemen worry about it, either," he said with a magnanimous gesture. "A little problem for the Securities Exchange Company, that's all. It won't interfere with your work in the least." He turned to Santosousso, whose pencil was busy.

"Hey," he called, "did you get who's named for the job? Edwin L. Pride! You can't get better than that, right?"

The newsman nodded. Pride headed an accounting firm that had been used by the government in several major investigations, most notably the Stuyvesant Fish Trust affair in 1906. "It's a good outfit, Ponzi."

"Nothing but the best for me, right? And that's the way it should be. When Edwin Pride says I am completely solvent, no one will be able to deny it!"

He was on his way down the front stairs now, smiling and waving his cane at a few of the agents and investors who lounged against the walls on either side. The *Post's* reporter trailed along.

"You're pretty sure that's how it will come out? That you're completely solvent?"

"Pretty sure?" Ponzi laughed. "*Positive*! *I* instigated the whole investigation, remember? You think I'd do that if there was any doubt about it in my mind? The examinations not only will prove my solvency, but will show that I have carried out every promise made to my investors." Outside now, blinking momentarily in the brilliant afternoon sunlight, he moved toward a waiting automobile at the curb. The car's rear door swung open and he stepped lightly inside, extending his right hand to greet the figure there.

"Mr. Pride!" he said jovially. "Glad to meet you! I'm Charles Ponzi!"

If Monday morning had not come so quickly, the weekend would have been nothing short of marvelous.

There was Saturday, when the Boston *Traveler* ran an eight-column headline, "Wall Street Calls Ponzi Wizard," over a lengthy story in which various financial authorities explained how he had made his millions legitimately. "If he has imitators," one of the experts said, "the entire financial world may be rocked to its foundations." The *Post* reported his response to Barron in full, and ran an amusing cartoon showing "The Wiz" talking a stream of dollar-signs into his telephone while, across the desk, his secretary "checked out millions" to a crowd of investors.

"Oh, Mr. Ponzi!" said the flattered Miss Meli, "Look! They called me 'Pretty *Julia* Meli!' Now where in the world did they get that from?"

He had laughed, tried to appease her by noting that the papers were not referring to *him* as "pretty," and had pointed out that the *Post* had made so many errors in its coverage of the Securities Exchange Company to date, "it will probably get one of those new Pulitzer Prizes for mistakes."

And there was Sunday, when his picture appeared on one paper's front page, showing him smiling with Rose at his side as they attended the dedication of the Home for Italian Children the previous afternoon. The picture was large enough to draw any reader's attention away from the small story adjacent to it, which noted that the governor of New Hampshire had ordered the branches of the Securities Exchange Company in Nashua, Manchester, and Portsmouth closed completely. "The Manchester office alone," said the article, "has taken in at least $350,000 from local citizens."

After breakfast, several reporters and photographers had been a willing audience. A female writer from the *Post* had quizzed Rose at length, and Ponzi had been delighted by his wife's skill in answering the familiar questions.

"It's such a burden," Rose had said. "I mean, all this wealth and everything. We used to have such a nice family life. Now, in spite of our beautiful home, there's no time for a home life. There's no privacy, and my husband is so busy—"

He had interrupted her in response to a photographer's request that they pose together, and had suggested that Rose sit on his knee "just for a moment, dear, to show them how happy we are together." Rose had blushed, of course, and refused. "No, Charles, it wouldn't be decent." His mother, looking on, had told the newspaperwoman in careful English that she could hardly believe the life that she and her beloved children had found. "Sometimes I think it all a dream, and I wake up, and it all be gone," she said.

Grinning, Ponzi had knelt at her feet to smooth her skirt for a photograph. "That's why we're taking all the pictures, mother," he told her. "So you can look at them and see if it's a dream, or if it's real."

In the afternoon, a phone call had informed him that Mr. Herman and several of his associates had checked into the Copley Plaza for their meeting, but he had pleaded fatigue. "I'm not conducting business on the Lord's day," he had said, glad for an excuse to delay things until he had more time to think the consequences through. "I know you'll understand. The papers are calling me 'the most widely discussed character in the United States,' and I haven't had a moment to myself all week." Then, after scheduling the meeting for later in the week, he ordered out the Locomobile for a leisurely drive to Suntaug-by-the-Sea, where Rose and his mother marveled at the fireworks display.

It was, all in all, a thoroughly delightful weekend.

☆

But Monday came.

"The sonofabitch! The goddamned sonofabitch!" Ponzi roared. "That bastard! That bastard!" Shirtless, his shoes not yet on, he sat on the edge of the bed, the copy of the morning *Post* across his lap, staring down at the headline:

PONZI HOPELESSLY
INSOLVENT

"It's by McMasters, goddamn him!" he cursed, ignoring Rose's look of bewilderment. "I should have suspected something when he wasn't around all weekend. Christ, Grozier must have offered him a fortune!"

Rose would never understand, he knew. She would never understand how one of his own employees could write such an article. Even after he pointed out the byline in large type—"BY WILLIAM H. McMASTERS"—she did not understand. And the words that Ponzi read to her, vehemently and in loud tones, could hardly be comprehended. "After this edition of the Boston *Post* is on the street there will be no further mystery about Charles Ponzi. He is unbalanced on one subject—his financial operations. He thinks he is worth millions. He is hopelessly insolvent. Nobody will deny it after reading this story."

Then, in twelve-point type, two columns wide, the article filled almost an entire page as McMasters detailed what he had learned about the operations of the Securities Exchange Company. He noted that a casual inspection of the stubs of Ponzi's vouchers showed that from June 8 to June 18, they had been issued at the rate of two hundred a day; during the next month, some five hundred a day had gone out, and during the last week when notes were issued, they were passed out at the rate of sixteen hundred daily. Under normal circumstances, the publicity agent wrote, the line of investors waiting to collect their principal and interest would grow longer each day as an increasing number of notes matured. Then, he said: "Ponzi is over $2,000,000 in debt even if he tried to meet his notes without paying any interest. If the interest is included on his outstanding notes, then he is at least $4,500,000 in debt."

The telephone was ringing loudly downstairs, and Rose was making soft sounds of dismay. But Ponzi was conscious of nothing other than the words on the paper before him.

McMasters! Goddamn spy! Goddamn double-crosser!

The publicist took credit for setting up the meetings with Pelletier, Gallagher, Allen! He took credit for the suggestion that Ponzi stop taking in any more money until his operation was approved! He had talked to Swig—*Birds of a feather!*—who debunked Ponzi's claim that he had been sending millions of dollars overseas! He reported how *his* advertisements in the papers and *his* warnings to speculators had helped slow the run on the office!

Why, goddamn it? Why? Ponzi's eyes were tired, his vision blurred as he sought the reason for the betrayal. He knew it had to be in the story somewhere.

There it was. The bail-out: "As a publicity man, my first duty is to the public. I want it distinctly understood that my responsibility for Ponzi closed when I took him into District Attorney Pelletier's office, and arranged to have him stop receiving money from the public."

"Christ, Rose, he's scared! He's yellow! That's all! He saw how tight things were getting, and he jumped out. He's saving his own skin, and he doesn't give a hang what happens to anybody else!"

He threw the newspaper to the floor. Then, with short, feverish strides, he began to pace across the bedroom, trying to think, trying to ignore the insistent telephone. All over town, he knew, people would be studying the last paragraphs of McMasters' article: "Numerous schemes to defraud the public, using the Ponzi story as the basis for operations, are springing up all over the country. These fake schemes must be stopped. The quickest way to stop them is to stop Ponzi. . . . It would seem like a joke if there were not 25,000 note-holders involved, thousands of whom have put their last dollars into the scheme and think that because Ponzi hasn't been arrested that he must be all right."

"Charles—"

He stopped pacing, looked at Rose. *Arrested!*

At her side now, looking down at her, his hand gently on her long dark hair, he smiled and said with great assurance, "The man's a liar, Rose. A damned liar. I'll prove it to you! To everybody! I'll sue him and the goddamned *Post* for every cent they have! Don't you worry about it. Don't even mention it to mother. It's nothing to fret over." He looked straight into her eyes. "Believe me," he said firmly. "Believe me."

The phone rang once more, and this time the maid scurried up the stairs to tell him that Miss Meli would not be put off again. Nodding, he pulled on his shoes and ran swiftly downstairs.

"Mr. Ponzi, the people—the crowds! They were lined up at six-thirty this morning! They're making all kinds of threats. The police are here, but I'm afraid! Everybody's shoving—"

He tried to keep his voice calm. "Don't worry, don't worry. Pay everybody what they have coming! Have some of the boys announce that everyone will get his money. Tell them the goddamn *Post* is a lying yellow sheet! I'll be there in a few minutes."

This time, this morning, he sensed the mob and its anger from almost two blocks away. And when his car appeared, tried to force its way through the mass of people, tomatoes and fruit splattered off its windshield and sides, and an occasional stone dented the doors. It was difficult to keep the smile on his lips as he surveyed the scowling faces around the car and heard their curses, but he managed to do it, holding it firmly in place until a ring of policemen and newspapermen shoved their way through the mob and surrounded him.

Then he opened the door and balanced precariously on the running board so that he could look out over the heads of the hundreds of people. The smile, the perfectly calm manner, the excellent cut of his suit—all served to create a ripple of silence around him, a ripple that rolled backward over the mob. He waited, feeling the attention riveted on him, and then began to speak in a loud, distinct voice.

"Friends," he said. "Friends, I have only one word for you this morning. Come for your money if you want it, but come in orderly fashion. You will get it. I may run out of checkbooks, but I will never run out of money."

He heard the laughter, and felt the mood of relaxation that settled onto the crowd. And he grinned.

"You've read the *Post*, and I'm here to say the story is so filled with inaccuracies that I don't know where to begin to refute it. But let me say that he laughs best who laughs last. And for the *Post*, the worst is yet to come." There was laughter once more, applause.

"People have admired me for my nerve. My smile, which has become so well known through cartoons and photographs, will be much broader after I'm through with Grozier and his paper." He waited for the applause now, and then waved a sheet of paper in the air, knowing that every eye followed the blur of white in his hand.

"I have here a statement from one trust company which shows that up to and including Saturday, I have paid out a total of $1,827,334.12, and out of my personal account I have paid $900,000, and another statement showing payments of $50,000. Does that sound like Charles Ponzi is short of money? I have other statements here—despite what the *Post* says about my not sending money to my banks overseas—that prove just the opposite! Insolvent? I absolutely deny the allegation!"

A cheer went up, a cheer that began among those closest to him and then washed backward to the farthest stragglers at the distant edge of the crowd. He wanted to say more. He wanted to tell the public about the pain and tears that the *Post*'s libelous and misleading article had brought to his lovely wife. He wanted to say that if his aged, ill mother should even catch an inkling of the malicious report, her heart would break and her health might fail to the point of death. But the cheer dropped a natural curtain between him and his audience, and he decided to let matters rest for the time being. The reporters, he knew, would follow him up to the office.

Santosousso caught up with him on the stairs and asked a question he only half-heard in the confusion. But it didn't matter. "I shall never say anything to a *Post* reporter again," he called out loudly. "The *Post* is a rotten paper."

In the front office of the madhouse that had been the headquarters of the Securities Exchange Company, clerks behind the barred windows were passing checks, one after another, to dozens of people who pushed, shoved, jostled their way to the front of the line. In the back room, Miss Meli, Miss Lacarno, and two other girls were busily checking the notes handed them by a stream of runners, and handing out signed checks in exchange.

"All kinds of phone calls for you, Mr. Ponzi," the secretary said. "I haven't had time to write some of them down. They'll call back."

Seated at his desk, the telephone in his hand, surveying the frenetic activity that he had set into motion so many months ago, Charles Ponzi suddenly felt the mood of exhilaration settle over him once more. *This is mine*, he thought. *These people! The hustling and bustling! All mine!*

And no one's going to take it away from me!

Throughout the afternoon, throughout the next day, he blustered and joked and promised and sneered his way through the onslaught of questions from reporters and the investigators. He laughed with the newsmen over the way that the McMasters article had set District Attorney Pelletier and Attorney General Allen against one another, with each official claiming that Ponzi had given him information that had been withheld from the other—and neither wanting to let the other in on the secrets. When the reporters wanted proof of his transactions with foreign banks, he blithely produced the receipts that showed he had sent hundreds of thousands of lire to Italy in favor of Imelda Ponzi, John Dondero, and himself. And when one astute newsman pointed out that the hundreds of thousands of lire "comes to only about $7,500 in American money, Mr. Ponzi, while you claim $5 million in banks overseas," he turned the accusation aside with a quick grin.

"I've said all along that there are secrets about my operation," he explained. "There are things that I haven't told my bankers, or the attorney general for that matter, for the simple reason that I am now being offered millions by people anxious to learn them. You all know that a group of New York bankers wants to give me $10 million for my company. If I give out too much free information, the deal might fall through. Remember, others are already trying to copy my methods—and there are only so many postal coupons available. If everyone knew what I know, the value of my company might decline. I've shown these receipts only to prove that what McMasters said about my not sending funds abroad—and what that liar Swig said—is obviously false!"

He looked at the newsmen scribbling away in their notebooks. "Now, if any of you want to know my real secrets," he said furtively, grinning as their eyes focused on him, "and he has $10 million to pay for them—" His smile widened in the swell of laughter, and he joined the merriment as the reporters slapped each other on the back and one turned his pockets inside out to show their emptiness.

By Wednesday, the crowds in Pi Alley and School Street had thinned once again to manageable levels. Captain Sullivan of the City Hall police detail called off the two patrolmen who had been stationed on the roof with binoculars to search out pickpockets in the mob, and Ponzi found that his comings and goings were greeted with as many cheers as jeers again. He had time—between the never-ending sequence of interviews and the conferences with lawyers and an increasingly nervous Chmielinski—to find considerable amusement in the situation.

When the *Post* ran a cartoon showing a caricature of himself, perspiration pouring from his forehead, peering into a huge crock labeled *Ponzi's Pot of Gold* and shouting, "I am still solvent!," while a crowd of "Boston's Get-Rich-Quick Investors—25,000 Strong" rushed at him with outstretched hands and empty tin cups, he was so delighted that he dropped into the newspaper offices to compliment the editorial cartoonist. He also dropped in to see Dunn.

"I heard that you weren't talking to us anymore," said Dunn in honest surprise.

"A spur-of-the-moment decision," Ponzi replied. "I know you fellows are just doing your job. Besides, if it hadn't been for you, the whole country would not be talking about me today." The confusion on the city editor's face only made his own amusement grow.

Someday, perhaps, he would tell Dunn about the favor that the paper and McMasters had done for him. He had realized it, of course, once he had a few moments to think logically about his plan to prove that he had more assets than liabilities. The renewed run on the office only meant that millions more would go back to investors at once, and that he would be relieved of the obligation to pay 50 percent interest on their notes. There had been great danger, he was aware, that the article might have brought in the police—closing him down on the spot, and leaving him with untold millions owed. But that danger seemed past now.

He had returned nearly $3,500,000. "I doubt whether any other individual or group of individuals could weather a run like that in five days!" he told the reporters. And the people were still with him to a large degree. If he could hold them, keep them on his side until he proved to Pride and Allen that his assets outweighed his liabilities, Charles Ponzi would rise higher than ever!

He had to be amused. And he displayed his amusement everywhere.

"Rose," he called one evening when he returned home early from the office, "put on your prettiest dress. We're going to the theater."

His wife was surprised, thrilled. She hurried to dress, and at Keith's Theater, she sat proudly beside her husband in a box near the stage. She smiled shyly when the master of ceremonies for the variety program introduced "The man all Boston is talking about, the man all the United States is talking about—Mr. Charles Ponzi, the Wizard himself!" Ponzi rose to acknowledge the applause and waved to the audience. Then he sat back to watch the film program, which began with a newsreel that showed him smiling and strolling in front of his home, arm in arm with Rose and his mother. Again the audience applauded. Then, as if in answer to an on-screen title that asked his image, "How much money do you have, Mr. Ponzi?," he called out loudly in the darkness:

"So much that they didn't break me yesterday, and they won't break me tomorrow!"

The roar of laughter and applause filled the theater. When the variety program began, he and Rose laughed aloud at two comedians who mentioned his name several times in their routine. The act was followed by a violinist, and he left Rose sitting alone to enjoy the music while he stepped into the lobby for a cigarette.

He discovered several newsmen and the assistant manager of the theater waiting there for him. "Mr. Ponzi," the manager said, "so glad you came out. These newspaper gentlemen thought we might arrange a meeting between you and our headliner—"

"Mr. Corbett?" he said. "I'd be delighted to meet Gentleman Jim anytime. I've not seen his performance, but I understand he's

as good an actor as he was a fighter." With the manager leading the
way backstage, and trailed by the group of reporters, he went to
shake hands with the former Heavyweight Champion of the World.

"I was a bank clerk myself for six years," Corbett told the
newsmen, "but Ponzi here must have stumbled onto something I
missed." Ponzi laughed, and pointed out that a lot of bankers were
trying to discover his secrets. "If they pick on you," Corbett said,
lifting a huge fist, "you just let me know."

When he returned to the box, he gave Rose's hand a reassuring
squeeze in the darkness. Then he turned to her, his teeth gleaming
in the bright stage light, his eyes sparkling. "Rose," he said, "I
promise you, everything's going to be just fine."

Late in the week, he learned that the *Post* was looking into his background in Montreal.

Cassullo brought him the news. "Dammit, Charlie, I don't know how they found out! This guy Santosousso, he picked up a rumor from some woman in the North End, I think. Anyway, the paper sent a reporter up there. If you ever thought o' getting' out, now's the time, Charlie!"

The two men were in the private office above the Hanover Trust after nightfall. Ponzi tapped a pencil slowly on the surface of his gleaming mahogany desk while he thought the situation over.

"It's too late," he said after a moment. "If the *Post* has been tipped off, you can bet that the authorities have, too. Somebody who has it in for me probably picked up a nice piece of change for giving out information—"

Cassullo waved a nervous hand. "Charlie, there's no time to talk about how they got onto it. I don't know about you, but I'm takin' a boat out of here tomorrow."

Just like McMasters, he thought. *Run! Keep your own nose clean!* But his words were slow and steady. "Louis, you're making a mistake. I've told you I intend to come out of all this clean as a whistle. So they find out about my past? Hell, I won't be the first great man to have served time! Look at Charlie Morse. He was there in Atlanta with me. Look at him now, mingling with bankers, dealing with the government!"

"Yes, but he's—"

"There are a dozen more I can think of. Look, just because they know I made a mistake once doesn't mean they can prove anything now. I'm telling you, I have kept every promise to my investors! That has to mean something!"

Cassullo was unconvinced. He shook hands, wished Ponzi good luck, stepped through the door—and vanished for all time.

Once the man was gone, Ponzi briefly wondered how much of his cash had gone with him. He had thought to accuse Cassullo of cheating him, of stealing him blind during the last few weeks, but he knew that it would only waste valuable time. He had no proof, of course—only Miss Meli's frequent declarations that peculiar-looking notes were showing up after each day's payouts.

Some of the notes had been made out to obviously fictitious names, and the stubs for them had been filed with the others, so that payment was made to an unknown person or group of persons. Other notes appeared to have been paid two or three times, somehow managing to escape the cancellation stamp wielded by the clerks. Others had been presented for payment long before maturity, but had their dates altered so that full interest was paid.

There was a plan behind it all, Ponzi knew. But to slow his payments while he investigated every note—that would only increase the chance of riot by the investors. Which, in turn, would bring in the police once more. "Pay everything," he repeated to Miss Meli, although he felt sure that a half-million dollars was being stolen from him in the rush.

Let Cassullo go! At least his departure might stop the unexpected drain on the capital of the Securities Exchange Company. The amount of cash still held by the company—that was the immediate worry. Chmielinski had brought the matter to Ponzi's attention: except for the $1,500,000 tied up by the certificate of deposit, the Hanover's balance in his name was almost depleted.

And still the faithful Miss Meli and Miss Lacarno were signing checks for withdrawals. Checks that added up to thousands and tens of thousands of dollars.

"Soon, Ponzi, any day now, those checks are going to start bouncing," the frightened banker warned. "Unless you get some money in here to us!"

One check. That was all it would take. One check refused, returned for insufficient funds—and the run would wash him away in a flood of indictments. The crowd at his cashiers' windows was down to a few hundred people a day now, but let one investor fail to get his money back—*as Ponzi had promised*—and it would be all over.

He had to find cash, that was the first priority.

His spies in the *Post* pressroom would keep him informed of developments as Grozier's men prowled through dusty Montreal records. At the local Western Union office, two clerks had agreed to accept a hundred dollars weekly for a copy of any telegram sent in or out that mentioned Ponzi's name, and they would see that he received the copy before the original was delivered. With luck, any exposure of his criminal past could be delayed until after his showdown with the auditors.

No, the only real problem was the one of cash.

He reached for the telephone. When the gruff voice of the furniture dealer answered, he said only one brief sentence: "Daniels, this is Ponzi, and I want you to meet me tomorrow after lunch, here, at the Hanover, my office." He hung up before Daniels could ask any questions, certain that the man would do as he was told.

He was correct. Mean-looking as ever, but with a suspicious grin on his lips, Daniels showed up promptly at two o'clock. His eyes shifted swiftly to take in the rich furnishings of the office, the thick carpet, the heavy curtains, before coming to rest on Ponzi, who sat easily in his leather-covered chair.

"You're doin' all right, Ponzi. Better 'n I thought, even."

Ponzi's eyes were cold. His voice was brittle. "I have no time for pleasantries, Daniels. I'm a very busy man. How much do you want to settle your suit?"

"Well, now," Daniels said, "I should o' brought my lawyers, I reckon."

Ponzi's voice snapped across the office. "Dammit, man, I want you off my shoulders now. If I wanted to wait years, I'd let my lawyers battle yours, and they'd both wind up with more money than either one of us. Let's settle this like gentlemen. Believe me, you'll come out ahead."

Daniels thought it over, and slowly nodded. "You're probably right. But I don't know—it's a million-dollar suit . . ."

"Name a price, Daniels. I've got plenty to do this afternoon."

The furniture dealer squinted at him, measuring, judging. "I'll settle for $200,000—" he began.

"$50,000, and not another cent!" Ponzi said in iced tones.

Daniels started to say something in protest, took a step forward. Then he nodded. "Done!"

Ponzi picked up his phone. "Fowler," he commanded, "bring in whatever we need Daniels to sign to release his attachment." He listened to the sounds at the other end of the wire for a moment. "I don't give a damn about your court proceedings! He's in my office now and we've made a settlement. Get those papers in here."

The lawyer appeared shortly afterward, grumbling about not having been consulted, but waving a sheaf of documents. While Daniels obligingly signed his name to them, Ponzi reached for the phone and ordered Chmielinski to bring to the office immediately

$10,000 in cash and a certified check for $40,000 made out to the furniture dealer.

"Christ, that's $50,000 all at once, Ponzi," gasped the bank president. "If you take out that much—?"

"It will release a half-million that I'll put back in, Henry! Don't argue with me. Just get up here with it. I've got a lot to do."

He made Daniels go with him to the Cosmopolitan Trust, where harried officials—just getting ready to lock up the vault—handed over $389,000 in cash. Carrying the heavy case of bills jauntily out onto the sidewalk, Ponzi grinned at the circle of reporters waiting for him. "Boys, I'm glad to see you! There's nearly half a million in here and I'd hate to meet a holdup man now."

"Hey, Ponzi," one of the newsmen shouted as he stepped into his car, with Daniels at his heels, "how much did you pay to get out of the suit?"

He leaned out the open door of the Locomobile. "I'm not sure that Mr. Daniels here would want me to tell that. His wife might want a bigger piece if she knew how much he got. Let's just say I paid him one dollar and other considerations!" The car sped off down the street in a trail of exhaust smoke and laughter.

He had intended to put the money into the Hanover account, then move on to the Tremont Trust to pick up the $186,000 there. But an angry Isaac Harris was waiting in his Hanover office.

"I don't know what you're up to, Ponzi, but as Daniels' lawyer, I'm not letting you get away with it!"

He took in the situation at a glance. His own lawyers—Leveroni, Bailen, McIsaac, and all the rest—would also be furious about his out-of-court settlement that cut their workload and their fee at the same time. "Goddamn you, Harris, what's your price?" he said bitterly.

The negotiations took several minutes. They ended with the lawyer accepting $14,500—$5,000 in cash from Ponzi's thick wallet and $9,500 from the angry Daniels.

"Cheer up, Daniels," Ponzi said, grinning at the furniture dealer, "he's left you $500 for carfare. I've seen lawyers do a lot worse for their clients."

"My client," said Harris haughtily, "also has a certified check for $40,000. I could have gotten him more if he had continued to enlist my services, but if he's satisfied—"

The interruption had taken too much time. He arranged to meet Daniels the following morning at the Tremont Trust, and stepped out once more into the crowd of reporters and the mob of curious, cheering people. As he pulled away he looked through the rear window at the crowd, and grinned as he saw towering over them the massive structure of the Hanover Trust Company.

It now had more than two million dollars of Charles Ponzi's money in it!

The question was whether it was enough.

Rose and his mother, aware for the first time in months that Ponzi was worried about money, learned how great his concern was that evening. The two women had been shopping and were in and out of department stores all afternoon. They told him what had happened at one store where Rose had not paid cash but had written a check. The clerk had recognized the name and must have said something, because all of a sudden the two women were surrounded by a crowd of people. "They followed us all over, Carlo!" said his mother. "We couldn't walk."

At any other time he would have laughed along with them. Now his only interest lay in how much they had spent. When he learned that it was a few hundred dollars, the slightest of frowns appeared on his face.

He knew that Rose saw his worry, but he could not conceal it from her. He no longer seemed to have the strength to make the effort. Saturday afternoon, he tried: He took his wife and his mother for a long drive through the countryside and kept up a continual chatter, telling them about what he had done that morning.

"After I collected my money from that villain Swig, I took it straight to the Hanover and deposited it, and then I went upstairs. Well, my office was so crowded with reporters and visitors, I went on up to the construction company, figuring I'd get some work done there. I was on the phone an hour or so later, and I heard these newsboys on the street. Do you know what they were shouting? 'Extra! Extra! Ponzi Disappears!' Rose, I couldn't believe it! Some reporter must have looked for me downstairs and couldn't find me. When he told his boss, they rushed the paper onto the street! Well, I went down and bought a copy so I could read about it!"

His laughter caused the two women to smile, but he saw that Rose's eyes were looking into his own with a complete absence of humor. Almost wildly, he looked around him, searching for something on the landscape to distract her. He found it.

"Turn the car!" he called to his driver. "There! At the airport! I've always wanted to take a ride in a plane!"

At Lynnway Field, while his wife and mother stared in fright from the ground, Ponzi flew swiftly overhead as a passenger in a small biplane. The pilot at his urging put the craft through a series of stunts. A pair of loops, an Immelman turn, and two wing-overs—and then he was back on the ground, breathless with excitement, his face flushed, and his hair uncharacteristically windblown across his forehead.

"Did you see me? I waved to you. Did you see me?"

The women nodded, seeming to catch some of his enthusiasm. But after he had paid the pilot thirty dollars for the brief ride and had tipped him an extra ten dollars, the mood of exhilaration rapidly faded. He was silent on the trip home.

Somehow, merely handing the money to the airplane pilot had served to bring him down to earth.

"I'm sorry, but Mr. Ponzi is very tired," the maid told the callers waiting on the broad front porch of the home that newspapers everywhere were calling "the Ponzi mansion." For a moment Ponzi thought she was merely shooing away some of the perennial crowd of reporters, but then he saw an agitated Chmielinski waiting outside for him. Beside the banker stood McNary, the treasurer, wearing a grave expression.

"It's all right," he told the girl as he came to the door. "Run on in and see about dinner. I'll talk out here in the air for a few moments." He watched her move into the house, and then he turned to the bank officials.

He had a fair idea of what the bank officials were going to say.

"Ponzi," Chmielinski sputtered, "I told you it was going to happen, and it has! Your account is overdrawn by—"

"Several hundred thousand," McNary said.

Instantly, he was all cool deliberation. Relaxed. Ready to fend off the attack. He spread his hands placatingly. "That can't be. I have your certificate showing that I have at least $1,500,000 in the Hanover. That, plus the cash I put in yesterday and this morning, should certainly—"

"It's not enough, Ponzi. It's not enough! Your office here has been issuing checks like mad, and so has every other office in New England. The $1,500,000 is tied up—you know that—and your other reserves are gone. We've paid all the checks we could, figuring you'd come up with more cash, but we can't handle any more!"

More cash. Always, more cash. "There are some Liberty Bonds, some stocks that could be sold—borrowed against, if need be. I know—"

McNary shook his head. "I've looked into that for you. Not more than $50,000 at most."

"We need more," Chmielinski said, almost pleading. "Ponzi, the bank examiners are all over us! They came in this morning like a swarm of bees! You have to shore us up! How much cash can you transfer from your European accounts?"

Ponzi felt a slow smile creep across his lips. *European accounts. My $5 million in the banks of Europe. God, Chmielinski believes it, too!* He shook his head. "No, Henry, I can't touch that money. Not on short notice, anyway. It would take days to get it here for you." He bit his lip to keep from laughing out loud as he watched the banker nod his head vigorously, seeming to understand.

"But—but—what are you going to do for us? The examiners will jump all over us when they see how much we've overpaid on your account—"

The night air was cool on his forehead, and his shirt felt damp with perspiration. But there was no reason for concern. The solution was simple.

"Henry, let's look at things realistically. I have a million and a half dollars deposited in your bank, right? But the certificate won't let me touch it for another three weeks. Now, suppose we do this: I'll make out some notes to various people—let's say I make one out for $80,000 to Lucy Meli—and they'll bring them to you for discounting. You take out your interest and pay them—"

"Goddammit, Ponzi, we're not paying out another cent for you!" McNary barked.

"No? What if I endorse the certificate of deposit over to you as collateral?"

Chmielinski's eyes widened. "You want us to lend you money against your certificate? We credit everything to your account?"

"Exactly. There's no risk. You have my million and a half, and you're lending me—what—a few hundred thousand, at most. You've both seen what's happened this week. The run is petering out fast. There won't be many more checks going out to investors, so you have nothing to lose."

He studied the bankers' faces, and decided to sweeten the pot. "I'll pay you $20,000 each as a bonus. For handling." He saw McNary's eyes meet Chmielinski's—and he knew it was a deal. Swiftly, he wrote out the notes, several hundred thousand dollars worth in varying amounts. "There," he said, "that should more than hold things."

"For how long?" asked a skeptical McNary.

"Why, until after the auditor's report next week! When he declares that I'm as solvent as old John D., we'll raise the deuce with the whole banking world, boys. Just let's all hold on tight until next week."

The bank officials nodded soberly. They started toward their car, then hesitated. Chmielinski said, "Ponzi, if there's anything wrong—"

"Wrong? Henry, do I look like a man who thinks there's anything wrong?" He smiled broadly. "If you had more than a million dollars in a single bank account, would *you* worry, friend? Gentlemen, trust me!" He waved them away, then snapped his fingers in afterthought. "Henry," he called, "as soon as you've transferred the cash to my account, make out a check for $50,000 to Dan Coakley, and send it over to his office."

He stepped inside the house before either man could react fully. "Coakley?" he heard Chmielinski gasp in surprise, and then the *bang!* of the screen door drowned out the banker's voice.

He was in an excellent mood once more. Disaster had been staved off yet another time. What an ability he possessed, to think faster than men who had studied finance all their lives! Even the thought that Coakley might be needed shortly did not depress him. *Hell*, he thought, *at least I can afford the best!*

He was chuckling when he came into the dining room, where Rose and his mother waited for him. His wife, he knew, was puzzled by the up-and-down swings that his moods were taking these days. *It's been weeks since I bought her a trinket of some sort*, he thought. *I must remember to get something Monday!*

Monday, however, was yet thirty-six hours away, and Sunday evening—with its note of impending disaster—came first.

After a long afternoon of jousting and joking with a half-dozen reporters who had maneuvered their way past the friends and relatives acting as "guards" on the estate, he settled in his study to catch up on newspaper reports of his success. He was particularly amused by an article in the New York *Evening World*, which had tracked down old '520 Percent Bill Miller" to comment on the newest celebrity in the get-rich-quick ranks. Miller—long out of prison and now the owner of a small grocery store in Rockville Centre, Long Island—had told a newsman: "Say, this Ponzi must be a wonderful bird! As far as I can see from the newspapers, he's carried out every promise he made to his customers. His methods may not seem reasonable, but only time will tell if his investors have placed their confidence in the right man. I wouldn't take $10 million and be in that young Italian's place, if he is not doing this thing on the square. In fact, even if he is, I would much rather own this grocery store, where I have few worries and breathe God's free, pure country air."

I'll say you would! Ponzi thought. *You'd change places with me in a minute if you knew how!*

And then the phone rang.

"Ponzi, is that you?"

He recognized the voice immediately—and the trouble that it meant. He looked around the room, making sure that Rose was safely outside. "Yes," he said, "who's this? Dunn?"

There was a cough of surprise at the other end of the line. "That's right, at the *Post*. You were expecting us to call, then?"

"No, not at all." He knew that his voice was absolutely level, perfectly normal. "It's just that I'm so used to having some of your reporters around, that a call from you at any hour of the day or night does not surprise me."

Dunn coughed again, clearing his throat. "What I have to say might surprise you." There was a long pause. "I want to read you something. This came in by wire from our man in Montreal." He cleared his throat again.

By wire! Goddammit, why didn't I get a copy of it? Those crooks at Western Union— He realized that the newspaperman had begun reading:

" . . . was arrested and charged with forgery August 31, 1908, and served almost three years, St. Vincent de Paul Penitentiary. Used alias Bianchi. Involved failure Zarossi Bank."

Ponzi counted to himself. *One. Two. Three. Four.* Then he said, "Dunn? Are you still there?"

" 'Course I'm here."

"Well?"

"What d' you mean? What d' you have to say about it?"

"About that wire? What should I say? It means absolutely nothing to me."

Dunn hesitated for just a fraction of a second. "Do you mean to deny that you're this man?"

"I certainly do. I'm afraid, friend, that you've fallen victim to a case of mistaken identity that's trailed after me for years. There was a fellow named Bianchi in Canada at the same time I was there, but I'm certainly not him."

He knew that there was not the slightest trace of doubt in his voice, and Dunn knew it also. "This Zarossi Bank, Ponzi. Did you ever work there?"

"I might have. As I told your reporters, the ones doing my life story—for tomorrow's edition, isn't it?—'considerable portions of my life must remain a mystery.' But I'll say one thing, Dunn, and there's no mystery about it: You print that the man arrested and convicted in Canada and Charles Ponzi are one and the same, and it will be the last issue of the *Post* that will ever leave the presses! You won't dare print it! And we both know it!"

Dunn's tone became placating. "All right, Ponzi, there's no need to get upset. The *Post* has t' check out everything, you know that. We're a responsible paper, and we don't go with rumors."

He breathed deeply, steadied his voice. "Sorry if I flew off the handle. I haven't had much sleep these past few days"—he laughed—"thanks to you and your boys. If you have any other questions—?"

"No," Dunn said, "nothing now, and thanks for the time. I'll probably be gettin' back to you in a day or so, though. You see, our man Baldwin—the one we sent up to Montreal—he's waitin' to get some pictures of you we shipped up this afternoon. If they don't match this Bianchi guy, maybe we can help clear up your 'mistaken identity' thing once and for all."

A day or so. The words echoed inside his head. He had a day or so—before the truth came out of Montreal, before the added funds ran out at the Hanover, before the auditor produced the long list of liabilities that could only be offset with stolen assets from the bank.

When he came out of the study, his face was unnaturally pale. His mother asked if he were ill, if he were tired, if something were wrong. He shook his head, and walked to the bedroom.

All through the night, he lay awake, staring at the dark ceiling. *I'm going to make it!* he thought.

"Well, goddammit, Ponzi, those are my figures!"

Through a thick cloud of Turkish-tobacco smoke, Ponzi smiled at the angry, frustrated human being who ordinarily was Edwin L. Pride, a very calm and very collected auditor. Now Pride was pacing about his well-appointed office, occasionally stopping to pound his fist on the gleaming desktop or to stare moodily out his window.

"Those are your *preliminary* figures, Mr. Pride," said Ponzi with evident control. "And I'm saying they are so far off the mark as to be worthless."

Pride shook his head in violent disagreement. He started to say something—then halted and strove to get a grip on himself. It was only Monday morning, too early in the week to get into a strong argument; there would undoubtedly be plenty of those later. He wondered if he had done the right thing by inviting Ponzi in for an initial presentation of his findings. But the little Italian had always been so cocky, so confident! Perhaps some kind of mistake *had* been made by one of the subordinates who pored wearily over the stubs and file cards of the Securities Exchange Company. It just did not seem possible that Charles Ponzi could go on insisting that he was completely and absolutely solvent when the staff had concluded that he owed nearly $6 million! What if those findings were reported to the district attorney and the attorney general, what if warrants were drawn up—and then what if Ponzi proved that he was indeed solvent and the celebrated Pride organization was wrong?

No, presenting the preliminary conclusions to Ponzi was a proper move. Pride felt certain of that. He turned inward from the window, and sighed. "Could you go over the estimates, Ponzi, and state your objections—slowly, this time?"

Ponzi nodded, gesturing casually with the long cigarette holder at the sheet of paper on Pride's desk. "To begin with," he said, "there's your figure that I've paid out exactly $7,924,059.17 to date. It's much too low, as McNary at the Hanover or his assistant, Farrell, can tell you—"

Pride interrupted him. "I don't deal with what people tell me. I deal in figures."

"Certainly, you can take—if you'll pardon the pun—pride in that, Mr. Pride. But there is certainly evidence that up until several weeks ago, before the Boston *Post* wrote me up, I had checked in $5.9 million. Then, there were accounts of about $400,000 each in the Merchants National Bank of Manchester and the Lawrence Trust Company of Lawrence, Massachusetts. It is also a fact that I carried accounts in about thirty other banks. Now, as you know, most of those accounts are largely depleted, so it stands to reason that I've paid out about $8 million in just the last few weeks."

The auditor slammed a large ledger on his desk. "But your books, Ponzi!" he shouted. "Your books don't show anything like that. At least, not so any intelligent person can find it." He tossed a handful of file cards onto the ledger, and a half-dozen fluttered to the floor.

Ponzi shrugged. "Perhaps not so *you* can find it, and I mean no discourtesy," he said. "But surely the fact that I have one bookkeeping system and you have another is no crime. Perhaps, in my anxiety to accommodate as many investors as possible, I neglected to install some accounting procedures that you might wish. But, at most, that's an inconvenience." He noticed Pride's rapt attention, shrugged, and continued, his words flowing in an unbroken stream.

"Obviously, from the start of my business until mid-July, I made a large number of payments. I admit that it's difficult to tell how much, because many investors immediately reinvested both their original principal and the 50 percent interest. But let's say it's about $1.7 million. That indicates that I've paid out about $9.7 million, or several million more than you say."

Again, Pride held up his hand. "Ponzi—" he said. Then, he gestured for him to proceed.

"It's hard to say—as long as you have the stubs and records there—but out of the total amount, I'd estimate that only $3.5 million was for notes that had matured. Notes, that is, on which I paid both the principal and the fifty percent. So, approximately

$6 million was refunds, and those refunds relieved me of the obligation to pay the fifty percent interest. Therefore, if each hundred dollars paid out eliminated $150 in liabilities, I should be credited with having paid not $7.9 million, as you say, but rather with $12 million, perhaps $12.5 million."

There was absolute stillness in the office now. Pride sat back in his chair, fingered the lobe of his left ear, and stared at the ceiling. The argument, he had to tell himself, was a novel one. But so far as all basic accounting principles went—

"What it comes down to, Pride, is that if I paid out $12.5 million and my liabilities are less than $15 million, as you surmise, my outstanding liabilities should not be over $2.5 million. Point two: You estimate that the total amount of investments into the Securities Exchange Company is under $10 million—"

"$9.9 million, and that's according to your stubs!" Pride's eyes were flashing.

I had him, but he's off the hook! "Yes, according to my stubs," he went on easily. "But the stubs do not show actual *cash* received. They show only the investment and the amount due. As I said, many investors did not take out cash or give me any when their notes came due. They simply let their original investments ride, so to speak. Take John Dondero, for example. He had an original investment of $2,000—and, after four or five months, he claims he is owed $16,500. But I only *received* $2,000. So your figure that I took in $9.9 million should be reduced by a third or more. I only received in cash less than $6 million, maybe $5.5 million."

"Ah, then," snapped Pride, leaning forward across the desk, "you're saying you paid out several millions more than you took in?"

"I've told everyone," said Ponzi, fitting a fresh cigarette to his holder, "that it's a highly profitable enterprise." He saw the cloud of confusion pass over the auditor's eyes. "One thing more, and then I must really be getting over to the office. I don't think there's any question about my having refunded $6 million to the public in these last weeks, is there? No? Well, under my terms with my agents, they were entitled to ten percent commission on all investments accepted. It stands to reason that I am now entitled to refunds from them on the money that Gallagher and Allen and the others have made me give back. Therefore, in my tabulation of my assets, I include $600,000 owed me."

"Owed by your agents? Do you have an agreement that they'll forfeit their commissions, after having done the work of getting money to you?"

Ponzi spread his hands and let the smile widen. "An unwritten agreement, perhaps, but one that I'm sure my men will respect. After all, Mr. Pride, I deal with honest men. They will understand that the problems which have been created were not of my doing." He bounced easily to his feet, held out his hand. "I'm sure that you will want to correct your figures before we meet with Mr. Gallagher—tomorrow? Wednesday?"

Pride was rubbing his chin now, looking down at the file cards on the desk and floor. He raised his head, appearing not to see Ponzi's proffered hand. His voice was hesitant. "It—uh—might take a bit longer than that. You've given me some things to think about, I'll admit. But I'll have final figures by the weekend for certain."

The weekend was too far away. The *Post* might get a lead in Montreal long before that. In his anxiety to get his liabilities down to the point where they could easily be covered by the securities in the Hanover's vaults, Ponzi wondered if he had confused Pride too much. He thought up an immediate lie, then snapped his fingers, as if suddenly remembering something.

"Oh, the weekend. I'm afraid that I may have to leave the city Friday. A Mr. Herman is in town and wants me to motor back to New York with him. If it's at all possible, I'd like to have this matter cleared up before I go."

The auditor looked at him steadily, trying to peer behind his unruffled expression. Ponzi knew what the man was thinking: *"Leave the city, is he? Mexico, probably."*

"I'll tell you what, Ponzi," Pride said. "If I keep my men at these books of yours, I should have a final report ready Thursday morning. Let's count on it."

Thursday! Better! Not good, but better. If I just get a bit of luck—! He turned to leave, but was stopped by Pride's call.

"Oh, just one thing. I've told Gallagher that it's almost impossible to come up with a final figure as long as you're still paying out cash down at your place. He authorized me to insist that you put a stop to it immediately."

Ponzi tried not to laugh, and succeeded with an effort. "I'm being shut down?" he managed to gasp, as if dismayed. "But that's illegal! The government can't treat an honest businessman like that! I'll go to court—"

Pride held his hands up, palms outward. "Now, now," he said soothingly. "No one said anything about closing you up. It's just to help us clarify things. After the audit—"

"*After!* What about my character *now?* You know what happens when a bank is closed up, Pride. You know the runs that

233

start, the riots! I'll be branded a crook! Hanged in effigy, or worse! I'm trying to give people back their money, not take it in! The newspapers will swear I'm closed up, and I'll be ruined."

"Hold on, Ponzi, I'm sure that Gallagher will give a statement to the press. He can make it very clear that this is just a precaution, just a temporary ac—"

"He goddamned better!" He appeared to be breathing hard now, his face red. "You just tell him that he goddamned better. If he ruins a business I've worked nearly forty years building up, he's going to be a very sorry man! You tell him that!"

He flung the office door open and stormed out, swinging his gold-headed cane almost viciously as he strode past startled secretaries and clerks. He was out on the street before he let his tightly held lips slip into a grin. Gallagher had stopped his payouts just when the cash was running low!

He found out only a few hours later how close a call the Securities Exchange Company had had. Barely had the sign been posted to inform the stunned and muttering crowd that payments were temporarily suspended "by official order," when the patient Miss Meli handed Ponzi the telephone. It was Chmielinski, and his voice was quavering.

"Ponzi, get over here quick. We've got problems."

In the bank president's office, an attorney was in close consultation with Chmielinski, McNary, and several other executives. When Ponzi hurried in, they turned to him with looks of desperation on their faces.

"The bank commissioner wants to close us down," Chmielinski blurted.

"What for?" The words were calm, but his mind was racing. If the bank closed before he could make use of the securities in the vault—

"He claims that the Hanover's conditions are not sound. It's these damn manipulations you've been asking us to do."

McNary's words were hurried. "We've told him that we're sounder than ever, that we've doubled our deposits in the last two months!"

"I've explained, Mr. Ponzi, that the problem is not the value of the bank's deposits," the attorney said. "The commissioner feels that there are some bad loans on the books."

"Oh," Ponzi said, as if dismissing the roomful of worried men. "You go tell him that he is mistaken. This bank has no bad loans, and cannot have any. Tell the commissioner that when I bought control of this bank, I told its officials that I would personally guarantee all loans. I have more than enough money to cover any

234

loans—good, bad, or otherwise—that the bank makes, and the Hanover is authorized to charge to my account any that the commissioner deems unsafe."

"That's true," McNary said quickly. "We've got it in writing."

"But the bank has made loans to you, Mr. Ponzi," said the attorney, "and the commissioner knows about it. It's those loans that I think he's concerned with."

Ponzi drew a breath. Someone had been talking, certainly. Otherwise, the examiners would not have already uncovered the deal made with Chmielinski and McNary less than forty-eight hours before. How had Allen found out about it so quickly? Someone in the bank—Pizzi, perhaps?—was probably looking to save his own neck.

His voice was steady. "Any loans to me are more than secured by a certificate of deposit for $1.5 million!"

The attorney shook his head. "National banks can make loans against a time deposit, but the attorney general ruled that Massachusetts trust companies can't do it."

The bank president spread his hands in a gesture of hopelessness. "We wanted to give Ponzi time to transfer some funds from his European accounts—"

Ponzi waved an impatient hand at the lawyer. "Look," he said, "you go up to the State House and tell Allen that when I bought control of this bank, it was in sound condition. If it was then, it is more so now. Further, tell him that I have informed Mr. Gallagher that until his audit is completed, there will be no further withdrawals from the Hanover. And I still have more than a million dollars in this bank to take care of any bad loans. Finally, I have been promised that the investigation into my finances will be completed by Thursday. For the commissioner to take any action before then would be a disservice to this bank's depositors and its stockholders. You tell him all that."

The lawyer checked his gold watch, and sighed. "I'll see him first thing in the morning. That gives you another twenty-four hours, Chmielinski."

A reprieve of twenty-four hours! Somehow, the time would have to be stretched. *I'll get Coakley and McIsaac onto it*, Ponzi thought. *Lawyers! Set them at each other, and nothing gets done!*

He was grinning when he stepped out of the bank's front door and found Santosousso and two other newsmen waiting in front of the Locomobile. "Well, boys," he chuckled, "I've been giving you a merry chase, haven't I? You're not getting much sleep with me around."

The *Herald's* reporter nodded, and suggested that he might

save the press trouble if he could give out a printed itinerary each morning. Ponzi laughed.

"I'd do that, if I knew from one minute to the next where I was going to be called, and what I'm going to be doing. Just about everybody wants to see me, boys. And all at the same time."

"They're keepin' you on the run, eh, Ponzi?" said Santosousso. "That doesn't mean you're in trouble, does it?"

Ponzi reached for the handle on the car and turned it with a strong movement of his hand. "Trouble?" he scoffed. "Not a bit!"

"We got word about your stoppin' payments. Some of your customers are plenty sore."

"Some of 'em are plenty frightened," added the *American* representative.

He felt the color creeping into his face. "Dammit, I was ordered to stop paying on my notes! You boys tell your readers that. And as soon as Pride reports that I'm absolutely solvent—like I've been saying all along—I'll go right back paying anyone who wants his money!"

The newsmen's pencils were busy as he stepped into the car. He rolled down the window and leaned out for a final statement. "If you boys want to get any more dope on what's going on, catch up with me at intermission tonight at the Park Square. Harry Frazee has a new comedy, and he asked me to bring Rose along to the opening. She's a real fan of Jack Norworth, and I owe her a treat." He pointed a finger at Santosousso. "Hey, you tell Grozier and Dunn that Ponzi's taking his wife to a show, and ask them if that sounds like I'm in trouble."

Striving to recall the play the next morning, Ponzi vaguely remembered that it had to do with a millionaire publisher of Bibles who tried to "spread a little sunshine" by giving his money freely to several young women. He had laughed several times, he knew that much, but for the life of him he could not think why. Rose, he remembered, had retreated into worried silence after several attempts to make conversation. Once—no, twice—he had thought to offer a word of comfort, but had been relieved when a joke or some activity on stage drew her attention away. At the first intermission, he felt that Rose was about to question him, but then the producer announced his name from the stage and pointed to him in the side box—and the entire theater burst into applause. By the time he had finished bowing and waving to the crowd, the show was on again.

He had barely finished breakfast when the call came from Chmielinski.

"It didn't work, Ponzi, goddammit! Allen's closing us!"

He felt very, very tired.

"When?" he asked. "When?"

The bank president told him. At once. The legal papers were being drawn up. The bank had been ordered to halt payment on any checks or withdrawals, to cease taking deposits, to stop making loans.

"The securities—" Ponzi said. "The assets in the vaults—"

"What about them?" replied Chmielinski angrily. "We can't touch them. Not yours, not anybody's! Goddammit, Ponzi, don't you understand? The state's taking over everything. God, I knew when you first walked in that you were trouble. This whole damn mess is your—"

Ponzi hung up the phone, cutting the banker off in midsentence, and called the office, where the loyal Miss Meli told him that she was the only person working. With no money coming in from investors, and no payouts to be made, most of the clerks had been dismissed. A few people, she said, were hanging about the outer office, but they were merely curious, eager to get a look at the Wizard of Finance. "There's some mail, Mr. Ponzi. Nothing important. A few checks—one for $300 and some smaller ones."

The public was still sending in its money! Despite the stories in the papers, despite the statements of the officials, despite the anxious hordes fighting to get their investments out, there were still people in New England and elsewhere throughout the country who would trust him with their life savings. People who wanted him to apply his Midas touch to their cash. People who would believe in him, and support him in anything he did because they were certain he could make them rich.

"Mr. Ponzi? What should I do with them, the checks? Deposit them, or—"

His mind had been wandering, he realized. "No, no," he said, "let's just hold onto them for awhile. Put them in a safe place, Miss Meli, until I get there."

But, he realized after he hung up the phone, there was little point in going to the office on School Street. There would just be reporters there, ready to waste his time with stupid questions. And he did not have much time—*what, forty-eight hours?*—to plan a new escape route, now that the Hanover was closed.

There was Herman's offer of $10 million for the company. Tainted money, perhaps, blood money—it was money. Accepting it meant taking a chance, but plenty of chances had been taken this far. He dialed the number of the Copley Plaza.

"Herman," he said, "I'd like to discuss your offer. I think we can come to terms."

The heavy voice rumbled back at him from the receiver. Yes, it said, a certified check for $10 million could be produced almost immediately. By Thursday morning? Certainly. A meeting at the hotel? At 9 A.M. precisely.

He felt somewhat better after he completed the call. His brain was working once more. If he could only get his hands on a certified check, made out to Charles Ponzi, for $10 million! That would be an acceptable substitute for the securities he had planned to borrow from the Hanover.

And after Pride and Gallagher had seen with their own eyes that his assets outweighed his liabilities many times over, the check could be returned to Herman and his mysterious friends! They would not like it, of course. They would not like his backing out of the deal, and they would be dangerous. But, with money flooding in from the public once again, he could hire bodyguards. Dozens of bodyguards if need be!

At noon he addressed the local Kiwanis chapter on "Finance," and he felt certain that the members enjoyed his speech far more than the hotel luncheon they were served. The applause was generous and the laughter frequent as he outlined his complex views on the right and wrong ways to make money through investments, and steadily attacked the "traditional" bankers who resented his success. During the question period that followed his remarks, he fielded queries with ease.

Q. "Mr. Ponzi, why can't the postal authorities find some evidence that you have been dealing in large amounts of International Reply Coupons?"

A. "Because the governments that have furnished me with coupons—and made my fortune possible—have made a profit on the transactions themselves. Naturally, they would not care to reveal the amount issued, whether they are friendly or unfriendly toward this government."

Q. "Mr. Ponzi, if you had to state it in the simplest possible way, what would you say your business is?"

A. "Getting people's money and bankers' goats!"

The response was enthusiastic even though he knew he was not really at his best. His mind had kept wandering to thoughts of a certified $10 million check and of Pride's imminent report. Once, focusing on Pride, he told himself that it was highly possible that the auditor might find him solvent, even without the addition of new funds. *The problem*—he had thought while looking out at the upturned faces of the Kiwanis—*is that I don't really know myself how much cash I've taken in, and how much I've paid out.*

If only he dared to include that in his speech, it would stun the

238

audience all right! What fools they were, to sit through an entire address on finance by someone who did not know how rich or poor he was himself!

The triumph helped him to relax when he came home early in the afternoon. He stretched out on a sofa for a nap before dinner, but was obviously more weary than he realized. It was nearly midnight when he woke up. Rose had opened the door to two men. One of them he recognized at once.

Eddie Dunn crossed the room toward him, not bothering to extend a hand.

"Sorry to call on you so late, Ponzi," he said, "but we have something to show you." He drew a thick, flattened roll of paper from his pocket. "These are the galleys on a story for the first edition."

"Dunn! Good to see you, any hour of the day or night!" he exclaimed. "And your friend, too. Anyone from the *Post* is always welcome here." He turned to Rose, noting gratefully that the cheer in his voice had calmed her. "Dear, why don't you put some wine out on the table, and maybe a slice or two of that fine cake of yours? I might be talking to these gentlemen for awhile, and if I know newspapermen they're probably thirsty. And then perhaps you'd best go on up to bed."

It was still for a long moment after she had gone. Then Dunn held out the papers in his hand. "I didn't want to read this over the phone," he said. "There are so many people listening in on your line that the *American* or some other paper might've picked it up."

Ponzi looked at the print on the first page.

CANADIAN "PONSI" SERVED JAIL TERM
Montreal Police, Jail Warden and Others Declare That Charles Ponzi of Boston and Charles Ponsi of Montreal Who Was Sentenced to Two and a Half Years in Jail for Forgery on Italian Bank are One and the Same Man

He went on reading, without expression. Not a muscle in his face moved.

The *Post* had it all, all right. Its man in Montreal had shown photographs to everyone—the police, Italians who had given their money to Banco Zarossi, even a steamship agent who had dealt with the bank and claimed to remember "Bianchi, the snake!"

He read on in the silence. The paper printed the Rogues

Gallery 1908 description of Charles Ponsi side by side with the 1920 data provided by Charles Ponzi to obtain his pistol permit. Except for the difference in ages, twenty-six and thirty-eight, all of the details of height, weight, color of hair and eyes, and nationality were identical.

It was a long story, and it took him several minutes to get through it. Finally, he looked up at the city editor.

"Your men have worked hard, Dunn," he said. "But there are no pictures."

The newsmen opened their mouths in amazement, simultaneously. Dunn found his voice first.

"You mean, you're denying that you're this Ponsi or Bianchi? You've got to be kid—"

"I'm not denying anything. If that's your story, print it. I merely pointed out that you have no pictures."

Dunn pressed his lips together in a tight smile, and shook his head in wonder. "We have pictures, the same ones from the prison file that are in the hands of the Boston police. We'll run them Wednesday, Ponzi, after one of our artists puts a mustache on one of those shots we took of you last week."

Ponzi's voice was absolutely steady. "Oh," he said, "that's quite interesting. I must remember to get the paper and see how I look."

The reporter at Dunn's elbow looked at him, his eyes narrowing. "Ponzi, do you want to make a statement? The public deserves it, don't you think?"

Ponzi laughed. "The public deserves exactly what it gets, no more, no less." He took out his watch and studied it. "It's very late, gentlemen. You'll forgive me if I don't offer you a drink after all. I have much to do tomorrow." He moved toward the door.

"You're not saying anything?" asked Dunn.

"I compliment you on your enterprise. Outside of that, I really can't think of anything else. Goodnight." He held the door open for them.

When he closed it, Rose was at his elbow. He turned and saw the fright in her eyes.

He had dreaded this moment, dreaded it for the two years that he had known and loved her. But now—now that it was here, now that it was time—he realized that it could be turned into an opportunity. Tomorrow, he would have to make a statement to the press. Now he saw a chance to rehearse and perfect his story.

He held out a hand to her, guided her into the living room, and seated her on the sofa. Then, while her eyes followed his every movement, he paced the floor and spoke quietly more to himself than to her.

"Rose," he began, "the morning paper will carry an ugly story about me. Full of vicious lies and spiteful gossip. But one thing is factual. Dear, it is bitterly painful for me to tell you this, but I must." He held his gaze on her for a lengthy period of absolute silence. "In Canada," he said, "many years ago, I was in jail."

She made no sound, no movement.

He went on quickly, explaining how he had been fooled by Salvati into taking the blame for Zarossi's flight, detailing how Salvati had turned on him for revenge. "When Zarossi was brought to trial, I exonerated him, Rose! I assumed the blame. He vanished. I don't know what happened to him. I'm not saying that I was a hero, but I can produce witnesses who will bear me out."

Perched on the edge of a large sofa cushion, Rose looked small and defenseless. Still, she said nothing, asked no questions.

"I was released from prison without a friend. Without a dollar. Without credentials. They didn't give me anything. I tried to earn a living as best I could. I was asked to escort some Italians across the border. I put them on a train, openly, and was immediately arrested. The charge was smuggling! It was impossible! *Smuggling!* But I was ignorant—innocent!—and never thought to dodge the consequences. Two years! That's what they gave me, Rose, after I pleaded guilty to a misdemeanor!"

He shook his head angrily. Then he reached out to take her hands, and knelt before her.

"Rose, dear Rose. I meant to tell you. I *wanted* to tell you. But I didn't know how. I feel so much better now I've made a clean breast of it all. I sinned, dearest, but I paid for it. That's what I'll tell the press tomorrow. People will understand. I know they will. And they'll know by your love for me that I've paid the full penalty. Anyone can look at you and understand that you could not love a man who does wrong."

He pressed his lips against the back of her cold hand, then looked into her eyes.

"Everything is going to be all right, Rose. I promise you that. If only you stand by me. If only you and mother help me show them all!"

He waited, breathing deeply. Then he saw Rose raise her chin slowly. There was something she would say now, that she would tell prying reporters later. "I've known all along about my husband's past," she would say to them. "When we were engaged, his mother wrote to tell me that he had been in prison. She wanted us to start life as man-and-wife honestly. I never told my husband about it. I thought that he would bring it up in time, when he was ready." That was what she would say, when she was asked what it was like to discover a long-hidden secret!

He buried his face in the coolness of her palms, trying to force tears into his eyes, and shielding his face from her. "Oh, my dear Rose," he said, "you are such a lovely, lovely person! I am so damn lucky! So damn lucky to have you!"

He looked up into his wife's eyes. "You tell the reporters exactly that, dear. That you've known all along. You tell them the truth, just like I'm going to do tomorrow. And you'll see, everything will be fine."

He could tell from the brightness in her eyes, from the way the corners of her mouth moved upward ever so slightly, that she believed him.

And the public would believe it, too!

He intended to stage his "confession" on Tuesday with the same aplomb he had shown before the Kiwanis members. For more than an hour, the group of newsmen hastily summoned to the law offices of Daniel McIsaac on the tenth floor of Barristers Hall were kept waiting. Behind the locked door, the reporters were told, Ponzi was discussing business with his lawyers and the treasurer of the Hanover Trust Company.

"Probably talkin' 'bout the Hanover closin' down," one of the reporters said, lighting a cigarette.

"You been over there today?" asked another. "I was there with a photographer this morning. There's practically a riot goin' on! People running all over tryin' to figure out how to get their hands on their money."

"Some I talked to," murmured a young man with a cynical smile, "want to get their hands on Ponzi."

The brief chorus of agreement ended abruptly as the office door opened. Immediately the newsmen crowded inside, their eyes searching out Ponzi.

He sat behind McIsaac's large desk, the familiar cigarette in its long holder between his fingers, the smile wan on his face, but there. He waited patiently until the reporters had positioned themselves around the room, then took them all in with a slow movement of his head.

"Boys, I can still smile," he said.

A murmur went up from the reporters, and one started to ask a question. Ponzi cut him off with a gesture.

"Let me finish first. If there's time, I'll answer questions. You boys know that I haven't ducked any up to now." He glanced around, smiling more broadly as the newsmen nodded. "All right," he said. "There's a stenographer here who will get my exact words, just in case any of you can't keep up with me. Okay?"

There was no response. He began:

"The statement that I am about to make I should probably have made before, in view of the notoriety given me by the press. However, I felt that my past had no bearing on the present situation. If several years ago I sinned—if I made a mistake and paid for it—I had every reason to believe that society owed me another chance."

He went on, then, to tell the group about men who had paid their dues to the American system of justice, and who had gone on to prosper. Charles W. Morse, he noted, was one, and there were others. He paused for breath, then smiled at the stenographer.

"New paragraph," he said light-heartedly. And he began to unreel the tale of his heroism in Montreal—"It is important for the people at large to know that I am the man who was convicted and sentenced in Montreal for a crime, but I am not the man who perpetrated that crime"—and he quickly explained the mistake that had landed him in a cell. Then he shrugged. "There isn't much more to be said. The public knows the facts, and whether they are such to make me unworthy of their confidence is for the people to decide."

A barrage of questions shot from the newsmen. Ponzi singled one out and looked the man who had asked it straight in the eye: "The Hanover closing? Yes, I heard about it, and I regret it. I feel that it's merely a new attempt on the part of the bank commissioner to prevent me from gaining possession of $1.5 million that I have in that institution. He hopes that I will not be able to meet my obligations to my noteholders. Well, I put my money in a state trust company, approved year after year by the bank commissioners, and I received a certificate of deposit that's good anywhere—but not good now because of the commissioner's action! What banker or merchant could stand the strain of being compelled by the public authorities to meet obligations before they came due, and at the same time be deprived of all liquid assets? It's obvious that there is an organized plot to ruin me, a plot that originates with jealous financial men of this city, state, and government!"

Others shouted questions. He started to reply, then stopped. Suddenly, he stood up, gripping the gold-headed cane so tightly that his knuckles showed white. "No more! My nerves can't last forever, boys. I've got to rest. That's all the statements for awhile."

Tight-lipped, with fatigue showing in his eyes, he hurried out of the building. A contingent of reporters followed, piling into a large touring car and chasing after the Locomobile. Ponzi's chauffeur tried vainly to lose them, circling Harvard Square three times before heading toward Somerville. At an intersection, the newsmen's car drew alongside, and a reporter called out, "What's your hurry, Ponzi? You're not thinking of takin' a trip, are you?"

"If I planned that—and I know you boys hear rumors—I would not have done what I did today," he called across the road. "I am going home, and I am going to stay home. If you want proof, well, just follow along, I guess. But you'll have to excuse it if I'm not much of a host tonight."

There was little rest in Lexington. The telephone—continually ringing with calls from reporters and lawyers and frightened investors—finally had to be left off the hook. Still, the hot and humid August air all too clearly carried the sound of automobile engines from the road, where a steady stream of cars passed back and forth as their occupants craned to glimpse the famous and infamous Ponzi. And, as evening fell, he imagined that he could hear the cynical comments of two newsmen who sat beneath a tree some fifty yards away.

"Angelo," Ponzi called to one of the laborers he had hired to stand guard about the house, "tell those reporters to come over here." While the man scurried off on the errand, he paced along the gravel walk at the side of his home. He stopped when the reporters came near and shouted at them.

"You men, get away from here!"

The reporters slowed, a questioning look on their faces. "The guard said you wanted to see us," one said.

"To tell you to get away from here!" Ponzi replied. He reached quickly under his coat and pulled out his small revolver. "My guards' power is limited, but mine isn't! You see this? When I shoot, I hit. Now get away or there's going to be some tall shooting around here!"

Hastily, the men backed off. Ponzi waited until they were across the roadway before he returned the pistol to his coat pocket.

He was smiling as he came through the door to Rose. "Now everything is fine, dear," he said. "Just fine, dear. We'll have some peace and quiet around here now, I think."

The strength in his voice, the calm expression in his eyes reassured her. For awhile, there might be no questions and no visitors. Just the two of them.

But then Ponzi walked slowly past her. Alone in the living room, for long hours, he sat in an armchair reading the front page of the newspaper over and over.

Tired, he thought. *I'm tired.*

But he was not worried. He had kept his promises to investors. He had explained his time in prison. And he was ready to prove his solvency.

There was no reason to worry. None at all.

On Wednesday, even after the *Post* ran his photographs—full-front and profile—from the Montreal police files, he felt no greater concern. He had admitted that he had been in jail, so the pictures proved nothing. Dunn and Grozier, desperate to prove him guilty of something, had resorted to printing "heart-rending tales" of investors who stood to lose everything—or so the *Post* claimed. Ponzi had to smile at the syrupy prose about "a printer down in the North End" whose dream of a new house from his $4,600 in savings had "turned into a dog house now." A couple who planned to return to their native Italy wept over a worthless note for $2,000. A Beachmont woman who had mortgaged her home for $8,000 and invested it, was quoted as saying, tearfully, "Not in a lifetime can I pay back that mortgage again."

His mother heard some of the stories, and tried to speak to him about them. Her words were halting, barely audible. "Carlo—these people—"

"Mother, reporters dig up these things, or make them up. Half these people haven't even invested with me! They're just trying to get a handout. Everyone who's given me money and wanted it back has gotten it. And as soon as I talk to the attorney general tomorrow, I'll see to it that these people get their money, too. I'd give it to them now if the bank commissioner would let me! After tomorrow morning, you'll see—I'll be right back in business!"

The telephone rang Thursday at eight, just a few minutes before he intended to leave to meet Herman at his hotel. Ponzi noticed that his palm was slick with perspiration as he put the receiver to his ear.

"Ponzi," said the hoarse voice. "The—uh—developments make me think we better hold off for a couple of days."

It took an effort, but he held his voice absolutely steady. "I understand, Herman. Just let me say that I'm seeing the district attorney this morning, and I expect a clean bill of health. Why don't you call me Saturday or Sunday? I think we'll both be ready to make a deal then."

The mysterious figure from New York somewhat reluctantly

245

promised to call back, and then clicked off. Ponzi replaced the receiver in its cradle and sat waiting for the phone to ring again.

With Herman, he realized, had gone his last plan. Now all that remained was the slim chance that Pride's calculations would not show a wide difference between the assets and liabilities of the Securities Exchange Company.

When the phone sounded, he caught it up quickly, before a second ring could disturb Rose or his mother.

"Fine, Mr. Pride," he said. "I'll be right down."

The straw hat in place, a fresh carnation in his lapel, and the cane swinging lightly in his right hand, he strode smiling into Gallagher's office a half-hour later. In a glance, he took in the others in the room. Pride. Hurwitz. Bank Commissioner Allen. Two large men who were obviously detectives.

Gallagher wasted no time. "Ponzi," he said, "the auditors report that the total of your outstanding liabilities comes to about $7 million. Can you produce assets to cover that amount?"

Ponzi cocked an eyebrow in disbelief. "$7 million? My liabilities are nowhere near that. Not half of that."

"But you agreed to accept Pride's figures."

He nodded. "Yes, but I assumed that as a professional accountant, he would not be more than a quarter of a million dollars off the mark." Then he smiled. "Well, be that as it may, I shall live up to my part of the agreement."

"Then," Gallagher said with an incredulous note in his voice, "you are ready to produce $7 million in assets?"

"I'm ready to produce what I can, Mr. Gallagher. But I don't believe my total assets come to more than $3 million right now."

He sensed the surprised silence in the room, and he grinned at the officials. Pride was the first to find his voice.

"But that means you're $4 million short, Ponzi," he said.

"Gee," Ponzi said softly, turning to the auditor and feeling the smile spread from ear to ear. "Then I guess I'm not solvent."

Out of the corner of his eye, he saw Gallagher gesture to the detectives and he knew that something was being said about arresting him. But he was only aware of one thing for certain. He had given the financial world the most brazen example of sheer nerve ever witnessed, and he had taken the people of Boston on a fifteen-million-dollar ride that would never be equaled.

With the handle—the gold handle—of his cane, he shoved back the brim of his straw skimmer until it rested at a jaunty angle on his head. Then he turned to the U.S. marshal who had moved alongside him. "Okay," he said, "I'm your prisoner."

246

EPILOGUE

Charles Ponzi died, penniless and virtually alone, in the charity ward of a hospital in Rio de Janeiro on January 15, 1949. He was sixty-six years old, partly blind, partly paralyzed as a result of a blood clot on the brain, but in the last photographs of him— propped up in bed in the anonymity-making white hospital gown— his lips are parted in a wide grin and his eyes look bright with the familiar dream of imminent fortune.

His arrest that hot August day in Boston, 1920, in no way signaled the end of his fight to realize the American Dream of every immigrant. To the very last, he battled with wit and intelligence, and the long, long struggle was over only when his body—not his mind—failed him.

Treated as something of a celebrity in the East Cambridge jail, where he was placed immediately after his arrest by federal authorities, Ponzi quickly laid plans with his lawyers to extricate himself from his trouble. All around him banks were crashing—the Hanover, the Tremont, Chmielinski's Polish Industrial Association Bank—while court-appointed receivers sifted through the assets of his bankrupt company to see what could be returned to his investors.

A final bankruptcy report was filed eleven years later, in 1931, after the weary officials managed to piece together the incomplete and muddled records of the Securities Exchange Company. It concluded that Ponzi's assets, including sixty-one dollars worth of postage stamps found in the School Street office, were $1,331,703.11. His liabilities totalled $3,986,179.77, including $16,075 "borrowed" from his wife and eight of her relatives. Investors who turned their notes over to the state—and many did not, holding onto the belief that Ponzi somehow would yet make good on his promise of 50 percent interest—received less than thirty cents for each dollar invested.

The plan constructed by Ponzi with attorney Daniel Coakley to get off as lightly as possible involved pleading guilty to a federal charge of using the mails to defraud. Although he could have argued that his only use of the mails had been to send postcards to investors advising them to come in and collect their interest, Ponzi hoped to accept a light federal sentence on two indictments rather than face more than fifty charges of grand larceny (each with a possible penalty of five years) brought against him by the Commonwealth of Massachusetts. Coakley, who was to be disbarred in 1922 for perjury and unethical legal practices, reasoned that his client would spend a few years in federal prison—and would be released after State Attorney General Allen's term in office had expired.

On November 1, Ponzi pleaded guilty to one of the government's two indictments ("in a firm voice, but with evident reluctance," said the Boston *Post*, which was given a Pulitzer Prize for its work in exposing the dapper swindler). In a brief statement before sentence was handed down, Coakley argued that his client "had $7 million in banks at one time, and a passport to Italy that he could have used if he had not expected to pay dollar for dollar. Wild and reckless though he was, he had no intent to defraud. He wasn't the garden variety of criminal. His wife has only three suits of clothes. You ought not to deal with him as a man who did this maliciously."

Somewhat to the surprise of Ponzi, William McMasters—the publicity man he had hired initially for $2,000—made an impassioned and carefully worded plea for mercy, claiming that Ponzi's sudden wealth had unbalanced him. Coakley objected to the tense of McMasters' statement: "He was nutty then, but he isn't now, your honor," the publicist told the judge.

Noting that "The court is impressed with much that has been said," the judge ruled, however, that "it will not do to have the world understand that such a scheme can be carried out through the United States' instrumentality, without receiving substantial punishment." He placed the sentence at five years—an announcement received stoically by Ponzi, but which caused his wife to faint.

As Massachusetts had no federal penitentiary, Ponzi was incarcerated at Plymouth Jail, from which he could readily be brought to Boston to assist the bankruptcy trustees in their effort to wind up his affairs. At Plymouth, the former "Wizard of Finance" was a model prisoner and a star attraction for Sheriff Earl P. Blake, who frequently allowed him to visit the public library in town to check out lawbooks. Visited regularly by his wife, attorneys, and friends, Ponzi continued to protest his innocence and to claim that jealous financiers had brought about his downfall. Rose—who had returned to work as a bookkeeper after accepting a payment of $2,500 dollars to quit claim to the Lexington home, automobile, and other assets—backed him up with frequent statements to newsmen:

"Of course, his mother is as certain of his innocence as I am. Why wouldn't we be? Who knows Charlie any better than we? . . . A chance to pay! If they'll only give him a chance to pay and let him come home! He would not want to do anything but make people happy. I know that he will show them yet that this is so."

Perhaps irate at having been taken in by Ponzi's early promises, or angered that the cheerful Italian was seemingly content at Plymouth (where for a while he bred white mice in the prison pharmacy), Attorney General Allen decided to prosecute Ponzi immediately on half of the state's charges. Ponzi's lawyers argued that their jailed client was exclusively under federal jurisdiction and could not be tried by Massachusetts courts. This manuever, however, was finally vetoed by the U.S. Supreme Court when Chief Justice William Howard Taft ruled, "The penitentiary is not a place of sanctuary." Still, a year's delay had been gained, and Allen's term was nearly over.

Hastily, the state rushed Ponzi to trial. The defendant arrived in court each day after a leisurely drive from Plymouth Jail in Sheriff Blake's personal automobile, and radiated confidence throughout the proceedings. The famous Ponzi smile widened further when, after the jury became deadlocked at an eight-to-four vote for acquittal, it returned a verdict of not guilty on all counts. With a wave to the crowd, Ponzi returned to Plymouth. He served three and a half years of his term, dining well enough on prison food to add nearly twenty pounds to his tiny frame before he was released on parole in mid-1924.

He could not resist making charges that he had been persecuted by the attorney general of Massachusetts in conspiracy with the bankers. "If they had let me out on bail when the trouble first started," he told the Boston *American*, "I could have made three million dollars for my creditors. I was offered that much by the movies to film my story. But would I be let out? Not at all." His insistence that he was blameless, and growing support from the public (particulary the Italians in the North End of Boston), led Attorney General Allen's successor, J. R. Benton, to order Ponzi's prosecution on the state's remaining charges.

Too poor now to hire an attorney, Ponzi used the legal knowledge acquired during his latest prison term to defend himself. The trial began on November 6, 1924, and ended two weeks later with the jury deadlocked on four indictments. The judge dismissed a number of other charges for technical reasons, but agreed to a third trial on the four controversial points. Early in 1925, Ponzi and his stunned wife heard the jury pronounce him guilty on each count. Judge James H. Sisk promptly sentenced the "common and notorious thief" to a term of seven to nine years in the Massachusetts State Prison.

Out on bail while the verdict was appealed, Ponzi hurried to Florida in a desperate attempt to raise money for his legal battles. As the manager of the Charpon Land Syndicate, he joined numerous confidence men selling Florida swampland to gullible buyers. His failure to file a necessary business certificate, however, brought an investigation by local officials, and a Jacksonville court quickly found him guilty of fraud. While a local paper ran gag photographs of "Ponzi's prospects" surveying their property from a rowboat and studying a sign that said, *No lot under more than 30 feet of water*, a judge gave him a year in jail.

Ponzi appealed the Florida sentence and was again free on bail in May, 1926, when word reached him that the Supreme Judicial Court of Massachusetts had upheld his earlier conviction. He fled to Texas, with two states now on his trail. In Houston, he signed aboard an Italian freighter as a seaman, but—despite a new mustache—was recognized and taken off the ship when it docked in New Orleans on its way to Genoa. He fought extradition for three months, then was returned to Massachusetts to begin his sentence at the State Prison at Charleston.

His mother, looked after by the loyal Rose, died during Ponzi's seven and a half years in Charleston prison; his wife remained steadfast. She secured a job as a secretary and bookkeeper at Boston's famed Coconut Grove nightclub (and was still employed there, but off-duty, the night of November 28, 1942, when a fire destroyed the club and killed 491 persons). Several times each month, she visited her husband in prison, taking him lawbooks and materials he needed to write endless appeals to the governor for commutation of his sentence.

When he emerged from jail on February 14, 1934, Rose was waiting for him—but so were immigration officials armed with a deportation warrant to send him back to Italy as an undesirable alien. White-haired, with much more of his high forehead and scalp showing now, and weighing a portly 150 pounds, Ponzi discarded plans for a homecoming party at a hotel and restaurant in Boston. Instead, he and his wife hurried to the home of her sister in Somerville for a subdued celebration. "Let me alone for awhile," he told the trailing crowd of newspapermen who followed his taxi in a sixty-mile-an-hour chase.

He had ninety days of liberty ahead, only ninety days to prepare an appeal and fight off deportation.

He managed to stretch the period to eight months, but it was not easy. He displayed humility: "I left prison in the humble spirit of a man who has much to be forgiven for." He accepted a job as a wholesale grocery salesman in Boston's market district for twenty-five dollars a week. He and Rose called on Massachusetts Governor Joseph B. Ely to plead for a pardon. When the governor denied the request, Ponzi asked that his deadline to leave the country be delayed one week more—just until October 15. This, too, was denied. Ponzi, the immigration service ruled, would leave the United States aboard the S.S. *Vulcania* on October 7, voluntarily or otherwise.

To prevent another attempt at escape, federal authorities arrested him at the end of September and held him in the detention pen at the East Boston immigration station. There he told newsmen that he had decided that Rose would remain behind "although she is ready to sail with me now." Once he had found employment in Italy and could afford to send for her, he would do so. Rose, in an interview, agreed: "I would go with him without a moment's question. Charles is a brilliant and kindly man, and whatever he has done, it must be clear to anyone that he has suffered enough. I am blaming no one. It is useless to talk of injustice or persecution. Charles is a victim of circumstance . . ."

The deportation scene, despite its tragic overtones, in many ways resembled a farewell party for a successful industrialist. Accompanied by seven uniformed immigration inspectors, several of whom carried his luggage, Ponzi was ferried by government motor launch to the cruise liner in Boston Harbor. Dressed immaculately and waving his cap in salute, he came aboard while newsreel cameras whirred and flash bulbs exploded all around him. In a press conference held in one of the ship's larger suites, he settled his rotund figure into a thick velvet-covered armchair and explained that friends had provided ninety-five dollars in addition to the $105 paid by the government for a third-class ticket, so that he might travel to Italy first-class. He also had been given some fifteen hundred Italian lire (about $500) to make a new start abroad.

Rose was not among the crowd of cheering relatives and friends who saw him off. The previous evening, she had brought a cold chicken dinner to her husband at the immigration station, but neither had eaten during a two-hour meeting. "She's everything I've got," Ponzi said in answer to a newsman's question. "Of course I'll send for her."

At noon, wiping tears from his eyes with a large white handkerchief, he was taken to the *Vulcania's* brig—to be held there until the ship was three miles at sea. His final statement for the reporters, after he had admitted that "I went looking for trouble and I got it," was to wish "success to President Roosevelt and his recovery program."

Ponzi's arrival in Rome was less spectacular than his departure. He came off the ship as a grey, stoutish, respectable gentleman returning from the fabled Eldorado (like so many other Italians) with empty pockets. He managed to find work as a bookkeeper with a movie company, then left for a slightly better job as a salesman of construction materials. Earning about a hundred dollars a week, he lived in a furnished room on a street of cheap new houses on the outskirts of the city. There, he began work on his autobiography, *The Rise of Mr. Ponzi*. Frequently, he wrote his wife and asked her to borrow from friends so that he might publish the story himself.

It was not until two years later that Rose filed suit for divorce, on the grounds that her husband was a convicted criminal. When the news reached Ponzi, he could only stammer, "I suppose it had to happen sometime. There is nothing I can say at the moment." But a few weeks later, he was angry enough to call a press conference and tell newsmen that he would contest the action if the government would permit his return to the United States. Bitter and distraught, his eyes red with tears, talking excitedly and almost incoherently, he threatened to write a second book, *The Boston Merry-Go-Round*. In it, he warned, he would name persons high in the Boston and Massachusetts governments who had profited at the time of the Securities Exchange Company. "I'm going to pieces," he shouted. "I'm going to hell, and I'm going to take a lot of people to hell with me."

Once the divorce was granted, however, he lost interest in revenge. He had to agree with Rose's statement to an interviewer: "When he had millions, when he had a mansion, when he had cars, I stuck with him. When he was down, when he was in prison, I stuck with him. I feel that I have proved my loyalty through thick and thin."

Admitting that the *Boston Merry-Go-Round* project was but a bluff to coax "hush money" out of worried Bostonians—a bluff that failed—Ponzi turned to Italian friends for funds on which to live. His chief source of income was Colonel Attilio Biseo of the Italian Air Force, commander of the Green Mice Squadron, and the personal pilot of Benito Mussolini. Biseo, a second cousin of Ponzi, provided enough cash for the aging swindler to get drunk frequently and gamble at penny-ante card games in a neighborhood bar.

To finance publication of his autobiography, Ponzi offered shares in it—one thousand shares at twenty dollars each. He gravely told prospects that he could promise 100 percent interest—"I don't think I'm under an illusion that twenty-five thousand copies should sell in New England alone." When this plan failed, he arranged with a friend in the United States to have a Brooklyn printshop run off one thousand copies of his book—but the printer would not release them until $235 due on the printing bill was paid. Ponzi did not have the money, but told a newsman that if a hundred Americans who wanted to read the book would each send two dollars and fifty cents to the printer, they would get the book at a bargain price, and he would have the other nine hundred copies to sell.

Eventually, Ponzi returned to work, this time as an interpreter for hotels in Venice and in Rome. Then, in 1939, a new career opened for him. Leading his squadron, Colonel Biseo flew to Rio de Janeiro to lay plans with authorities there for an airline between Brazil and Italy. Biseo offered his cousin the job of business manager of the line, called LATI, and Ponzi promptly departed for Rio by steamer. Solvent once more, he checked into the expensive Gloria hotel, then moved to a pleasant two-story house in the exclusive Spanema Beach area. Two servants and a chauffeur were at his disposal, and his close associates were the Italian ambassador and Colonel Vicenze Coppola, who headed the airline.

Briefly, the twice-monthly flights to Rome were hailed by local businessmen and government alike, but the spread of war in Europe brought on an investigation into the airline's activities. Authorities in Rio determined that the planes were being used to smuggle Brazil's diamonds and strategic minerals to the Axis, and were carrying two-way traffic in spies, microfilm, and escaped military figures. In December, 1941—as the United States entered the war—the government cut off supplies of gasoline to LATI, and Ponzi was out of a job.

He tried to raise money by selling his story of the LATI affair to the newspapers, but found little interest. With his savings, he bought a small rooming house, then was forced to sell it when neighbors complained that roomers there appeared to be primarily prostitutes. He next opened a hot-dog stand, boasting that he would start a chain of them across the country. After a few months, he closed the stand and bought a shabby apartment on Copacabana Beach. There he made a precarious living as a teacher of English and French. In 1947, he sold his apartment and moved to a rented room in a squalid working-class suburb far from the sea. He obtained employment at $300 a month as an interpreter for an Italian importing firm, but his eyesight began to fail and a stroke early in 1948 produced a partial paralysis.

Friends arranged for his admittance to the free government hospital of São Francisco de Assis, intended for employees of the Ministry of Education. Ponzi's only income now was sixty-two dollars and fifty cents monthly, a social insurance benefit that he qualified for as an employee of the importing firm. An operation for a cataract in one eye improved his sight somewhat, enough so that he could write occasional letters to Rose in distant Boston. "She did not answer," said a half-blind Brazilian workman, Ponzi's closest companion in the four-bed hospital ward. But the one-time millionaire was cheerful—frequently tipping the workman fifty cents for bringing him his favorite Continental cigarettes which he continued to smoke in a long holder, and speaking positively of getting well so he could start a new business.

On Friday afternoon, January 14, 1949, his ward companion looked across to the window bed where Ponzi lay, waiting for an operation on his other eye, and looking out at a patio where sunlight danced off shrubs that moved gently in a mild breeze. "Is everything all right, Señor Ponzi?" the workman asked.

Ponzi turned his head and grinned cheerfully. "Yes, yes," he replied.

The words—positive, as always—were his last.